An Anthology of European Neo-Latin Literature

BLOOMSBURY NEO-LATIN SERIES

Series editors: William M. Barton, Stephen Harrison, Gesine Manuwald and Bobby Xinyue

Early Modern Texts and Anthologies

Edited by Stephen Harrison and Gesine Manuwald

The 'Early Modern Texts and Anthologies' strand of the *Bloomsbury Neo-Latin Series* presents editions of texts with English translations, introductions and notes. Volumes include complete editions of longer single texts and themed anthologies bringing together texts from particular genres, periods or countries and the like.

These editions are primarily aimed at students and scholars and intended to be suitable for use in university teaching, with introductions that give authoritative but not exhaustive accounts of the relevant texts and authors, and commentaries that provide sufficient help for the modern reader in noting links with classical Latin texts and bringing out the cultural context of writing.

Alongside the series' 'Studies in Early Modern Latin Literature' strand, it is hoped that these editions will help to bring important and interesting Neo-Latin texts of the period from 1350 to 1800 to greater prominence in study and scholarship, and make them available for a wider range of academic disciplines as well as for the rapidly growing study of Neo-Latin itself.

An Anthology of European Neo-Latin Literature

Edited by Daniel Hadas, Gesine Manuwald and Lucy R. Nicholas

BLOOMSBURY ACADEMIC
LONDON • NEW YORK • OXFORD • NEW DELHI • SYDNEY

BLOOMSBURY ACADEMIC
Bloomsbury Publishing Plc
50 Bedford Square, London, WC1B 3DP, UK
1385 Broadway, New York, NY 10018, USA

BLOOMSBURY, BLOOMSBURY ACADEMIC and the Diana logo are trademarks of Bloomsbury Publishing Plc

First published in Great Britain 2020

Cover design: Terry Woodley
Cover image: Abraham Ortelius, Map of Europe, Wikimedia Commons

A catalogue record for this book is available from the British Library.

Library of Congress Cataloging-in-Publication Data
Names: Hadas, Daniel, 1979- editor. | Manuwald, Gesine, editor. | Nicholas, Lucy R., editor.
Title: An anthology of European Neo-Latin literature / edited by Daniel Hadas, Gesine Manuwald and Lucy R. Nicholas.
Other titles: Bloomsbury Neo-Latin series. Early modern texts and anthologies; v. 2.
Description: London, UK ; New York, NY : Bloomsbury Academic, 2020. | Series: Bloomsbury Neo-Latin series. Early modern texts and anthologies volume 2 | Includes bibliographical references and index. | Texts in Latin and English translation, with introduction and commentary in English. |
Summary: "Compiled by a team of international experts, this volume showcases the best of the huge abundance of literature written in Latin in Europe from about 1500 to 1800. A general introduction provides readers with the context they need before diving into the 19 high-quality short Latin extracts and English translations. Together these texts present a rich panorama of the different literary genres, styles and themes that flourished at the time, and include authors such as Erasmus, Buchanan, Leibniz and Newton, along with less well-known writers. From the vast array of material available, a varied and meaningful sample of texts has been carefully curated by the editors of the volume. Passages not only exhibit literary merit or historical importance, but also illustrate the role of the complete texts from which they have been selected in the development of Neo-Latin literature. They reflect the wide range of authors writing in Latin in early modern Europe, as well as the importance of Latin in the history of ideas. As with all volumes in the series, section introductions and accompanying notes on every text provide orientation on the material for students"— Provided by publisher.
Identifiers: LCCN 2020022266 (print) | LCCN 2020022267 (ebook) |
ISBN 9781350157293 (paperback) | ISBN 9781350157286 (hardback) |
ISBN 9781350157309 (epub) | ISBN 9781350157316 (ebook)
Subjects: LCSH: Latin literature, Medieval and modern–Europe. | Latin literature, Medieval and modern—Europe—Translations into English. | Latin language, Medieval and modern—Readers.
Classification: LCC PA8114 .A58 2020 (print) | LCC PA8114 (ebook) | DDC 870.8—dc23
LC record available at https://lccn.loc.gov/2020022266
LC ebook record available at https://lccn.loc.gov/2020022267

ISBN: HB: 978-1-3501-5728-6
PB: 978-1-3501-5729-3
ePDF: 978-1-3501-5731-6
eBook: 978-1-3501-5730-9

Series: Bloomsbury Neo-Latin Series: Early Modern Texts and Anthologies

Typeset by RefineCatch Limited, Bungay, Suffolk

To find out more about our authors and books visit www.bloomsbury.com and sign up for our newsletters.

Contents

List of Contributors

Laurynas Adomaitis is a doctoral student (*perfezionando*) at the Scuola Normale Superiore di Pisa. He has also recently been a visiting fellow at the École Normale Supérieure in Paris, the Leibniz-Forschungsstelle at the Westfälische Wilhelms-Universität Münster and the Université de Montréal. His research covers Gottfried Wilhelm Leibniz's logic and scientific methodology as well as a variety of themes in early modern philosophy and science, especially the philosophy of Anne Conway.

William M. Barton is Key Researcher at the Ludwig Boltzmann Institute for Neo-Latin Studies, Innsbruck. His research focuses primarily on engagements with the natural environment and landscape in Latin literature. Within this broad field, his interests have centred on the shifting attitudes towards the mountain in early modern Latin literature, the representation of nature's creative power in the post-classical period and the depiction of the natural world in early descriptions of *la Nouvelle-France*. Barton's more recent published work in these fields includes the monograph *Mountain Aesthetics in Early Modern Latin Literature* (2016) and a critical edition with introduction, translation and commentary of the late antique *Pervigilium Veneris* (2018).

Emma Buckley is Senior Lecturer in Latin and Classical Studies at St Andrews University. She works on the poetry and literature of the early Roman Empire and on classical culture in early modern England. She has published on Neo-Latin supplements, academic drama and early modern translation, and is, with Edward Paleit, co-editor of *Thomas May, Lucan's Pharsalia (1627)* (2020).

Jacqueline Glomski is Honorary Senior Research Associate in the Centre for Editing Lives and Letters at University College London (UCL). Her present work focuses on seventeenth-century Neo-Latin prose writing. She is a contributor to and the co-editor of *Acta Conventus Neo-Latini Monasteriensis: Proceedings of the Fifteenth International Congress of Neo-Latin Studies* (with A. Steiner-Weber, K. A. E. Enenkel et al., 2015) and *Seventeenth-Century Fiction: Text and Transmission* (with Isabelle Moreau, 2016), and has also contributed to *Der neulateinische Roman als Medium seiner Zeit / The Neo-Latin Novel in its Time* (2013) and *A Guide to Neo-Latin Literature* (2017). She is a fellow of the Royal Historical Society and a fellow of the Society of Antiquaries.

Paul Gwynne is Professor of Medieval and Renaissance Studies at The American University of Rome. He is the author of three monographs and a number of articles on the diffusion of Italian humanism and the reception of the classical tradition.

Daniel Hadas is Lecturer in Medieval Latin at King's College London (KCL). He has published an edition and commentary of St Augustine's *Epistulae ad Romanos Inchoata Expositio* (*Augustin d'Hippone: Commencement de Commentaire sur l'épître aux Romains*, 2019).

Stephen J. Harrison is Professor of Latin Literature at the University of Oxford and Extraordinary Professor at the University of Stellenbosch. He has published extensively on Virgil, Horace, Apuleius and their reception, is engaged in an international project to edit the works of George Buchanan and is co-editor of the texts and anthologies strand of Bloomsbury's Neo-Latin Series.

Alfred Hiatt is Professor of Medieval Studies in the Department of English at Queen Mary, University of London (QMUL). His research interests include forgery and the reception of forgeries, maps and geographical writing, and the reception of the classical tradition in the Middle Ages. He is the author of *The Making of Medieval Forgeries: False Documents in Fifteenth-Century England* (2004) and *Terra Incognita: Mapping the Antipodes before 1600* (2008).

Astrid Khoo is a doctoral student in Ancient History in the Department of Classics of Harvard University. Her recent publications include the chapter 'Dream Scenes' for the compendium *Structures of Epic Poetry* (2020) and (with Martin T. Dinter) '"If Skin Were Parchment . . .": Tattoos in Antiquity' in the edited volume *Tattooed Histories* (2019). She is interested in a wide range of topics, from dress history to medieval conceptions of 'otherness'; she is currently working on an edition with translation of the Neo-Latin didactic poem *De rusticis Brasiliae rebus* ('*On the Agriculture of Brazil*', José Rodrigues de Melo, 1781).

Fiachra Mac Góráin is Associate Professor of Classics at University College London (UCL). His research focuses mainly on Virgil and the Virgilian tradition. He is co-editor (with Charles Martindale) of *The Cambridge Companion to Virgil, Second Edition* (2019), editor of *Dionysus and Rome: Religion and Literature* (2020) and has published articles on Virgil and the reception of his works, and on the representation of religion in literature.

Jan Machielsen is Senior Lecturer in Early Modern History at Cardiff University. He is the author of *Martin Delrio: Demonology and Scholarship in the Counter-Reformation* (2016) and the editor of *The Science of Demons* (2020).

Gesine Manuwald is Professor of Latin at University College London (UCL) and President of the Society for Neo-Latin Studies (SNLS). She has published widely on classical Latin authors (including Cicero, Ennius and Valerius Flaccus) as well as on Neo-Latin literature. Publications in the latter field include several articles on Thomas Campion as well as the edited collection *Neo-Latin Poetry in the British Isles* (with L. B. T. Houghton; 2012). She is co-editor of the texts and anthologies strand of Bloomsbury's Neo-Latin Series.

Lucy R. Nicholas is a teaching fellow in the Classics department at King's College London (KCL) and at the Warburg Institute. She has published extensively on the mid-Tudor humanist Roger Ascham. The Latin works of Walter Haddon, Johannes Sturm and Gabriel Harvey represent the focus of her current research.

Lucy Sheaf is a member of the Philosophy department at King's College London (KCL). Her research is focused on Leibniz's writings on the Philosophy of Religion, particularly his work on the problem of evil.

Pablo Toribio is tenured researcher at the Institute for Mediterranean and Near Eastern Languages and Cultures (ILC) of the Spanish National Research Council (CSIC), Madrid. He has held post-doctoral fellowships at the Leibniz Institute for European History (Mainz), the Ludwig Boltzmann Institute for Neo-Latin Studies (Innsbruck) and the universities of Louvain, Fribourg (Switzerland), Geneva, Erfurt and Rostock. His research focuses on the edition and study of Neo-Latin sources related to early modern antitrinitarianism. His work on Isaac Newton's theological manuscripts has led to a number of publications, notably the critical edition *Isaac Newton: Historia Ecclesiastica* (2013).

Paul White is Associate Professor of Classics at the University of Leeds. He works on Neo-Latin poetry, commentaries and print culture, with a primary focus on the French sixteenth century. He has published articles on poetry, education, authorship and print culture in Latin and French vernacular contexts, and is the author of books on the early modern reception of Ovid's *Heroides* (2009), on the classical editions and commentaries of the Paris-based printer and author Jodocus Badius Ascensius (2013) and on the reception of the elegist Gaius Cornelius Gallus in the Renaissance (2019).

Gareth Williams is Anthon Professor of Latin Language and Literature at Columbia University. His research interests cover classical and imperial Latin poetry, Seneca's philosophical prose and Renaissance humanism. He has recently published *Pietro Bembo on Etna: The Ascent of a Venetian Humanist* (2017) and is currently working on the writings of Ermolao Barbaro.

Bobby Xinyue is British Academy Postdoctoral Fellow at the University of Warwick. He works on Latin literature of the Augustan age and its reception in the early modern period. He has published articles on Virgil, Cicero and Propertius as well as on a number of Neo-Latin poets. He has recently co-edited a volume entitled *Reflections and New Perspectives on Virgil's Georgics* (2019). His current research focuses on the reception of Ovid's *Fasti* in the Renaissance.

Preface

This book serves as a companion piece to the first volume in this new series, the *Anthology of British Neo-Latin Literature* (edited by L. B. T. Houghton, Gesine Manuwald and Lucy R. Nicholas). Although it follows closely the principles and aims of the first anthology, the scope of this volume is extended from Britain to Europe. A more ambitious geographical spread with no corresponding lengthening of the page count carries with it additional challenges regarding the selection of texts. It was inevitably not possible to include examples from all literary genres and all relevant periods from all European countries. Still, the sample texts provided will give a representative insight into the breadth of Neo-Latin writing in Europe, its variety and interconnectedness, its literary quality as well as its association with major scientific, political, philosophical and religious developments. If this compendium encourages users to read more of the vast body of Latin from this period, the book has achieved one of its aims.

The excerpts have been prepared by scholars based in different countries and from a range of disciplinary backgrounds; accordingly, a variety of approaches and interests are on display. So it is hoped that the volume also illustrates the interdisciplinary nature of Neo-Latin studies as well as the wealth of issues and questions raised by the primary texts.

Since the book is intended as an introductory volume, each entry offers a fairly literal translation, contextual information, and guidance concerning literary and linguistic details. Hopefully, the texts will speak to a wide range of readers, including advanced school pupils and university students, interested lay people and scholars.

The editors would like to thank all the contributors for their dedication and support from the outset and for their cooperation, flexibility and quick responses throughout the editorial process. Warm thanks are also due to Bloomsbury, especially to Alice Wright and Georgina Leighton, for their early enthusiasm for this project, and the energy they have applied in bringing it to fruition.

D. H. / G. M. / L. R. N.
London, March 2020

Introduction

Lucy R. Nicholas and William M. Barton

European Neo-Latin and its development

Given the marginal place of Latin today, it is difficult to imagine a world in which this language was a dominant force, as either a spoken or a written phenomenon. In fact, within Western history it is the last two centuries that are anomalous; for Latin was viewed as a perfectly natural linguistic option, and often the most obvious medium, for a vast gamut of subjects, right through the medieval era and up to the end of the eighteenth century. Indeed, the period from 800 to 1800 CE has been referred to as Europe's 'Latin millennium'.[1] It is tempting to compare the status of Latin in that period with that which English now enjoys. A still better analogy is modern standard Arabic, which is rooted in the classical period, and so divorced from any spoken vernacular, but is used throughout the Arab world as the language of education and of formal speech and writing.

The term 'Neo-Latin' denotes the Latin employed during the second half of this Latin millennium, so from *c.* 1300 to *c.* 1800, and, more specifically, a use of this language that attempted to revive the 'real' Latin of the ancient world. The expression 'Neo-Latin' has its detractors: some prefer descriptions such as 'early modern Latin' or 'Renaissance Latin'. Of course, none of these labels were used at the time in which this kind of Latin flourished; they were coined at a much later stage.[2] Furthermore, any claim that writers of this period were resurrecting an 'authentic' Latinity is susceptible to challenge. Nevertheless, here the term 'Neo-Latin' shall be adopted throughout, as it at least has the advantage of signalling that early modern Latin was of a different order to the Latin of the Middle Ages that preceded it.

With the arrival of humanism in the period we know today as the Renaissance (*c.* 1350–1600), there was a resurgence in the production of Latin literature throughout Europe, and the Latin language was quickly recalibrated along strictly classical lines. This is not to suggest that medieval Latin should be viewed as an independent language without any relation to the Latin of the Romans or indeed to Neo-Latin.[3] Many medieval orthographical and syntactical conventions find their way into Neo-Latin texts. Nor was the classicizing impetus of the Renaissance entirely new: the medieval period also witnessed attempts to reform Latin in accordance with classical and early Christian norms, during what is sometimes dubbed the Carolingian Renaissance (*c.* 750–815) and again in the twelfth century, above all in France and England. However, from the thirteenth century onwards, reverence for the classics increasingly yielded to other tendencies in the development of Latin: on the one hand, assimilation to the vernacular and, on the other, the growth of new, specialized vocabularies in the courts, chanceries and universities.

In reaction, the early humanists then attempted to overhaul what they perceived as the decayed status of the Latin language, which they held to reflect a wider decay in European culture. Aiming to base themselves exclusively on classical and patristic models, authors such as Petrarch, Giovanni Boccaccio and Gian Francesco Poggio Bracciolini – to name but three – sought to recreate the Latin of an ancient past, just as their contemporaries in the visual arts similarly pursued their craft in accordance with ancient models. In literature, Virgil and Cicero quickly emerged as the principal models for poetry and prose respectively.[4] In a cultural atmosphere now hypersensitive to questions of language and literary 'elegance', European authors spilt much ink over questions of appropriate vocabulary, grammar, syntax and style. Here Lorenzo Valla's zealously classicizing work, the *Elegantiae linguae Latinae* ('*The refinements of the Latin language*', composed *c.* 1449, first published 1471), emerged as one of the most important studies of the Latin language to date. The work continued to circulate long after its author's death in numerous edited and abridged versions.[5]

Valla's philological focus made him an important figure in the development of Latin style, and his approach spread to numerous areas of study.[6] But his strong opinions on the correct and tasteful use of Latin, as well as his ideas about the areas appropriate for philological enquiry, contributed to numerous quarrelsome exchanges with his contemporaries in Europe. In particular, Valla's mid-fifteenth-century clash with Poggio Bracciolini saw the nature of the humanist project as a whole come under dispute:[7] Valla's critical approach to the Latin language, and thereby its literature, placed even the works and style of ancient authors under the philological microscope. Moreover, he was prepared to subject ecclesiastical documents and Scripture to the same sort of critical investigation.[8] Poggio, on the other hand, felt that Valla's fierce philological criticism often went too far. He preferred to see Latin as a more flexible tool for the expression of literary ideas and insisted that the work of theology and of philology should remain separate.[9]

The reverberations of the contemporary debates over Latin language and style inspired by Valla and Poggio, among many others, could be felt all over Europe, and the ideals of the Neo-Latin project continued to gain ground. Responses to their discussions over style, imitation and the value of 'good' Latin were subsequently expressed in various literary guises. Among the most important interventions were those of Erasmus of Rotterdam. His *Ciceronianus* ('*The Ciceronian*', 1528), for example, staged a satirical dialogue over writers' slavish imitation of Cicero's language and promoted a more moderate, yet still largely 'classical' Latin style. The same author's *Colloquia familiaria* ('*Familiar Colloquies*', 1518) presented examples of suitable, cultivated conversation for training pupils' Latin skills. This collection's combination of pleasant style and characteristic humour made it an early modern bestseller. Again, on the satirical side, for example, the anonymous collection of letters from fictitious German scholastic writers, the *Epistolae Obscurorum Virorum* ('*Letters of Obscure Men*', 1515–19), sought to mock opponents of the humanist Johannes Reuchlin by giving their voices a distinctively out-of-date, that is to say non-humanist, style.[10]

The relative linguistic and stylistic cohesion of the Latin that emerged from this early debate was based, then, largely on ancient models, while rejecting scholastic forms and neologisms rooted in the vernacular. This Latin admitted, however, classicizing neologisms where necessary and allowed, in moderation, innovative syntactic arrangements according to taste. The resulting unity, which still provided room for individual authors to express themselves in a distinctive style, encouraged the steady, widespread adoption of Neo-Latin across Europe and beyond. The rapid dissemination of printing technology based on moveable type after its development in Germany and later arrival in Italy both aided and promoted this process immeasurably. As an early form of mass communication, printing made Latin books more easily accessible to a wider range of readers across the continent.[11] The subsequent advances in the book trade (for example, Aldus Manutius' easily portable classics in small octavo format) quickly transformed the humanist register of Latin into a standard. These developments established Neo-Latin as an international tool for diverse groups: ecclesiastics, merchants and soldiers, authors, diplomats and royalty across Europe were now able to communicate in Latin – though not always seamlessly![12]

The ensuing formation of a *res publica litterarum* ('Republic of Letters'), which emerged in the fifteenth and became cemented throughout the sixteenth and seventeenth centuries, served as an important means of establishing networks and a more consistent literary style.[13] Swiss polymath Conrad Gessner, for instance, maintained throughout his career lively exchanges with colleagues in France, Italy, Austria and Germany, on botany, chorography, medicine and zoology. He was thereby able to collect the data necessary for his efforts towards encyclopedic knowledge. Well into the mid-eigheenth century, European intellectuals (especially natural scientists) still relied on Latin for their correspondence, between centres as far apart as Sweden and Sicily or Portugal and Hungary / Romania.

While Latin thus took precedence over vernacular languages in its role as a European lingua franca for the larger part of the early modern period, it was nonetheless instrumental in the establishment of linguistic study of Europe's national languages and of their own structural development. Andalusian scholar Elio Antonio de Nebrija, for example, published the first recognized grammar of a modern Romance language in 1492. His approach to Castilian in the *Gramática de la lengua castellana* ('*Grammar of the Castilian language*') drew almost exclusively on the philological apparatus of Latin grammar, as established among early humanists.[14] Indeed, European expansion saw the subsequent 'Latinization' of vernacular languages across the globe. This process meant that languages as far removed from Indo-European, let alone from Latin, as Innu (Montagnais) and Japanese, for example, were described according to Latin's grammatical structure.[15]

Latin's role as a stimulus for the development of European vernaculars through the production of grammars depended heavily on its position as the language of education.[16] Following the medieval tradition of grammar schools, Latin continued to operate as the main – ideally exclusive – language of instruction from the first school classroom all the way to the university lecture halls. Indeed, the fundamental place of linguistic skills within the first stage of the *artes liberales* ('liberal arts'), the *trivium* (grammar, logic and rhetoric), underlines the central role of Latin and language in Renaissance and early modern education: students were expected to master these three fields before moving on to the later stage of the *quadrivium* (arithmetic, geometry, music and astronomy). The three great university disciplines of law, medicine and theology were also largely taught in Latin. Moreover, the development of a new curriculum – the *studia humanitatis* ('humane studies') – on the back of the medieval *artes dictaminis* ('treatises on letter-writing') meant that good Latin and thorough knowledge of the Greek and Roman classics came to symbolize not only proper linguistic and intellectual training but the acme of moral and cultural polish.[17] The place of Latin as the primary tool and subject of this pedagogical system ensured the progress of a recognizable humanist style across Europe. Diplomats, tradesmen, businessmen and representatives of the church from all corners of the continent were exposed to this idiom as part of their basic and continued education.[18]

Once established, the uses, forms and areas of life for which this Latin register was required remained remarkably stable across the continent until around the middle of the eighteenth century. Latin was employed in areas well beyond the realm of belles-lettres, in literary and non-literary productions, including in political, philosophical, religious, technical and more personal, everyday writing of all kinds. With the growth of writing in Europe's vernacular languages, the role of Latin dwindled slowly until the end of the nineteenth century.[19] Today, the use of Latin is limited to a small number of specific fields: alongside occasional verse, for example, Latin is still used in accordance with isolated academic traditions and for the formalized descriptions of plants within the field of botany. It also remains the official language of the Vatican: papal encyclicals, for instance, continue to be published in Latin, alongside their vernacular versions. Meanwhile, contemporary writing associated with a rise in interest in *Latinitas viva* ('living Latin') has contributed to the recent resurgence of new Latin titles.

Neo-Latin as a literary medium

Neo-Latin was central to the activities of the intellectual elite, but also to many of the significant contemporary cultural developments at all levels. It is not an overstatement to claim that the history of early modern Latin runs parallel to the history of the Western mind. Latin was a vital medium for articulating the period's religious upheaval, Europe's expansion through exploration, military conflicts and warfare, and the appearance of the 'new science' that set the path towards the eighteenth-century Enlightenment. Martin Luther's ninety-five theses of 1517 were, for instance, formulated in Latin, and, notwithstanding the valid association made between the Reformation and the rise of the vernacular, the ensuing controversy continued principally in Latin. Erasmus proposed his moderate approach to the Church's schism exclusively in Latin. John Calvin's systematic Protestant philosophy in his *Institutio Christianae Religionis* ('*Establishment of the Christian Religion*', 1536) was set down, too, first in Latin. The subsequent Catholic Counter-Reformation also found expression predominantly in Latin: the Jesuit order, for example, framed its influential programme of study, the *Ratio studiorum* ('*Plan of Studies*', 1599), which in turn relied heavily on a foundation of classical learning, in Latin.

Latin was likewise a key means to communicate news of pioneering discoveries. European powers, bent on expansion, commissioned expeditions in every direction and, for example, among the earliest reports of the European explorations that would eventually facilitate the Jesuits' missions across the world was Peter Martyr's Latin *De orbe novo decades* ('*Decades on the New World*', 1511–25; first printed together 1530). This collection of letters and reports, on the back of Amerigo Vespucci's earlier Latin pamphlet *Mundus novus* (*'New World'*, 1503), paved the way for an intensive Neo-Latin literary production on the theme 'New World' across Europe.[20]

The onset of the Thirty Years' War (1618–48) in central Europe was the beginning of one of the most destructive periods of European history. The Treaties of Westphalia, which sealed the peace after the conflict, were formulated in Latin (*Instrumentum Pacis Monasteriensis, Instrumentum Pacis Osnabrugensis*; *'Peace Treaty of Münster' 'Peace Treaty of Osnabrück'*, 1648). Throughout the tragic events that devastated large parts of central Europe, literary responses emerged across the continent. There was, from Sweden, for example, the epic *Adolphid* (*'On Adolphus'*) (1629), written by French Huguenot Antoine Garissoles to the glory of the Swedish king, Gustavus Adolphus; from Germany, Cyricacus Lentulus' didactic poem *Europa* (*'Europe'*) (1650) cast in poetical form an image of the continent in the wake of the war; while Petrus Lotichius' *Austria parva* (*'Little Austria'*, 1653) presented a history of the war in the form of an encomium of Ferdinand IV, Archduke of Austria.

The European 'scientific revolution' was another widespread cultural event in which Latin played a crucial role. From the famed early foundational publications in Latin (e.g. Nicolaus Copernicus' *De revolutionibus orbium coelestium*; *'On the revolutions of the celestial orbs'*, 1543), Latin remained the primary language of the natural philosophical project until well into the eighteenth century. Isaac Newton's 1687 *Philosophiae naturalis principia mathematica* (*'Mathematical principles of natural philosophy'*) reached its international public through its author's choice of Latin, and Carl Linnaeus' *Species plantarum* (*'Species of plants'*) changed the face of scientific botany in 1753.[21] Indeed, such was the prevalence of Latin in the fields of science and philosophy that important works published in vernaculars were quickly translated into the ancient language to ensure their international circulation. Galileo Galilei's controversial *Dialogo sopra i due massimi sistemi del mondo* (*'Dialogue on the two chief world systems'*, 1632) was translated under the title *Systema Cosmicum* (*'World system'*) for an international audience by 1635, and Newton's influential *Opticks* (1704) was translated into Latin by 1706.[22]

The Latin of the Renaissance and early modern period played a significant part in the major historical events of the age and participated fully in the associated cultural shifts and ruptures that formed the Europe that we know today.[23] The extent, variegated uses and wide appeal to contemporaries of literary and intellectual discourse in Latin can also be illustrated by the sheer number of works that continue to surface as interest in this literature grows and library catalogues are digitized. The number of German books only overtook those in Latin at the Frankfurter Buchmesse in 1681 – then as now the world's largest book fair – this gives some idea of the sheer size of Latin literature's 'lost Atlantis'.[24] Likewise, the continued rediscovery of Neo-Latin publications of every sort, from poems on tea to intensive scholarly studies of Oriental poetry, underlines the amount still to be learned about the Latin of early modernity.[25]

Neo-Latin literature and its genres

Overview

The corpus of European Neo-Latin literature as treated in this anthology was produced over a period of about 350 years and is as vast as it is varied. One way to marshal such a voluminous body of material is through division into different types or classes of work. Most early modern works of Neo-Latin can, at least superficially, be assigned to a particular literary genre. Indeed, in recent Neo-Latin surveys, generic classification has been adopted as a useful organizing principle.[26] Modern scholarship has thus helped to delineate frameworks, while highlighting a need for the continued evaluation of genre as a concept and of the practices used within certain genres. As useful as such studies can be, their focus is often exclusively on the literary categories of poetry and belles-lettres. Yet, as suggested above, much, if not most Neo-Latin output belongs to less purely literary fields: science, theology, philosophy, law, administration, etc. While it is not possible to be comprehensive in the space permitted, this anthology intends to be representative of this true generic variety.

The genres covered in this volume have been determined either by content or form. They are: historiography, epistolography, satire, drama, dialogue, epic poetry, pastoral, love elegy and occasional verse, medicine, philosophy, theology, commentary and scholarship. These are not purely anachronistic designations imposed by modern scholars; the original authors would have recognized them. Genre was a major concern throughout early modernity, with early modern critics demonstrating a consistent interest in formal generic distinctions, not least because so many Neo-Latin writers looked back to the classical canon and were attentive to the generic forms established in antiquity.[27] However, before examining these genres in detail, a few caveats must be registered.

The first relates to the ancient canon. While this canon undoubtedly provided models and parameters that gave definition to the genres of the early modern period, Neo-Latin productions often transcend the generic confines of the classical tradition. Such developments were arguably *imitatio* on a grand scale, encompassing all the subversion, deviation and change that the longstanding practice of imitation entailed. Thus genre, even when based on classical models, was far from a static entity; early modern genres evolved and bifurcated, while new ones flourished as the world changed. The Reformation, the growth of the universities, advances in science and the ensuant new perceptions of the world and the universe, new ideologies and pan-European upheavals had a direct impact on modes of Latin expression. Regional developments could also influence shifts in generic structures, and the notion of a circumscribed European Neo-Latin genre *tout court* may be challenged by any number of local variations.[28]

Furthermore, as well as adhering to classical systems, Neo-Latin genres evolved in parallel, and sometimes in tension, with other more contemporary forms. These included a number of medieval genres. For example, hagiographical works and hymns are often also found composed in the humanist Latin idiom. Neo-Latin works likewise interacted with early modern works in the vernacular, to which Latin writers, who frequently wrote both in Latin and their native tongue, responded. On the face of it, generic groupings of vernacular writings tended to take the same shape as those in Neo-Latin. However, the substance of each could diverge radically. First, Latin was a far more natural linguistic channel for classical allusions and rhetorical forms. Secondly, assumptions about intended readership could result in quite different tones and approaches.[29]

Early modern genres also overlapped. While the genres of antiquity tended to be strictly separated (at least from a modern point of view), each genre having its own history, lexicon, main features, metre (in the case of verse) and principal representatives, for Neo-Latin texts the situation is less clear-cut. We may attribute a work to a specific genre, but the vast majority contain elements that defy such tidy taxonomy. Take, for example, Newton: this towering thinker was a scientist but also a biblical exegete, and his theological considerations were wholly bound up with his mathematical investigations. The history of Neo-Latin is peopled by creative thinkers who astonish our own world of specialism with their extraordinary command of several disciplines at once.[30] Neo-Latin literature was thus dynamic and constantly shifting in its aspirations, fields of reference and scope. Given the scale of research still to be undertaken on the Neo-Latin corpus, it seems certain that generic categories will be added to and refined as scholars examine them more closely, and that further permutations will emerge.

Genres covered in this volume

As for the genres featured in this volume, let us begin with those that may appear most familiar today. The first is historiography. The early modern period abounds with Neo-Latin works dealing with the history of peoples and places from all over Europe, Asia and the New World, and there are a range of subdivisions, including chronicles, biography and numismatics. Many regard Leonardo Bruni's *Historiae Florentini Populi* ('*History of the Florentine People*'), written over the space of a quarter of a century between 1415/16 and 1442, as the first in a bountiful succession of humanist histories, many very large in scale.[31] These emerged at the same time as systematic manuals on the *ars historica*, which prescribed the requisites of the historian's art: these generally centred on veracity and rhetorical elegance. However, even though the term *historia* was widely applied, all such productions tended to be a blend of several genres, incorporating elements of classical and medieval historiography, along with, for example, geography, panegyric and philology.[32] Pietro Bembo's monumental *History of Venice* of the early sixteenth century is a fine example of such variety (Text 4). Bembo composed this work in his capacity as Venice's official historian, a post awarded primarily on account of his Latin style,[33] and the work's stylistic underpinnings are immediately in evidence. His coverage of Christopher Columbus and his discoveries in the New World engaged with contemporary geographical, scientific and sociological interests.

Epistolography or letter writing is another genre that sits at the heart of the Neo-Latin oeuvre and played a crucial role in the *res publica litterarum*. A fashionable activity in antiquity, literary epistolography was also given fresh impetus in the Renaissance when in 1345 Petrarch discovered a manuscript containing a large number of Cicero's letters.[34] The letter form, as it had developed through the medieval *ars dictaminis* ('the art of writing letters'), had, in the early modern mind, a close correspondence to rhetoric, and there was a fine line between *oratio* and *epistola*.[35] Letters composed in Latin tended to have a literary character and often constituted a form of self-fashioning, advertising as they could a person's intellectual calibre and capacity to operate on the international stage. Epistolary exchanges were often published and, even when they were not, were almost certainly composed with a notional public in mind. Correspondence can also offer an important window into wider historical developments. One of this anthology's entries presents letters exchanged between Cardinal St Robert Bellarmine and a Jesuit priest, Francisco Enzinas, writing to the cardinal in Rome from the Philippines, concerning the Catholic liturgy (Text 12). The letters are testimony both to the immense geographical distances such correspondence could cover and to the cohesion of Latin speech communities.

A second extract likewise contains the letter form, namely the *Epistulae Obscurorum Virorum* (*EOV*, Text 8). This entry similarly draws attention to features of the Neo-Latin Republic of Letters, but shows a very different goal from that of Bellarmine and Enzinas. These letters are in fact imaginary and deeply satirical, rooted in a wider quarrel between university faculties and humanists about the advisability of Hebrew learning and about traditional academic approaches more generally. Satire was an established genre in antiquity and likewise flourished in the early modern period: some of the best-known of all Neo-Latin texts are Erasmus' *Encomium moriae* ('*Praise of folly*', 1511) and Thomas More's *Utopia* (first published in 1516). The *EOV* can be considered alongside these and a number of other satirical dialogues, novels and even joke books of the time.

Drama was another genre reanimated by Neo-Latin, and plays written in Neo-Latin flourished across Europe for centuries. There is evidence of thousands of plays from this period, both published and unpublished, of which the vast majority were written for performance in schools and universities. While the classical playwright Terence was widely read throughout the Middle Ages, the early modern dramatic scene was further enriched by the resurfacing of Plautus and Seneca and by the Greek plays which were increasingly being translated into Latin. All this stimulated intensive emulation and innovative adaptation on the early modern stage. Many plays, such as the one featured in Text 13, were written in the manner of a Senecan tragedy. This play, authored by Matthew Gwinne and composed in iambic trimeters, centres on the life of the emperor Nero and, in this excerpt, the deaths of Seneca and his wife Paulina. Yet even as it cleaves to the Senecan model, its very title *Nero: Tragaedia Nova* ('*Nero: A New Tragedy*') points to innovation. It is in effect a historical chronicle clothed in verse and concerns itself as much with the historical works of Tacitus and contemporary topical issues, such as the conduct of women, as it does with the revenge themes inherent in Senecan drama. Indeed, by far the most pressing aim of most early modern drama was pedagogy rather than entertainment. This emerges especially clearly in Text 19, which was written by a teacher and school librarian, Gottlob Krantz, in order to educate students at a school in Wrocław about the contents of their library. The dialogic structure of the play served to assist the inculcation of spoken Latin as well as contributing to the cultural and moral instruction of pupils.

Dialogue, though strictly speaking a form, may be considered a genre in its own right. There exist numerous examples of Neo-Latin dialogues throughout this period, which drew on the prose dialogues of Plato, Lucian and Cicero in particular, the colloquia of Late Antiquity (such as the *Hermeneumata Pseudodositheana*) and even ancient stage comedies. A strong medieval culture of disputation probably helped sustain the form, however much humanists challenged the pedantry of much traditional dialectic. An overriding purpose of early modern Neo-Latin dialogues was to teach Latin conversation, while simultaneously inculcating an ethical code. The Latin could be pitched at a simple or a more advanced level, and content could range from the quotidian to more important religious, cultural and social issues. The most famous proponent of the dialogue was Erasmus, whose *Colloquia* became a landmark text, repeatedly reprinted and imitated. Yet the typology 'dialogue' hardly does this multilayered work justice: as Text 3 shows, it incorporated both satirical and philosophical content.

Neo-Latin poetry was a widespread and diverse pan-European phenomenon. The sheer quantity of early modern Latin verse dwarfs what survives from antiquity and what was produced in the Middle Ages. Various genres proliferated, and, given the extent of uncharted territory in Neo-Latin verse, it is likely that certain genres still await identification. Still, many poetic genres of this period did deliberately and self-consciously model themselves on ancient forms and their corresponding metrical schemata. Only a handful of genres may be discussed here. The first one, epic poetry, appears in surprising guises in this anthology. Epic verse was one of the most prestigious genres in the ancient literary canon and continued to thrive through the Middle Ages. Neo-Latin epic poets duly observed elements from the Greek and Roman compositions at their disposal (Virgil's *Aeneid* often standing as the paradigm form), including their metre, heroic grandeur, combination of narrative and direct speech, similes and ecphrases. Yet these ancient tropes blended with modern concerns: subjects could be taken, for instance, from the Christian Bible, contemporary warfare, international exploration and conquest, and Jesuit missionary work. The selections in Texts 2 and 11 illustrate these developments. Jacopo Sannazaro's epic *De Partu Virginis* ('*On the delivery / offspring of the Virgin*') was a religiously motivated treatment of the birth of Christ and imbued Mary, the mother of God, with heroic status. Francesco Benci's *Quinque martyres e Societate Iesu in India* ('*The five martyrs from the Society of Jesus in India*') was the first in a series of Jesuit epics of martyrdom. Both poems are unmistakably Virgilian in style, but the didactic dimensions of Virgil's writing are redirected towards specific religious causes and the provision of holy moral exemplars.

Another work by Virgil, the *Eclogues*, along with its own Hellenistic predecessors, above all Theocritus' *Idylls*, was central to the formation of another genre, pastoral poetry. Medieval interpretations and reworking of this material along Christian lines continued well into the early modern period. For Christian Neo-Latin poets of the Renaissance and beyond the polyvocalism of Virgil's *Eclogues* afforded the possibility for radical and creative experimentation,[36] and key elements of pastoral, such as the humble style, use of allegory and satirical digressions were reconfigured afresh. Sannazaro, in addition to epic, also wrote pastoral poetry; indeed, his Italian-language masterwork *Arcadia*, which instantiated an idealized pastoral world among the shepherd-poets, is one of the best-known vernacular manifestations of this genre. The *Adolescentia* (*'Youth'*) of Battista Spagnoli Mantovano ('Mantuan') here illustrates the development of this genre in Latin (Text 1): from this collection of ten eclogues, selections from one of these convey how Neo-Latin pastoral could function not just as a display of Latin virtuosity, but also as an important moral and religious tool.

Elegy is another poetic category, though one rather differently understood in its Latin incarnations than in its English counterpart, which tends to be a lament. In classical as well as Neo-Latin elegy the genre was defined less by its occasion or substance than by its metre, namely the elegiac couplet. The range of subjects thought appropriate for treatment in this metre was vast and varied, and love elegy – the best known of classical elegiac forms – should be regarded as only one branch of a much broader landscape. Joachim Du Bellay's *Amores* (*'Love poems'*, Text 10) have affinities with medieval erotic literature and vernacular love poetry. They also accommodate the devices, motifs and propensities of the amatory verse of Propertius, Tibullus and Ovid, including, most obviously, the construct of the elegiac *puella* ('girl' or 'beloved') but also the paraklausithyron ('lament by the closed door') and themes of enslavement and loss. Similarly in keeping with its pagan predecessors, these *Amores* draw attention to their own generic instability through frequent allusions to epic. But Du Bellay's experimentation extends yet further, for his poems also contain characteristics of the epigram which, despite metrical overlap with elegy, was generally considered to constitute a separate genre.

Another type of verse that burgeoned during the early modern period was what is often termed 'occasional' poetry, i.e. verse produced for a specific event. Such pieces sprang directly from a special set of social experiences, such as royal births, anniversaries or bereavements. Several established genres originated as occasional works, including epithalamia ('wedding songs') and victory odes. George Buchanan's epideictic poem marking the ceremonial visit to Bordeaux of Holy Roman Emperor Charles V in 1559 (Text 7) represents a type of such occasional poetry, one that also draws on the classical model of panegyric. The composition belongs to a larger collection of verse entitled *Silvae* (*'Forests'*). These look most immediately to the Roman poet Statius' *Silvae* as their model in terms of metre, length and topic, but are also informed by the fields of oratory and declamation.

Readers may be struck by the diversity of topics addressed in Neo-Latin poetry. There was seemingly no bar to the subject matter that could be treated in poetry. A huge diffusion of poems engaged with areas of science, for example, and many great scientists were also accomplished poets, such as the Danish astronomer Tycho Brahe.[37] Girolamo Fracastoro's poem in dactylic hexameter about syphilis (Text 5) is a prime example and constituted a significant contribution to the medical exploration of epidemic disease, even as it sought to maximize the expressive and denotive potential of Latin. Classical models for scientific themes were not lacking, and early modern poets who penned poems about plague would naturally look to writers like Virgil and Lucretius as well as to the prose account of the Greek historian Thucydides.

Fracastoro's *Syphilis* therefore takes us into a variety of genres that we might loosely place under the umbrella of science. Yet, as scholars have observed, it is misleading to speak of 'science' per se in the period from 1400 to 1800.[38] Rather, an intensified interest in answering the questions left open by earlier traditions, matched with a growing readiness to interrogate these traditions' long-held truths, resulted in a succession of critical advances in the fields we now know as the sciences. Latin was crucial to the pursuit and promulgation of all such research, not least because of the technical precision Latin offered and its role as a lingua franca between natural philosophers across Europe. A keen interest in medicine, but also in topography, geography and natural philosophy, is clearly on display in the works of the Swiss writer Conrad Gessner. In *Descriptio Montis Fracti sive Montis Pilati, iuxta Lucernam in Helvetia* ('*A Description of the Fräckmünt or Mount Pilatus, near Lucerne in Switzerland*', Text 9) Gessner describes the mountain terrain of Mount Pilatus, surveying not just the effect of the mountain air on the body, but also the area's flora, fauna and quality of spring water. Such approaches would, in time, give rise to the natural sciences, while the encyclopedic tendencies exhibited in this work have much in common with the genre of scholarship.

The discipline of philosophy as established and entrenched in antiquity had obvious relevance for the development of all subsequent philosophical writing. There has been no philosopher in the Western tradition who was not in some way or another indebted to classical philosophical systems.[39] In the first instance, early modern philosophers were profoundly influenced by late medieval philosophy and the Aristotelian ideas and methodologies that had been introduced during that period. This notwithstanding, modes of philosophical enquiry underwent a series of radical transformations. Humanist translations of newly discovered Greek philosophical materials (chiefly Plato and the Neo-Platonists) had a profound effect on the practice of philosophical writing and the concepts that were now broached. Philosophers also inhabited a world in which Christianity dominated, so that questions on the nature of God and man's relationship with God were central to many contemporary philosophical tracts. This is exemplified in Gottfried Wilhelm Leibniz's *Confessio philosophi* ('*The philosopher's confession*'), which interrogates the relationship between determinism and free will (Text 18). This counts as Leibniz's first substantial contribution to a lifelong interest in theodicy. Greater levels of sensitivity concerning historicity and cultural relativism, in parallel with profound shifts in metaphysics and epistemology, likewise had an impact on philosophical practices. In particular, the work of René Descartes (who wrote in Latin as well as in French) marked a significant break from the Aristotelian tradition. The importance of Cartesianism may be witnessed in the *Principia philosophiae antiquissimae & recentissimae* ('*Principles of the most ancient and modern philosophy*') by Anne Conway, a text that conveys a deep concern with the notion of existence and the relationship between body and spirit (Text 15).

Descartes' influence would be felt in a wide range of disciplines, including mathematics and physics, whose most famous early modern proponent, Isaac Newton, is also featured in this volume (Text 17). Newton's *Philosophiae naturalis principia mathematica* ('*Mathematical principles of natural philosophy*'), the foundational work of modern physics, opened with a devastating critique of Descartes.[40] While the physical world was the ostensible focus of this work, the ground covered in the section extracted in this volume, the General Scholium, was distinctly theological in flavour. Newton's explicit reconciliation of the role of God within Nature and his explicitly anti-Cartesian stance entailed a holistic conception of the fields of natural philosophy and theology, an approach that was very much in line with his great predecessors, such as Nicolaus Copernicus and Johannes Kepler.

Theology itself had a central place in the intellectual life of Europe. From the New Testament onwards, Christians have sought to combine faith with reason, and specifically with the classical philosophical tradition, in order to better understand God's nature and message, and to define orthodoxy. In the high Middle Ages theology had developed into a highly formal and complex university discipline, requiring extensive training in formal logic and in the works of Aristotle.

With the onset of the Reformation and the birth of printing, theology remained a vital genre, but its proper scope and methods became subject to vigorous controversy. Traditional approaches, such as the framework of dialectic that had shaped theological debates throughout the medieval period, and especially the use of the technical, 'scholastic' Latin of the university theology faculties, came under serious challenge. The theological output of the early modern period expressed this reaction and was especially marked by a new emphasis on historical consciousness and the appropriation of classical topoi, style and rhetoric. Reformers like John Calvin produced theological treatises that combined doctrinal *gravitas* with Ciceronian flair. Martin Luther, too, as illustrated in the extracts from his work *De abroganda missa privata* ('*On the necessary removal of the private mass*') harvested principles of classical oratory so as to inject his polemics with greater elan and eloquence

(Text 6). The Reformation is often associated with the demise rather than the resurgence of Latin, but many of the most important of the works produced in the Catholic–Protestant reformation controversy were written in Latin. Reformers on both sides of the divide, especially Jesuits, continued to view Latin as the foremost language of theological discourse and to use it as such.

Of the final two genres represented in this volume, the first is the textual commentary. A spectacular number of Neo-Latin commentaries were produced between 1400 and 1700. Writers used the form to meditate on and investigate a huge spectrum of texts and topics, from ethnography to jurisprudence, zoology to diplomacy. Medieval scholars commented on classical and indeed medieval literary texts, but the bulk of their efforts was devoted to canonical texts, such as the Bible and Aristotle. With the arrival of the Renaissance, there was an unparalleled diffusion of commentaries on classical texts, for example. In this species of commentary, the late antique commentator on Virgil, Servius, became an important point of departure, and had a significant influence on textual interpretation and the reception of classical works and also on the creation of a canon. Commentaries became so popular that ancient texts were often primarily accessed through these intermediary forms, such as the monumental work on Virgil by Juan Luis de la Cerda (Text 14).

The function and significance of the commentary involved more than simply textual criticism. Rather, the commentary stood as a medium for collating and transmitting information. Commentaries therefore fall into the larger genre we term 'scholarship', which also proliferated during the early modern period and is a key marker of the advances in historical and scientific learning. In this genre, Jean Mabillon's pioneering *De re diplomatica* ('*On diplomatics*', Text 16) was an ambitious and far-reaching investigation into different types of medieval documents and manuscripts, including scrutiny of their scripts, style and relevant comparanda, and the confirmation of authentic documentation and the detection of forgeries. The book is now viewed as the foundational work of palaeography and diplomatics.

Aims and coverage of this volume

The field of Neo-Latin has been described as a 'lost continent'.[41] Given the sheer scale of the body of Latin literature composed between the fourteenth and eighteenth centuries across the globe, all we can hope to do in this volume is offer an aperitif to whet a reader's appetite for further study. This anthology presents fourteen genres from nine modern European nations. The regions represented are those that have tended to be associated with a more traditional and conservative understanding of a western European bloc, but there is every reason that future Neo-Latin anthologies will place focus on the prolific Neo-Latin of, for example, eastern Europe, Scandinavia and Spain. To put our volume into some perspective – larger surveys of early modern Neo-Latin literature cover approximately thirty countries or regions and over a hundred genre-based divisions.[42]

Given this immense scale and variety, editorial decisions about what to include and what to leave out of this miscellany were difficult: there is no right way to select nineteen texts to represent 500 years of 'European' Latin. As the previous section sketched out, we chose generic division as, on balance, the most helpful organizational principle, and selected texts that seemed able to chart the core characteristics of the generic range. Such an approach has enabled us to widen the field of contributors, to include scholars from beyond the discipline of Classics and its hinterlands. We hope in turn to attract an interdisciplinary readership. We also feel that a selection by genre is preferable to one by 'nations', as it more accurately reflects the world of Neo-Latin and the nature of the Republic of Letters. While an overview of the Neo-Latin produced in a single geographical area, such as has been done in the anthology of British Neo-Latin literature in this same series, can helpfully chart a region's cultural and historical trends, categorizing according to national borders is contentious. It is not at all straightforward to speak of, say, Swiss Neo-Latin, whereas there certainly is such a phenomenon as theological Neo-Latin. Moreover, many of the authors featured in this volume, while they could in theory be assigned a single country of origin, spent much of their life elsewhere. Buchanan (Text 7), for example, though a Scot, was raised and educated in France and resided there for many years. Erasmus, a Dutchman by birth, was essentially an international scholar who travelled extensively, feted by courts across Europe for his humanist learning.

Division by genre also prompted us to offer space to less well-known authors as well as the more famous. While there can be no doubt that certain Neo-Latin figures were deeply influential in the standards they set, the textual blueprints they forged and their impact on the further development of genres, the very issue of 'familiarity' in modern times is a complex one. It is often the case that writers who were in their own time highly celebrated have fallen into relative obscurity precisely because fewer modern readers are able to access the works they wrote in Latin. On the other hand, a writer's lack of success in his/her own time does not necessarily imply a concomitant lack of historical or literary value. Furthermore, and perhaps surprisingly, the Latin writing of well-known authors does not always have a corresponding translation in English (parts of a treatise by Luther are translated for the first time in this anthology).

A further consideration for the editors was that of gender. Women's voices have tended to be rather muted in Neo-Latin digests, most immediately because the bulk of published texts was by men. Even so, as a spate of recent scholarship is powerfully demonstrating, there are numerous examples of women who knew Latin and were proficient in it.[43] A number of these were female royals or noble women who benefited from the privileged place of Latin at courts across Europe and who tended to be given the same instruction as their male counterparts. Queen Elizabeth I of England (1533–1603) was instructed in advanced Latin and Greek composition, as was Queen Christina of Sweden (1626–86). Nuns in convents often attained high levels of learning in Latin, and in the seventeenth century a number of women successfully secured entrance into academies and universities on the Continent.[44] Some women even had the unusual distinction of having their works in Latin published – for example, the English-Czech poet, Elizabeth Jane Weston.[45] This notwithstanding, the bilingualism of the early modern intellectual culture more often than not stood as a barrier rather than an opportunity for women. It is revealing that the one female author featured in this volume, Anne Conway (Text 15), wrote her *Principles of the most ancient and modern philosophy* in English (subsequently translated into Latin). While the potential for women to be versed in Latin may be inferred from another section of this anthology, namely the excerpt from Erasmus' *Colloquia* (Text 3), which benignly portrays a learned lady at the expense of a doltish abbot, this is a fictive female voice in a tract written by a man.

This volume also aims to provide a meaningful chronological snapshot. In this, we have decided to begin *c.* 1500, leaving out the first flowering of Neo-Latin in the Italian Renaissance. This implies no deprecation: rather, we consider that a wide selection of texts from that period is already more readily available, owing most notably to the vigorous Italian tradition of philological study of the Renaissance and to the wide range of translations into English provided by the *I Tatti Renaissance Library*. Still, our selections begin with two exuberant creations of Italian humanism, from the late fifteenth and early sixteenth centuries. We then move through a medley of texts from the sixteenth and on to the philosophical trailblazing and the explosion in knowledge acquisition of the late seventeenth and early eighteenth centuries.

The extracts also seek to convey a sense of the stylistic range of Neo-Latin. Many of the authors included in this volume adhered to a classically honed, rhetorically affective and elegant Latinity, often developed in self-conscious opposition to the drier Latin of the medieval schoolmen. The view that texts should both teach and delight had considerable currency. Bembo (Text 4), for example, cultivated an exquisite Ciceronian style in his work of history.[46] Stylistic trends were by no means static, and Cicero and Virgil were not always the supreme guides; other stylistic ideals emerged, some cleaving to other ancient authors like Tacitus and even to contemporary ones such as Erasmus, the Flemish humanist Justus Lipsius or (in poetry) the Italian Giovanni Gioviano Pontano.[47] Nor can talk of literary models do full justice to the linguistic reality of Neo-Latin. In many cases, Latin style remained utilitarian. For example, it is clear from Bellarmine's letter (Text 12) that Latin could be used simply as a convenient and economic medium for conveying a message. Newton's Latin (Text 17), too, is noticeably workaday. Although many who operated in the field of science also prized a refined Latin style, scientific Latin appears to have often been a working language rather than one of display.[48]

Nevertheless, the majority of the texts included in this anthology were composed by humanists whose primary agenda was to emulate and, if possible, to surpass the ancient models that they held in such high esteem. The practice of *imitatio* was fundamental, and occurred at both the macro level, in terms of generic reproduction and general themes, and at the micro level, as evidenced by the frequent classical syntax, diction and allusions in so many texts in this volume. For readers, knowledge of this classical legacy is necessary and illuminating, certainly, but compendia of classical parallels without further consideration of the contemporary context where they are used is an arid exercise. The contributors to this volume have instead attempted to address the different ways in which early modern texts worked in dynamic dialogue with the classical tradition. Pagan terms of reference can look to modern eyes highly incongruous, especially when, for example, woven into the overtly Christian framework of so many early modern works. So, for instance, in Sannazaro's orthodox Catholic poem on the Virgin Mary (Text 2), God is calqued onto Jupiter and the angel Gabriel onto Mercury. Yet such phenomena must be understood in light of early modern humanists' total immersion in classical writing, internalized to the point of perfect fluency of recall and recombination.[49] The writers of this era felt a deep level of comfort with the pagan past they had recreated and imagined: beyond easy comparisons, this led as far as reformulation of the idea of civilization itself in terms of the ancient models.

Despite the humanist origins of the Neo-Latin register and its related literary interests, works written in Latin were not merely focused on a classical past and, in this sense, somehow backward-looking. As individual entries in this anthology highlight, the more immediate contexts and purposes of individual authors could be very determinative of form and content. Engagement with other literatures, including Scripture and patristics, along with other contemporary works both in Latin and the vernacular, could also be instrumental in shaping the contours of a text. Indeed, within Neo-Latin research,[50] the nature of Latin's relationship with the rising vernacular languages is currently generating increased attention. While the focus of this volume is Neo-Latin, certain entries draw attention to the multidirectional exchanges possible between different linguistic repertoires – for example, as regards the translation into Latin of Anne Conway's philosophical tract (Text 15), the German counterpart of Luther's Neo-Latin *De abroganda missa privata* (Text 6) or the parody of vernacular-inflected Latin in the *EOV* (Text 8).

The texts can be read in the order presented. At the same time, they are all self-contained and may be studied selectively and individually. Each entry opens with an introduction, offering necessary background on the biography of the writer, the context of the work in question and important features of the selected passage. This is followed by the original Latin text accompanied by a modern English translation and attached commentary notes (keyed to line numbers for verse passages and to numerical references within the text in the case of prose texts). Beyond this standard structure, details vary between entries according to what is most appropriate for each author and text, and also what contributors, approaching these texts from different angles, have chosen to highlight. These differences of approach are integral to one of the overriding aims of this book, which is to introduce readers not simply to a broad range of texts, but also to the broad spread of possible ways to engage with the study of Neo-Latin literature.

Latin texts: sources and conventions

One of the pleasures of working with early modern texts is that it is possible to consult original editions (now often available online). Thus, some of the Latin texts in this book have been taken directly from early printed books; some of the popular ones were printed so frequently in the early modern period that a decision had to be made as to which edition should be used for reference. In the case of some entries new modern editions could be adduced, and their versions of the texts have then generally been compared with the original editions. The basis for the text given is identified in each instance.

Despite the standardization we have broadly adopted, the early modern layout of these texts is not unimportant to the study of Neo-Latin. Since authors often liaised closely with their printers, the arrangement of the words on the page, the use of marginalia, the choice of typeface or the decision to employ particular abbreviations have to be regarded as potentially meaningful details of a composition.

Early modern practices regarding the presentation of Latin texts can initially seem quite confusing. For the convenience of readers, the texts included in this book have been slightly adjusted and standardized to match modern conventions (often following modern editions of these texts where they exist). For instance, the medial <s>, <ſ>, has been replaced by <s>, and <ij> by <ii>; ligatures such as <æ> and <œ> have been written as two letters <ae> and <oe>, and abbreviations have been resolved. Medieval spellings have mostly been adjusted to their more classical forms, and we do not envisage there will be any difficulty with more obvious orthographical variants. The accentuation of words (diacritics), which was another common feature of the early modern presentation of Latin, has similarly not been reproduced. Capitalization has also been standardized. Moreover, readers of Neo-Latin cannot escape some outlandish (to modern eyes) uses of punctuation. For example, commas were often used (sometimes in order to assist with oral delivery) where they would not be in a modern text, and authors / printers would put an exclamation mark where nowadays a question mark is used. We have generally modernized the punctuation, at least where it was most likely to cause confusion. We have assumed readers are familiar with the practice of verbal contractions, which are common in Latin more generally, and these have accordingly not been systematically explained.

Neo-Latin texts often comprised more than the main text. Editions might include elaborate prefaces and dedicatory letters or poems (so-called 'paratexts'), which can offer intriguing information about the contemporary cultural and intellectual background. A good example is the General Scholium to Newton's third edition of his *Principia mathematica* (Text 17).

As for the translations, contributors have sought to produce felicitous renderings into English, but ones that remain faithful to the Latin. The translations are not intended to be definitive: their primary aim is to help readers make their way through the Latin.

This volume does not provide a word list or a glossed vocabulary; so, for the purposes of independent interpretations, other lexicographical resources may be necessary (for an overview of Neo-Latin reference works and tools see Knight / Tilg 2015: 575–9). Lewis and Short's *Latin Dictionary* should, for the most part, be sufficient, not least because of the classical configuration of so much of the Latin in the passages provided. Due to the broader chronological scope of its coverage of Latin usage, Lewis and Short can yield more helpful results than the *Oxford Latin Dictionary* for post-classical Latin texts and their sources. For later Latin coinages and for early modern linguistic nuances, additional sources of information are available, such as Johann Ramminger's *Neulateinische Wortliste* (http://ramminger.userweb.mwn.de). A number of Latin dictionaries useful for reading Neo-Latin texts, including Lewis and Short alongside Du Cange, are available via the Logeion website (http://logeion.uchicago.edu).

Notes

1 The concept of Europe's Latin millennium is borrowed from the title of chapter 3 in Leonhardt 2013: 122–244.
2 The coinage 'Neo-Latin' had its origins in Germany in about the 1760s as 'Neulatein' or 'neulateinisch' (Knight / Tilg 2015: 1).
3 A point robustly made in Sidwell 1995: preface.
4 For the place of Cicero and Virgil in the development of Neo-Latin as well as an overview of the register's linguistic characteristics see J. Ramminger, 'Neo-Latin: Character and Development', in Kallendorf / Ford / Bloemendal / Fantazzi 2015: 21–36.
5 On Valla and the *Elegantiae* and for a sketch of the work's wide-reaching influence for the Neo-Latin world see Korenjak 2016: 131–3.
6 For Valla's early contributions to the fields of historical, biblical and philosophical scholarship, within the history of Neo-Latin literature see Ostler 2007: 244–6.
7 Poggio's *Orationes in Laurentium Vallam* ('*Speeches against Lorenzo Valla*') and Valla's *Antidota in Pogium* ('*A remedy against Poggio*') (*c.* 1453) represent highpoints of these humanists' conflict.
8 Valla's *De falso credita et ementita Constantini Donatione declamatio* ('*Speech on the forged and falsely attributed Donation of Constantine*', *c.* 1440) and his *Adnotationes in Novum Testamentum* ('*Notes on the New Testament*') are examples of this philological approach to ecclesiastical and holy scripture.
9 The irony and humour of Poggio's *Orationes* showcases an approach to literary work very different from the dense, dry style of his opponent's *Elegantiae*.
10 On the debate over Latin style generally, and the opposition between camps of Ciceronianism and a more moderate, eclectic style, see T. Tunberg, 'Approaching Neo-Latin Prose as Literature', in Moul 2017: 237–54.
11 On the turn in literary culture after the invention of the printing press see Eisenstein 1979.
12 On Latin as a lingua franca for diverse groups all across Europe (and even outside of it) see Burke 2014: 45–8. Latin was already a medieval lingua franca, but in the early modern period Latin was increasingly standardized and used over a wider geographical area and by a greater range of socio-economic groups.
13 For a general introduction to the 'Republic of Letters', its various changes and impact even today in a digital world see van Miert 2016: 269–87.
14 On Nebrija's Latin philological work and his application of these techniques to Castilian within the context of contemporary European discussion of Latin see Ostler 2007: 256–9.
15 For Innu-aimun (Montagnais) see Jean-Baptiste de la Brosse, *Montanicae linguae elementa* ('*Rudiments of the Montagnais language*', 1768). For Japanese see Diego Collado, *Ars grammaticae Iaponicae linguae* ('*Grammar of the Japanese language*', 1632).

16 On Latin's general position in education early in the period see Black 2001: 1–5.

17 Korenjak 2016: 118–20. Works on the moral training of pupils by means of intensive engagement with ancient authors in the original included Juan Luis Vives' *Introductio ad sapientiam* ('*Introduction to wisdom*', 1524) and Erasmus' *De pueris instituendis* ('*On educating boys*', 1529).

18 On the spread of this learning style and its contact with various layers of society see Bloemendal 2016: 92–7.

19 A concise overview of Neo-Latin alongside increasing literary production in various European vernaculars is offered in Leonhardt 2013: 206–9; see also Winkler / Schaffenrath 2018.

20 For a detailed overview of this field see A. M. Blair, A. Laird, M. Mund-Dopchie and Z. von Martels, 'Latin and the New World', in Kallendorf / Ford / Bloemendal / Fantazzi 2015.

21 For a general introduction to Linnaeus' Latin, including the continued use of his system today, within an account of Latin's history as a whole, see Janson 2007: 152–6.

22 For a recent overview of Neo-Latin and the natural sciences see Korenjak 2016: 234–53; on the frequent translations from the European vernaculars into Latin in general see Korenjak 2016: 145–7. On the translation of works from the vernacular into Latin particularly to ensure their cultural status see Bloemendal 2016: 185–7.

23 For a statement of Neo-Latin's constant contemporary cultural relevance see Korenjak 2019: 14–15.

24 For the statistics see Würgler 2009: 40. For a 'lost Atlantis' see Cameron 1941: 403.

25 For a poem on tea see Pierre Petit, *Thia Sinensis* ('*Chinese Tea*', 1685); for a study of Iranian poetry see William Jones, *Poeseos Asiaticae commentariorum libri sex* ('*Six books of commentaries on Asian poetry*', 1774).

26 Most recently, Moul 2017, but see also Knight and Tilg 2015, which dedicates one of three sections to 'Language and Genre'; Kallendorf / Ford / Bloemendal / Fantazzi 2015; and IJsewijn and Sacré 1990–8.

27 Moul 2017: introduction.

28 As detailed studies of Neo-Latin works are increasingly demonstrating.

29 Although, as Peter Burke points out, there was 'an ever-shifting division of labour' between Latin and the vernacular ('"*Heu domine, adsunt Turcae*": A sketch for a History of Post-Medieval Latin', in Burke 1993: 56). Burke is rightly interested in the sociolinguistic frameworks in which Neo-Latin developed and in the 'politics of choice' about which language to write in (Burke 2004).

30 Knight / Tilg 2015: 3.

31 See Leonardo Bruni, *History of the Florentine People*, ed. and trans. by J. Jankins, 3 vols, Cambridge MA, 2001–7 (I Tatti Renasissance Library 3, 16, 27); and G. Ianziti, 'Challenging Chronicles: Leonardo Bruni's History of the Florentine People', in S. Dale, A. Williams Lewin and D. J. Osheim (eds),

Chronicling History: Chroniclers and their Historians in Medieval and Renaissance Italy, Philadelphia 2007.

32 F. Mundt, 'Historiography', in Moul 2017: 358–76, at 373.

33 C. Kidwell, *Pietro Bembo: Lover, Linguist, Cardinal*, Montreal / Kingston 2004: 360.

34 For the importance of Petrarch in the development of this genre see J. Glomski, 'Epistolary Writing', in Moul 2017: 255–71.

35 Glomski, 'Epistolary Writing', 258.

36 See E. Haan, 'Pastoral', in Moul 2017: 163–79, at 164.

37 IJsewijn / Sacré 1998: vol. 2, 59.

38 Knight / Tilg 2015: 263.

39 Kallendorf / Ford / Bloemendal / Fantazzi 2015: 659.

40 Kallendorf / Ford / Bloemendal / Fantazzi 2015: 661.

41 J. Hankins, 'The Lost Continent of Neo-Latin Literature and the Rise of Modern European Literatures; Catalog of an Exhibition at the Houghton Library, 5 March – 5 May 2001', *Harvard Library Bulletin*, 12 (2001): 1–92.

42 IJsewijn / Sacré 1990–8.

43 For example: J. Stevenson, *Women Latin Poets*, Oxford 2005; L. J. Churchill, P. R. Brown and J. E. Jeffrey (eds), *Women Writing Latin*, vol. 3: *Early Modern Women Writing Latin*, 3 vols, New York / Abingdon 2002; and see also the bibliography in 'Gender', in Knight / Tilg 2015: 374–7.

44 'Gender', in Knight / Tilg 2015: 370–3.

45 D. Cheney, *Neo-Latin Women Writers: Elizabeth Jane Weston and Bathusa Reginald (Makin)*, London / New York 2016.

46 Kallendorf / Ford / Bloemendal / Fantazzi 2015: 926.

47 A point developed in Winkler / Schaffenrath 2018: 2 and *passim*.

48 Kallendorf / Ford / Bloemendal / Fantazzi 2015: 703.

49 P. Hardie, 'Vida's *De arte poetica* and the Transformation of Models', in *Apodosis: Essays Presented to Dr. W. W. Cruickshank to Mark His Eightieth Birthday*, London 1992: 47–53, at 48.

50 Deneire 2014; Bloemendal 2015; Winkler / Schaffenrath 2018.

Bibliography

Black, R. (2001), *Humanism and Education in Medieval and Renaissance Italy: Tradition and Innovation in Renaissance Schools from the Twelfth to the Fifteenth Centuries*, Cambridge.

Bloemendal, J., ed. (2015), *Bilingual Europe: Latin and Vernacular Cultures – Examples of Bilingualism and Multiculturalism c. 1300–1800*, Leiden / Boston.

Bloemendal, J. (2016), *Latijn. Cultuurgeschiedenis van een Wereldtaal*, Amsterdam.

Burke, P., ed. (1993), *The Art of Conversation*, Cambridge.

Burke, P. (2004), *Languages and Communities in Early Modern Europe*, Cambridge.
Cameron, A. (1941), 'Latin Literature', *Modern Language Quarterly*, 2: 403–20.
Deneire, T., ed. (2014), *Dynamics of Neo-Latin and the Vernacular. Language and Poetics, Translation and Transfer*, Leiden / Boston.
Eisenstein, E. (1979), *The Printing Press as an Agent of Change*, 2 vols, Cambridge.
IJsewijn, J. and D. Sacré (1990–8), *Companion to Neo-Latin Studies*, 2 vols, Leuven.
Janson, T. (2007), *A Natural History of Latin*, Oxford.
Kallendorf, C., A. Ford, J. Bloemendal and C. Fantazzi, eds (2015), *Brill's Encyclopaedia of the Neo-Latin World*, Leiden.
Knight, S. and S. Tilg, eds (2015), *The Oxford Handbook of Neo-Latin*, Oxford.
Korenjak, M. (2016), *Geschichte der neulateinischen Literatur. Vom Humanismus bis zur Gegenwart*, Munich.
Korenjak, M. (2019), *Neulatein: Eine Textsammlung. Latein / Deutsch*, Stuttgart.
Leonhardt, J. (2013), *Latin: The Story of a World Language*, Cambridge MA [translated by K. Kronenberg; original German - Munich 2009].
van Miert, D. (2016), 'What was the Republic of Letters? A brief introduction to a long history (1417–2008)', *Groniek*, 204: 269–87.
Moul, V., ed. (2017), *A Guide to Neo-Latin Literature*, Cambridge.
Ostler, N. (2007), *Ad infinitum: A Biography of Latin*, New York.
Sidwell, S. (1995), *Reading Medieval Latin*, Cambridge.
Winkler, A. and F. Schaffenrath, eds (2018), *Neo-Latin and the Vernaculars*, Leiden / Boston.
Würgler, A. (2009), 'Medien in der frühen Neuzeit', in *Enzyklopädie deutscher Geschichte*, vol. 84, Munich.

1

A Pastoral Exchange on the Treatment of Poets

Battista Spagnoli Mantovano (1447–1516), *Adolescentia* 5.1–23, 68–91, 111–25

Bobby Xinyue

Introduction

Battista Spagnoli (1447–1516) was one of the most prolific writers of Latin verse in the Renaissance, with a total output of around 55,000 verses to his name. Often referred to as 'Mantuanus' (or, in England since the Renaissance, 'Mantuan'), from his birthplace, Mantua (where his Spanish family had settled since 1435),[1] he began his education with Gregorio Tifernate and Giorgio Merula, before moving to Padua in the early 1460s to study philosophy. He entered the Carmelite order in early 1463 and, after spending two years as a novice in Ferrara, went on to have a distinguished career within the order, holding the role of vicar general of the Mantuan Congregation six times before becoming the prior general of the entire order in 1513. While Mantovano's life was spent mainly between Mantua and Bologna, he came to Rome on a number of occasions and was centrally involved in successful reforms to the Carmelite order.[2] A number of his works – for example, the *De calamitatibus temporum* (1479) and the *Parthenice Mariana* (1482) – were focused on religious and moral issues.

Mantovano's best-known work is the *Adolescentia*, a collection of ten eclogues, first printed in Mantua in 1498, and so called because (according to the author himself) it was written in his youth (*ab illa aetate Adulescentiam vocaveram*, 'I had called it *Youth*, from that period of my life').[3]

As scholars have established,[4] the 1498 edition of the *Adolescentia* consists of eight eclogues (poems 1 to 8), originally published as a collection sometime between 1471 and 1476 under the title *Suburbanus* ('*The Rustic*'), and two eclogues (poems 9 and 10) composed later in the 1480s. A date range of 1460 to 1463 can be given for the original composition of the first eight eclogues, which went on to have a gestation period in the 1460s before they were published as the *Suburbanus*.[5] What would eventually become eclogues 9 and 10 in the *Adolescentia* were composed separately: the first was written in the mid-1480s and dedicated to Falcone de' Sinibaldi, and the second sometime between 1486 and 1488 and dedicated to Bernardo Bembo.[6] The 1498 edition of the *Adolescentia* contains a dedicatory letter addressed to Paride Ceresara, in which Mantovano describes why he decided to publish the work. He claims that he encountered a manuscript copy of the original eight eclogues in Bologna in 1497 and wanted to destroy the work as it contained 'much that was too youthful' (*multa nimis iuvenilia*); however, finding that too many copies were already in circulation, he resolved to revise the eclogues and to append the two later eclogues to the original eight. The reliability of the letter's information is suspect. Mantovano's account has resonances of the stories of the near-destruction of Virgil's *Aeneid* and the revised publication of Ovid's *Amores*.[7] Moreover, it seems too convenient that Mantovano came across a copy of his early pastoral poetry at Bologna in the year 1497: in that year, an early printed edition of Petrarch's *Bucolicum carmen* was produced in the same city. Seen in this light, Mantovano's 'chance discovery' of his youthful work is best understood as an attempt to breathe new life into his earlier poetry at a time when there was heightened interest in pastoral poetry.

That the *Adolescentia* is the product of a creative process spanning over thirty years is reflected in the polyphony, thematic diversity and intertextual activities of the collection. The *Adolescentia* begins with four poems on the nature of love, culminating in a deeply misogynist portrayal of women in the fourth eclogue. Eclogues 5 and 6 then deal respectively with the greed of rich men and the contrasting ways of the city and the country. From eclogue 7 onwards the collection becomes more focused on religion, with the poet's involvement in the reform of the Carmelite order and his deep antipathy towards the corruption and decadence within his order and the Church at large prominently foregrounded. While the presence of Virgil's *Eclogues* can be felt throughout, there is 'an earthiness and workaday quality about Mantuan's shepherds more pervasive and striking than anything found in previous Latin pastoral'.[8] Conversing fluently with a wide range of ancient and early modern texts – encompassing Ovidian elegies, Juvenal's *Satires*, biblical literature, medieval debate poetry, Petrarch's and Boccaccio's pastoral poetry, *fabliaux* and *bergerie* literature, and the epigrams of Giovanni Gioviano Pontano and Ugolino Verino – the *Adolescentia* oscillates between Arcadian contemplation, Christian religiosity and rustic realism.[9] Enlivened by the frequent intrusion of elements extraneous to bucolic texture[10] and underpinned by a dynamic (and often ironic) engagement with literary conventions and moral and religious questions, the *Adolescentia* resists a narrowly biographical reading.

The immediate and long-lasting popularity of the *Adolescentia* is attested by the fact that, between 1498 and 1600, the work was reprinted more than 160 times. Mantovano's Latin gained a reputation for its succinctness and erudition, and the collection quickly established itself as a textbook in schools across Europe.[11] Mantovano was praised by Erasmus (see Text 3) as the *Christianus Maro* ('Christian Virgil'),[12] and the eclogues were especially popular north of the Alps.[13] In 1502, just four years after the first printed edition of the *Adolescentia*, Jodocus Badius Ascensius (Josse Bade) published a commentary on the poem;[14] two years later Mantovano's eclogues appeared alongside those of Virgil, Calpurnius Siculus and Petrarch in an edition printed in Italy.[15] The work became so well known in the second half of the sixteenth century that it appeared in William Shakespeare's *Love's Labour's Lost* (IV.2.112–19).

The passages presented here come from the fifth eclogue. The poem amounts to a complaint about the greed and dishonourable behaviour of patrons, a topic well treated by a number of ancient and Renaissance texts, among them: Theocritus' *Idyll* 16, Juvenal's *Satires* 1 and 7, and Poggio Bracciolini's *De avaritia*. Mantovano's poem is a dialogue between two shepherds, Sylvanus and Candidus, the latter suffering from the stinginess of the wealthy. Candidus' appearance here is the first of four in the *Adolescentia*. Badius suggests that Candidus is an authorial persona – the commentator clearly has in mind the well-established tradition of identifying Virgil with the *Eclogues*' Tityrus. However, just as that equivalence is fluid and multivalent, there is no reason to assume that Candidus is an accurate portrait of Mantovano or that the poem is singularly informed by personal experience.

Metre: dactylic hexameter

Notes

1 Hence the name 'Spagnoli' (also sometimes 'Spagnulo' or 'Spagnolo'). His paternal grandfather, Antonio Modover, came to Italy from Cordova.
2 See Saggi 1954.
3 Dedicatory letter of the 1498 edition.
4 See especially Piepho 1989 and Severi 2010, whose pioneering studies provide the basis of my summary.
5 We do not possess complete manuscript copies of earlier versions of eclogues 1–8 before they appeared as the *Suburbanus*. On the *Suburbanus* see Piepho 1989: 133–46 and Severi 2010: 63–85.

6 Earlier versions of eclogues 9 and 10 survive in manuscript copies: see Piepho 1986 and 1989: 146–59 and Severi 2010: 137–54.
7 Mantovano's account also evokes the prose epistolary preface to Ausonius' *Griphus ternarii numeri*.
8 Piepho 1989: xxxii.
9 Severi 2010: 208–10.
10 Fabbri 2005: 249.
11 Piepho 1989: xxvii.
12 See *Opus epistolarum Des. Erasmi Roterodami* (Oxford 1906–58), vol. 1, p. 163 (letter to Hendrik van Bergen, Bishop of Cambrai, 1496).
13 See Severi 2010: 391–475.
14 Baptista Mantuanus, *Adulescentia*, in: *Secundus operum B. Mantuani tomus*, Paris, ed. Badius Ascensius, 1513.
15 On the collection's printing history see Coccia 1960: 113–15.

Bibliography

Coccia, E. (1960), *Le edizioni delle opere del Mantovano*, Rome.

Fabbri, R. (2005), 'Le ecloghe di Battista Spagnoli il Mantovano', in P. Viti (ed.), *Letteratura, verità e vita. Studi in ricordo di Gorizio Viti*, 245–55, Rome.

Grant, W. L. (1965), *Neo-Latin Literature and the Pastoral*, Durham NC.

Hinds, S. (2017), 'Pastoral and its futures: reading like (a) Mantuan', *Dictynna*, 14 (https://journals.openedition.org/dictynna/1443).

Hubbard, T. K. (1998), *The Pipes of Pan*, Ann Arbor.

Mustard, W. P. (1911), *The Eclogues of Baptista Mantuanus*, Baltimore.

Nichols, F. J. (1969), 'The development of Neo-Latin theory of the pastoral in the sixteenth century', *Humanistica Lovaniensia*, 18: 95–114.

Piepho, L. (1986), 'Mantuan and religious pastoral: unprinted versions of his ninth and tenth eclogues', *Renaissance Quarterly*, 39, 644–72.

Piepho, L. (1989), *Adulescentia: The Eclogues of Mantuan. Edited and Translated*, New York.

Porter, W. (1981), 'Eclogue five of Mantuan (1448–1516), Candidus: on the treatment of poets by the wealthy', *Allegorica*, 6: 7–20.

Saggi, L. (1954), *La congregazione mantovana dei Carmelitani sino alla morte del B. Battista Spagnoli (1516)*, Rome.

Severi, A. (2010), *Adolescentia. Battista Spagnoli Mantovano: studio, edizione e traduzione*, Bologna.

Source of the Latin text

The Latin text has been taken from Severi 2010: 277–86.

Latin text

ECLOGA V

De consuetudine divitum erga poetas
Sylvanus Candidus

Sylv. Candide, nobiscum pecudes aliquando solebas
pascere et his gelidis calamos inflare sub umbris
et miscere sales simul et certare palestra.
Nunc autem, quasi pastores et rura perosus,
pascua sopito fugis et trahis ocia cantu.
Can. Vos quibus est res ampla domi, quibus ubera vaccae
plena ferunt, quibus alba greges mulctraria complent,
cymbia lacte nivent et pinguia prandia fumant,
carmina laudatis; si quid concinius exit,
plauditis ac laeti placidas extenditis aures.
Pro numeris vanas laudes et inania verba
redditis; interea pastor sitit, esurit, alget.
Sylv. Nonne potes curare greges et dicere versus,
cum vacat, et positis vitam traducere curis?
Can. Omnem operam gregibus pastorem impendere oportet:
ire, redire, lupos arcere, mapalia sepe
cingere, mercari paleas et pabula, victum
quaerere; nil superest ocii. Laudabile carmen
omnem operam totumque caput, Sylvane, requirit.
Grande utrumque opus est et nostris viribus impar.
Cum cecini, sitio; sitienti pocula nemo
porrigit. Irrident alii: 'Tibi penula,' dicunt,
'Candide, trita, genu nudum, riget hispida barba.'
. . .
Si vis nostras audire Camoenas,
erue sopitam de sollicitudine mentem:
vult hilares animos tranquillaque pectora carmen.
Torpeo, ut esuriem patiens et frigora milvus,
iam dudum squarrosa cutis, situs occupat ora,
nec pecus in stabulis, nec in agro farra, nec aurum
in loculis. Et vis positis me vivere curis?
Non facit ad nostros talis medicina dolores.
Fac alacrem, tege, pasce, gravi succurre senectae;
invenies promptum versu et cantare paratum!
Plena domus curas abigit, cellaria plena,

English translation

Eclogue V

On the conduct of rich men towards poets
Sylvanus Candidus

Sylv.: Candidus, once you used to graze your herd with us and blow on your pipe beneath this cool shade, and share jokes together with us and take part in our wrestling matches. But now, as if detesting shepherds and fields, you flee from [these] pastures and drag out your idle moments, having put your song to sleep.

Can.: You who have abundant means at home, whose cows have full udders, whose herds fill up the white pails, whose cups are whitened by milk and whose rich meals give off steam – you praise my songs; [and] if something more elegant [than usual] rings out, you applaud and happily extend a gentle ear. In return for my verses, you pay me in empty praises and hollow words; meanwhile [this] shepherd is thirsty, hungry and cold.

Sylv.: Surely you can look after your flocks and sing your verses when there is a free moment, and lead your life with your cares set aside?

Can.: A shepherd must devote all his effort to the flocks; [he must] keep coming and going, warding off the wolves, surrounding his huts with a fence, buying straw and feed, finding [himself] food. No leisure time remains. A praiseworthy song, Sylvanus, requires all my effort and the whole of my mind. Both [singing and herding] are substantial tasks and unequal to my strength. When I have sung, I get thirsty; [yet] no one holds out a cup to me in my thirsty state. Some mock me. They say: 'Candidus, your cloak is worn, your knees are bare, your beard is rough with bristles.'

. . .

If you want to hear my Muses, rescue my dulled mind from worry; a song desires pleasant thoughts and a tranquil heart. I am numb, like a kite suffering from hunger and cold. For some time now my skin is scaly, [and] my face is covered in dirt; there is neither herd in my stables, nor grains in my field, nor gold in my pockets: yet you want me to live 'with my cares put aside'? Such a remedy does not cure my woes. Provide me with joy, clothe me, feed me, help me in the weight of old age: [then] you will find me ready for poetry and prepared to sing. Anxieties are dispelled by a fully stocked home, a full pantry, a

plena penus plenique cadi plenaeque lagenae,
horrea plena, greges laeti, gravis aere crumena.
Tunc iuvat hybernos noctu vigilare decembres
ante focum et cineri ludos inarare bacillo,
torrere et tepidis tostas operire favillis
castaneas plenoque sitim restringere vitro
fabellasque inter nentes ridere puellas.
Tityrus (ut fama est) sub Moecenate vetusto
rura, boves et agros et martia bella canebat
altius et magno pulsabat sidera cantu.
Eloquium fortuna dabat; nos, debile vulgus,
pannosos, macie affectos, farragine pastos,
Aoniae fugiunt Musae, contemnit Apollo.

. . .

Sylv. Candide, vidisti Romam sanctique senatus
pontifices, ubi tot vates, ubi copia rerum
tantarum? Facile est illis ditescere campis.
Can. Deciperis me velle putans ditescere. Vesci
et lupus omne animal crudis existimat escis,
tuque putas alios quo tu pede claudere passum.
Non ego ditari cupio, sed vivere parvo.
Fac habeam tenuem sine solicitudine victum;
hoc contentus eam. Romana palatia vidi,
sed quid Roma putas mihi proderit? O Sylvane,
occidit Augustus nunquam rediturus ab Orco.
Si quid Roma dabit, nugas dabit; accipit aurum,
verba dat. Heu Romae nunc sola pecunia regnat!
Exsilium virtus patitur. Sperare iubemur
undique et in toto vates spe pascimur orbe.

full supply of food, both full jars and full flasks, a full granary, happy herds, [and] a purse heavy with coins. Then it delights [me] to stay awake at night before the fireplace in wintry Decembers and stir the ashes playfully with a stick. [Then I enjoy] roasting chestnuts and covering them with warm embers, quenching my thirst with a full glass, and laughing at idle stories among the spinning maids. Under the protection of ancient Maecenas, Tityrus (so they say) once sang more loftily of the countryside, of cattle and fields, and of the wars of Mars; and he struck the stars with his grand song. Good fortune gave him eloquence; but as for us – a feeble crowd, ragged, weakened by destitution, fed on scraps – the Aonian Muses flee us, and Apollo despises us.

. . .

Sylv.: Candidus, have you seen Rome and the bishops of her holy council, where so many poets, where so much wealth resides? It is easy to get rich in those fields.

Can.: You are mistaken in thinking that I want to get rich. Just as the wolf thinks that every animal feeds on raw flesh, so you think that others finish their step with the same foot as you do. I do not wish to be rich, but to live with little. Provide me with a slender diet free from care, and with this I should live content. I have seen Rome's palaces, but what do you think Rome can do for me? O Sylvanus, Augustus is dead, never to return from Orcus. If Rome will give anything, it will give useless trifles. It takes gold [and] gives only words [in return]. Alas, only money now rules in Rome! Virtue endures exile. Everywhere we go we are told to be hopeful, and all over the world we poets are fed on hope.

Commentary

1 The first two words, *Candide, nobiscum*, recall the opening of Virgil's first eclogue, where Meliboeus begins his song with *Tityre, tu*. Meliboeus, a dispossessed shepherd who is made to leave his land, remarks on Tityrus' secure and leisurely pastoral existence (*Tityre, tu patulae recubans sub tegmine fagi*, 'Tityrus, you lying under the canopy of a spreading beech . . .'). In Mantovano's eclogue, the roles are reversed: the poem's first speaker, Sylvanus, lives a trouble-free life, whereas his addressee, Candidus, suffers from poverty and worry.

2 *calamos inflare* has a Virgilian precedent: *tu calamos inflare levis, ego dicere versus* ('you blow on the slender reeds, I sing verses', *Ecl.* 5.2).

4 *pastores et rura perosus* echoes Petrarch, *Epistles* 3.5.103, *vallesque et rura perosus* ('detesting valleys and fields').

5 *ocia*, accusative plural of *ocium*, is a medieval spelling of *otium*; this spelling remained in common usage and appeared frequently side by side with *otium* in Renaissance Latin texts. *ocium* / *otium*, here translated as 'idle moments' but often meaning 'leisure', is a fundamental aspect of pastoral life. In Virgil's *Eclogues*, *otium* is the prerequisite condition for a shepherd's song and is desired by pastoral singers (e.g. 1.4–6 and 5.61). Shepherds are meant to enjoy *otium*, but here *trahis* ('you drag out') suggests that Candidus cannot take pleasure from his time spent in the pastoral world.

6 *res ampla domi*: Candidus shows his economic interest from the start. Mantovano reworks an expression that appears twice in Juvenal, *res angusta domi* ('scanty resources at home', 3.265; 6.357).

7–8 The anaphora of *quibus*, the quick succession of *alba, lacte, nivent* and the repetitive effect produced by *cymbia . . . pinguia prandia* combine to convey an overabundance of wealth. *alba greges mulctraria complent* evokes Virgil, *Georgics* 3.177, *nivea implebunt mulctraria vaccae* ('cows will fill the snowy-white pails').

9–10 *concinius* (or the classical spelling *concinnius*) is frequently used (by Cicero, in particular) in discussions pertaining to the aesthetic merit of speech. *extenditis aures*, as Mustard (1911: 135) observes, appears in Seneca, *Epistles* 40.3 (*nec extendat aures nec obruat*, 'one should neither have their ears outstretched nor block them'). But perhaps more relevant are the classical parallels for *placidas . . . aures*: (i) Virgil, *Aeneid* 4.440, *placidasque viri deus obstruit auris* ('and divine force renders deaf the man's gentle ears'), which recounts Aeneas' insusceptibility to Dido's desperate pleas; (ii) Ovid, *Epistulae ex Ponto* 1.2.127–8, *ergo tam placidas orator missus ad aures* | *ut propior patriae sit fuga nostra roga* ('and so, sent as an advocate to such gentle ears, ask for my banishment to be closer to home'), where Ovid asks Maximus to petition Augustus for the poet's return from exile. In both instances, as here, the men who can lend their 'gentle ears' are in a position to transform the lives of those who wish to be heard. And in both ancient cases they do not oblige.

11–12 As noted by Badius, these lines evoke Juvenal's complaint against stingy patrons in *Satires* 7, a substantial influence on Mantovano's poem: *didicit iam dives avarus | tantum admirari, tantum laudare disertos | ut pueri Iunonis avem* ('the miserly rich man has by now learned only to admire the eloquent, only to praise them, as boys do Juno's bird [the peacock]', 30–2). Candidus rejects praise as an adequate response to the merit of his artistic output and, in the process, commodifies his poetry. The issue of economic exchange is grafted onto the pastoral formula of song exchange. The subtle switch of Candidus' style of self-referral to the third person (*pastor*) drives home the point that he is an object of pity even to himself.

13–14 Sylvanus completely avoids the issue. Unattuned to Candidus' request and present condition, Sylvanus attributes Candidus' lack of poetic productivity to his poor time management. He dismisses Candidus' complaints of physical discomfort and economic exploitation with a coolly conceived ablative absolute (*positis . . . curis*, 14), a grammatical construction that insinuates that Candidus' worries about his well-being are a separate issue. The ablative absolute encloses *vitam traducere*: the word-positions mimic the contemptuous idea that the exploited individual is responsible for his own life (*vitam*), and that the initiative (implied by *traducere*) needs to come from within.

15–18 *sepe* (16) is the ablative singular of *saepes* ('fence', 'hedge'); the transformation of the diphthong -*ae*- into -*e*- is an orthographic medievalism that survived even into the eighteenth-century editions of some classical authors. The realities of a shepherd's working life are generally overlooked in Virgil's *Eclogues*. Indeed, Candidus' claim that rural labour uses up all his effort and leaves him with no time for leisure directly contradicts the convention that pastoral work and leisurely existence are symbiotic.

18–19 *Laudabile* is important, as later in the poem Mantovano distinguishes between good poetry that celebrates worthy things and corrupt poetry (*carmina . . . | perdita*, 149–50) that merely flatters its honorand, lacking integrity and artistry.

20 *nostris viribus impar*: declaring one's strength as being unable to cope with weighty tasks is a common trope, especially among Augustan poets

writing in 'lower' genres (e.g. lyric, amatory elegy, pastoral) and justifying why they are not embarking on an epic. But here Candidus literalizes the trope by explaining in the next sentence (21–2) that he lacks the actual physical strength and life's basic provisions to compose poetry.

21–2 *cum cecini, sitio; sitienti pocula nemo | porrigit*: at Virgil, *Eclogues* 5.45–7 a good song is compared to thirst-quenching water: *tale tuum carmen nobis, divine poeta, | … quale per aestum | dulcis aquae saliente sitim restinguere rivo* ('Divine poet, your song to me is … like quenching one's thirst in summer with the dancing stream of sweet water').

23 Echoed and expanded upon in Euricius Cordus' *Eclogues* 2.90–2 (published in 1514): *inauditi laceris in vestibus itis, | vix male defendit consutilis inguina cento, | nuda rigent genua, attrita pes exit aluta* ('without listeners you walk in torn clothes, a badly sewn-up rag barely protecting the groin, bare knees stiff from the cold, [and] your foot protrudes from the worn leather shoe').

68 *nostras … Camoenas*: the Roman Camenae have been identified with the Greek Muses since the third century BCE (cf. Livius Andronicus, *Od.* fr. 1).

70 This sentiment has two important ancient precedents: (i) Ovid, *Tristia* 1.1.39, *carmina proveniunt animo deducta sereno* ('poetry comes fine-spun from a mind at ease'); (ii) Juvenal, *Satires* 7.53–6, *sed vatem egregium … anxietate carens animus facit* ('but a mind freed from anxiety makes an outstanding poet'). The idea that sorrow and worry deprive the singer of his poetic creativity also underpins Virgil's ninth eclogue, especially 2–6, 53–4, 66–7.

71–4 *squarrosa* is very rare: Mantovano appears to have picked it up from Festus (*De verborum significatione* 17), who only cites its usage in Lucilius. But it matters to Mantovano that the word comes from a lost Latin poet who happens to be a pioneer in Latin verse satire and a generic predecessor to Horace and Juvenal. Note also the Virgilian colour of *situs occupat ora*: cf. *Aeneid* 4.499, *pallor simul occupat ora* ('paleness at once spread across his face'). The simile of the hungry and cold kite appears to have no ancient parallel, though it may be relevant that in Ovid's *Metamorphoses* 2.716–19 (another simile) the kite is depicted as a fearful creature feeding on scraps.

75 By referring to Sylvanus' advice (ironically) as *medicina*, Candidus further emphasizes his physical deterioration.

76 *Fac alacrem*: literally 'make [me] joyous'. 'Make my life cheerful' could also convey the sense.

80 *gravis aere crumena* finds a near-parallel at Virgil, *Eclogues* 1.33–5, where Tityrus complains that, even though his labour produced plenty of food for city dwellers, his 'right hand never used to return home heavy with gold' (*non umquam gravis aere domum mihi dextra redibat*, 35).

82 *cineri ludos inarare bacillo*: literally 'to plough games into ash with a stick'.

84 *sitim restringere*: see note on 21–2 above.

86–8 *Tityrus* means Virgil (see introduction, and Mantovano, eclogue 2.8–9, *noster | Tityrus est auctor, qui pascua dixit et arva*, 'our Tityrus is the authority, who spoke of pastures and fields'). The poetic subjects mentioned here – *rura, boves et agros et martia bella* – signify Virgil's three major poems: *Eclogues*, *Georgics* and *Aeneid*. The canonization of Virgil's generic progression is a well-established topos since the Middle Ages: see Hubbard 1998: 295 n. 81 with references. But here the emphasis is on Maecenas' patronage: *sub Moecenate vetusto* intervenes in the sentence's movement from poet (Tityrus / Virgil) to poetry. The choice to use Virgil and Maecenas as an example is mediated through Juvenal, *Satires* 7.69–71: *nam si Vergilio puer et tolerabile desset | hospitium, caderent omnes a crinibus hydri, | surda nihil gemeret grave bucina* ('for if Virgil had lacked a slave boy and decent lodgings, all the snakes would have fallen from the hairs [of the Furies], [and] the mute trumpet would have sounded no solemn groan'). The image of Virgil's poetic immortality (*magno pulsabat sidera cantu*), as Severi (2010: 282) observes, not only draws on Petrarch's praise of John the Baptist in *Bucolicum carmen* 1.70–1 (*hunc igitur, dulci mulcentem sidera cantu | illa tulit tellus*, 'therefore, that land gave birth to him, who stroked the stars with his melodious song'), an important intertext for Mantovano's eclogues 9 and 10, but also echoes the praise of Mantua and Virgil by Silius Italicus in *Punica* 8.593–4: *Mantua, Musarum domus atque ad sidera cantu | evecta Aonio* ('Mantua, home of the Muses and exalted to the stars by the Aonian song'). Mantovano's attribution of Virgil's poetic achievement to good patronage is later picked up by Edmund Spenser, who invokes these lines in the *Shepheardes Calender* (*Oct.* 55–60) and presents Virgil's career as a precedent for contemporary poets who are looking to try their hands at epic in order to secure patronage.

89 *fortuna* is ambiguous, capable of suggesting both (good) luck and (financial) prosperity.

91 The linked appearance of the Muses and Apollo has many ancient precedents. But here the double rejection by poetic divinities echoes especially Juvenal, *Satires* 7.59–61 (where we find the Muses and Dionysus together): *neque enim cantare sub antro | Pierio thyrsumque potest contingere maesta |*

paupertas ('for neither can sad poverty sing in the Pierian cave nor grasp the thyrsus').

111–13 The idea that Rome might rescue a shepherd-poet from his current predicament is embedded in Virgil's first eclogue, where Tityrus visited the city (18–35) and subsequently acquired a stable and leisurely life through the help of an anonymous Roman young man (44–5), whom Servius and many scholars identify with Octavian, the future Augustus. At the same time, however, the disruption to pastoral life in Virgil's first and ninth eclogues is also caused by forces within Rome. The ambiguous nature of Virgil's ancient Rome – a place of opportunities and dangers – is re-enlivened in Mantovano's portrayal of the Renaissance papal city. *illis . . . campis* both extends the poem's rural language and gestures at various places in or near Rome (e.g. Campus Esquilinus).

116 *pede claudere passum* refers to the composition of poetry. *passum*, 'step' or 'pace' (as a measure of length), here metaphorically refers to poetic rhythm, as does *pede* (a metrical foot). Compare with Horace, *Satires* 2.1.28–9, *me pedibus delectat claudere verba | Lucili ritu* ('it delights me to close off words in feet in the manner of Lucilius').

117–18 The language and imagery are philosophical. *vivere parvo* is influenced by Horace, *Satires* 2.2.1–4, *Quae virtus et quanta, boni, sit vivere parvo . . . discite* ('Friends, learn what and how great is the virtue of living with little'). *tenuem . . . victum* (118) appears twice in connection with Epicurus in Cicero's *Tusculanae disputationes* (*tenuem victum antefert copioso*, 'he prefers a spare diet to plenty', 3.49.3; *laudat tenuem victum*, 'he praises a slender diet', 5.26.4).

120–1 A resounding moment of 'self-conscious negotiation between ancient and modern Rome' (Hinds 2017: 8). The death of Augustus emblematizes not only the irretrievable loss of ancient Rome and its poetic culture, but also the frailty of riches and the emptiness of imperial pretensions.

122 *nugas* usually appears in conjunction with forms of *agere* or *dicere*; as the direct object of *dabit* it attains a material presence, which, however, only serves to emphasize its lack of physicality and practical use compared with *aurum* at the end of the line.

123 *Heu Romae nunc sola pecunia regnat*: this is indebted to Juvenal, *Satires* 1.112–13, *inter nos sanctissima divitiarum | maiestas* ('among us the greatness of wealth is most sacred'), and Petronius, *Satyrica* 14.2, *quid faciunt leges, ubi sola pecunia regnat* ('what can laws do where money alone reigns?'), as well as the Horatian image of the *regina Pecunia* ('Queen Money', *Epistles* 1.6.37).

The rule of money in papal Rome is also a favourite theme of medieval satirical poetry.

125 *spe pascimur*: see Jupiter's address to Juno at Virgil, *Aeneid* 10.625–7: *sin . . . totumque moveri | mutarive putas bellum, spes pascis inanis* ('but if you think the whole course of the war may be moved or altered, you are nursing a futile hope'). The evocation of this Virgilian expression perhaps hints at the inevitability of poets finding only empty promises.

2

The Pierced Ear: Divine Revelation and Impregnation

Jacopo Sannazaro (1458–1530), *De Partu Virginis*, Extracts from Book 1

Lucy R. Nicholas

Introduction

Jacopo Sannazaro (1458–1530) was a Neapolitan humanist and poet. His influence throughout the early modern period was considerable, with writers from across Europe deriving inspiration from his works. Sannazaro's verse is marked by its great delicacy and beauty, and is the product of an imagination burgeoning with sound, colour and ideas. His poems also capture well the fusion of classical literature and Christianity that was a feature of so many Latin poems from late antiquity onwards, albeit few managed to effect so successful a synthesis as Sannazaro's. Even as a young man, Sannazaro belonged to a wide circle of like-minded individuals, all of whom were steeped in classical learning. He was a talented protégé of Giovanni Gioviano Pontano, another famous Italian poet, whose Accademia Pontaniana (a sodality of intellectuals and one of the first formal 'academies') Sannazaro entered in 1478, subsequently becoming its principal in 1525. His network extended beyond the Republic of Letters: he was also closely associated with the king of Naples, Frederick IV, following him into exile in 1501 (until 1504), an act of loyalty that secured handsome gifts of patronage.

Sannazaro produced a number of major works in both Italian and Latin. His earliest enterprise was the *Arcadia* (1480/90), a pastoral poem composed in the vernacular, and an obvious inspiration for Sir Philip Sidney's later English-language *Arcadia*. Thereafter, however, Sannazaro opted to write in Latin. One reason may have been his increasing devotion to the Roman poet Virgil, whose Latin masterpieces held a privileged place in the contemporary mind, and cast a long shadow over early modern poetic practices. We can be in no doubt about Sannazaro's deep commitment to Virgil. His emulation of the Roman poet is evident in all his verse productions, so that, as the sections below illustrate, Virgilian formulae and motifs are ubiquitous. In addition to this stylistic debt, Virgil's poetic output and career progression may have stood as a model for Sannazaro's own. Following his *Arcadia*, Sannazaro wrote two great works, his *Piscatory Eclogues* (*Piscatoria*), first printed in 1526, an obvious nod to Virgil's *Eclogues*, and an epic poem about the birth of Christ, the *De Partu Virginis* ('*On the Offspring*' or '*On the Delivery of the Virgin*'), which Sannazaro considered to be his greatest project. *De Partu Virginis* had a long gestation period: Sannazaro began work on it in 1506, and it was finally published just before his death in 1527. It is 1,443 lines long, commensurate with many of the epic productions of the time. A tour de force, *De Partu Virginis* was widely read by Sannazaro's contemporaries and considered by several sixteenth-century critics to constitute the first modern Christian epic (Brazeau 2014: 225).

The influence of the *Aeneid* can be felt on every page of the poem, but the *Eclogues* and Virgil's didactic work, the *Georgics*, also have a presence. There was further proximity. Sannazaro's villa on the coast of Naples was located a short distance from 'Virgil's tomb', which he had in turn helped to restore.[1] Before he died, Sannazaro had a church (Santa Maria del Parto, an appellation with an obvious connection to his *De Partu Virginis*) built in Naples so as to ensure that he would be buried not far from his spiritual and literary mentor. The closeness of the two writers is evoked in Cardinal Pietro Bembo's (see Text 4) distich engraved on Sannazaro's tomb: *Da sacro cineri flores, hic ille Maroni / Sincerus musa proximus ut tumulo* ('Give flowers to holy ash. Here [lies] that man Sincerus,[2] nearest to Maro in his poetry as in his grave').

Virgil was an author of paramount importance to Sannazaro, but the frequent appropriation of Virgil and the other classical writers Sannazaro drew on (including Statius, Lucretius and Ovid) did not lead to literary mummification. Sannazaro was a devout Christian, and the aim of his poetry was not just to project a style or to engage in the politics of patronage, but to express an orthodox piety which could reinforce and build on the illumination of Gospel truth. In his sacred poem *De Partu Virginis* Sannazaro replicates a Virgilian tone and diction, only to then announce to Virgil in the latter's own prophetic words the birth of a miraculous child, in a sort of post-pagan challenge to Virgil's own messianic *Eclogue* 4 (Fantazzi 1997: 232).[3] He also reapplies descriptions of heroic virtue found in classical epics to Mary: whereas Aeneas' heroism is characterized by *pietas*, Mary's is by chastity.

Through the work's three books, the nativity of Christ is unfolded, but Sannazaro also encircles this narrative with a cluster of other stories, including the adoration of the shepherds and the prediction of the later events of Christ's life. The focus of the extracts below is the archangel Gabriel's

Annunciation to the Virgin Mary and the divine Conception. The primary biblical source for this was the Gospel of Luke (1:26–38). The birth is not covered in Mark's or John's Gospels and is only briefly narrated by Matthew (1:18–25), and in this last the annunciation is delivered to Joseph. The biblical accounts of the nativity episodes are brief, and a large part of the challenge for Sannazaro was to fashion an epic poem out of so little material.

Sannazaro's epic has been characterized as his version of Mary's Magnificat; indeed the poem's first word, *virginei*, advertises the importance of her role. The Marian focus is noteworthy. Sannazaro was composing at a time of hardening religious schism between Catholics and Protestants. Despite the scepticism of many of his contemporaries in Naples, Sannazaro held fast to the orthodox faith, and there is strong likelihood that the emphasis on the Mother of Christ in *De Partu Virginis* constituted a direct response to the Lutheran denial of her importance in the plan of salvation (Fantazzi 1997: 239). More generally, Sannazaro's poem foregrounded the redemptive impact of the birth of Christ, in contrast to a Protestant focus on the Fall and the degeneracy of sinful humanity. His verse also has a deeply devotional flavour, in tune with the increased focus on Mary in some branches of the Catholic Church. The ultimate dedicatee would be the Pope (the poem being initially intended for Leo X and then, upon Leo's death in 1521, for Clement VII). Prior to that, he sent manuscripts to Rome for inspection by Jacopo Sadoleto (Bishop of Carpentras), to the papal secretary, Giles of Viterbo, and also to Cardinal Pietro Bembo. Bembo was in no doubt about the confessional significance of this epic, comparing Sannazaro to the devout David who combats with his sling a heavily armed Goliath, and describing it as a work of 'divine providence' (Greene 1973: 160).

On the one hand, the poem is inescapably classical in its tenor, with the majestic rolling of its Virgilian rhythms and turns. Indeed, its constant application of pagan terms for Christian figures can sometimes be quite startling: for example, this epic does not incorporate the biblical names of 'Gabriel' and 'Mary', but instead uses terms such as *interpres* ('go-between'), *regina* ('queen'), and, for God, *numina* ('divine power') and *genitor* ('begetter'). Certain allusions, especially those that harness the violence of classical myth, can likewise be unsettling (see, for example, the note on line 187). Yet, Sannazaro also integrated within this stylistic framework material ranging from the Old and New Testaments to the depictions in Italian painting and frescoes of the Annunciation and the Virgin and Child. Indeed, the poem is as aesthetically affecting and eclectic as an artwork by Raphael.

Sannazaro was also working within a broader landscape of religious and epic poetry. It is clear that he knew, for example, Baptista Spagnoli Mantovano's *Parthenice Mariana* (of 1488; for Mantovano, see Text 1), a work dedicated to the life of the Virgin and one that influenced a whole generation of religious poets. In life, Sannazaro was a humanist who fused a myriad of material to create a poetic masterpiece. So, too, in death: the Santa Maria del Parto, which Sannazaro commissioned, still stands as a monument to his composite love of the classical and the Christian, with its mythological iconography and many biblical reliefs, and a tomb built for himself so as to be near that of Virgil.

Metre: dactylic hexameter

Notes

1 It was not in fact Virgil's tomb: see J. B. Trapp, 'The Grave of Vergil', *Journal of the Warburg and Courtauld Institutes*, 47, 1984: 1–31.
2 Like many humanists of the age, Sannazaro adopted a classical nom de plume, *Actius Sincerus*, words meaning 'littoral' or 'pertaining to the seashore' and 'pure / whole / honest' respectively, the former from the Greek noun ἀκτή and the latter being the Latin adjective *sincerus*. He may even have been casting himself as a sort of Apollo, *Actius* being one of that god's epithets.
3 On the Renaissance reception of *Eclogue* 4, see L. B. T. Houghton, *Virgil's Fourth Eclogue in the Italian Renaissance*, Cambridge 2019.

Bibliography

Brazeau, B. J. (2014), '"Emotional Rescue": Heroic Chastity and Devotional Practice in Iacopo Sannazaro's *De partu Virginis*', *California Italian Studies*, 5.1: 225–46.

Fantazzi, C. (1997), 'Poetry and Religion in Sannazaro's De Partu Virginis', in G. Tournoy and D. Sacré (eds), *Ut Granum Sinapis: Essays on Neo-Latin Literature in honour of Jozef Ijsewijn*, 231–48, Leuven (Supplementa Humanistica Lovaniensia XII).

Greene, T. M. (1973, 3rd ed.), *The Descent from Heaven: A Study in Epic Continuity*, New Haven / London (esp. pp. 144–70).

Kennedy, W. J. (1983), *Jacopo Sannazaro and the uses of the pastoral*, Hanover NH / London (esp. pp. 180–224).

Kidwell, C. (1993), *Sannazaro and Arcadia*, London.

Putnam, M. C. J., trans. (2009), *Latin Poetry: Jacopo Sannazaro*, Cambridge, MA / London (The I Tatti Renaissance Library 38).

Quint, D. (1983), *Origin and Originality in Renaissance Literature. Versions of the Source*, New Haven / London (esp. pp. 43–80).

Source of the Latin text

The text is taken from Putnam (2009), with some very minor orthographical changes.

Latin text

Passage 1 (1.73–90)

In this passage God makes his intentions for Mary and the imminent birth of Christ known to the archangel Gabriel, who then promptly, and in compliance with the Father's commandment, soars down to earth to disclose the divine plan to Mary.

'Hanc mihi virginibus iam pridem ex omnibus unam
delegi prudensque animo interiore locavi,
ut foret intacta sanctum quae numen in alvo
conciperet ferretque pios sine semine partus.
Ergo age, nubivagos molire per aëra gressus,
deveniensque locum, castas haec iussus ad aures
effare et pulchris cunctantem hortatibus imple,
quandoquidem genus e stygiis mortale tenebris
eripere est animus, saevosque arcere labores.'
Dixerat. Ille altum Zephyris per inane vocatis
carpit iter, scindit nebulas atque aëra tranat,
ima petens pronusque leves vix commovet alas.
Qualis, ubi ex alto notis maeandria ripis
prospexit vada seu placidi stagna ampla Caystri,
praecipitem sese candenti corpore cycnus
mittit agens: iamque implumis segnisque videtur
ipse sibi, donec tandem potiatur amatis
victor aquis: sic ille auras nubesque secabat.

English translation

Passage 1 (1.73–90)

'Long ago I singled out this one [woman] from all the virgins and, with foresight, settled in the deepest part of my mind that she would be the one to conceive in her chaste belly the sacred deity and carry a holy progeny, free of insemination. Therefore go! Set in motion your cloud-wandering course through the air, and as you descend to the place, announce, as you have been bidden, these [commands] to her pure ears. And, [although] she may hesitate, fill her with beautiful encouragement, seeing that it is my intention to snatch the mortal race from Stygian darkness, and to ward off dreadful sufferings.'

He [God] had spoken. [But] he [Gabriel], after summoning the Zephyrs, navigates his lofty path through the void, divides the clouds and swims through the air. Making for the land below and leaning downwards, he scarcely stirs his light wings. Just as when a swan, with gleaming white body, has espied from on high the Maeandrian shallows with their familiar banks or the teeming pools of the calm Cayster, purposefully propels itself headlong; and now it seems to itself to have no feathers and to be slow, until at last it triumphantly takes possession of its beloved waters; so he [Gabriel] was cleaving the breezes and the clouds.

Passage 2 (1.155–69)

Just before this passage starts, Gabriel has reached Mary, whom he finds (fittingly) reading 'books of the ancient Sybils'[1] *and meditating on the promised birth. She is, as yet, unaware of her own role in the incarnation. Gabriel announces (i.e.* dixerat*) that Mary has been chosen by God to give birth to his son, to a divinity. In what follows, Sannazaro outlines Mary's response and has Gabriel offer further natal news.*

Dixerat. Illa animum sedato pectore firmans
substitit, et placido breviter sic ore locuta est:
'Conceptusne mihi tandem partusque futuros,
sancte, refers? Mene attactus perferre viriles
posse putas? cui vel nitenti matris ab alvo
protinus inconcussum et ineluctabile votum
virginitas fuit una: nec est cur solvere amatae
iura pudicitiae cupiam aut haec foedera rumpam.'
'Immo istas (quod tu minime iam rere) per aures,'
excipit interpres, 'fecundam Spiritus alvum
influet implebitque potenti viscera partu,
flammifero veniens caelo atque micantibus astris.
At tu, virgineum mirata tumescere ventrem,
haerebis pavitans: demum, formidine pulsa,
gaudia servati capies inopina pudoris.'

[1] Sannazaro would have known about the tradition that Sibylline prophecies foretold Christ's coming – perhaps in particular from Lactantius, who was much read in the Renaissance, and whose explicit juxtaposition of Hebrew and Gentile prophets proved influential in the centuries that followed.

Passage 2 (1.155–69)

He [Gabriel] had spoken. She [Mary] stood still, becalmed in heart and fortifying her mind, and briefly spoke thus with calm voice: 'Pray, are you, holy one, announcing to me the advent of a pregnancy and a birth? Do you suppose that I am able to bear a man's touch, I whose unshakeable and immovable vow even on the point of [leaving] the belly of my mother in labour was [for] virginity alone? Nor is there any reason I should wish to overturn the duties of my beloved chastity or should break this bond.' The messenger responds: 'Rather, the Spirit, descending from flame-bearing heaven and the flashing stars will flow through those ears of yours (something you now [can] scarcely imagine) into your fertile belly and will fill your innards with a powerful embryo. Then, in wonderment at the swelling of your virgin's womb, you will be transfixed amid your trembling; yet at last, with fear banished, you will partake in the unexpected joys of preserved modesty.'

Passage 3 (1.185–202)

In this final extract, the Virgin Mary experiences impregnation, but not by normal means.

Tantum effata, repente nova micuisse penates
luce videt: nitor ecce domum complerat. Ibi illa,
ardentum haud patiens radiorum ignisque corusci,
extimuit magis. At venter (mirabile dictu!
non ignota cano) sine vi, sine labe pudoris,
arcano intumuit verbo: vigor actus ab alto
irradians, vigor omnipotens, vigor omnia complens
descendit – deus ille, deus! – totosque per artus
dat sese miscetque utero. Quo tacta repente
viscera contremuere. Silet natura pavetque
attonitae similis; confusaque turbine rerum
insolito occultas conatur quaerere causas,
sed longe vires alias maioraque sentit
numina. Succutitur tellus laevumque sereno
intonuit caelo rerum cui summa potestas,
adventum nati genitor testatus, ut omnes
audirent late populi, quos maximus ambit
Oceanus, Tethysque et raucisona Amphitrite.

Passage 3 (1.185–202)

That was all she [Mary] uttered. Suddenly she beholds that the hearth had flashed with a strange light. Look! A lustre had filled her home. Then she was yet more afraid, unable to endure the burning rays and flashing fire. But, marvellous to relate (I sing of things not unknown), her womb, without force, without stain to her modesty, swelled with the hidden word. A glowing energy impelled from on high comes down – an all-powerful energy, an energy penetrating all – that was God, God! – and gives itself to all her limbs and mingles with her womb. Touched by this, suddenly her innards quivered. Nature, as though struck by thunder, falls silent and quakes. And brought into confusion by this extraordinary convulsion of events, Nature tries to seek out their secret causes, but senses a very different order of strength and a greater divinity. The earth is shaken at its roots, and the Begetter whose power over [the nature of] things is supreme thundered on the left in a clear sky as he bore testament to the coming of his Son, so that all people far and wide, whom the mighty Ocean and Tethys and husky Amphitrite surround, might hear.

Commentary

Passage 1

73 *Hanc ... unam*: these two words frame the line to highlight the Virgin Mary's importance.

77 *Ergo age*: using a Virgilian formulation (*Georgics* 1.63 and *Aeneid* 2.707), God enters the poem, appearing in person as in the Old Testament, and urges Gabriel to deliver the news to Mary. Sannazaro makes him do so with all the elocutionary arsenal at his disposal (Kennedy 1983: 193), including *ergo age* and the threefold imperatives of *molire*, *effare* and *imple*. In Sannazaro's epic, rhetorical skill is presented as a force for good and constitutes proof of honest intent.

79 *cunctantem* is highly reminiscent of Virg. *Aen.* 8.387, applied to Vulcan when he is being seduced by Venus..

imple is possibly being used proleptically, for *implere* can also mean 'to impregnate' (e.g. Ovid, *Metamorphoses* 11.265, 4.698, 5.111 and 9.280 and, referring to animals, Pliny, *Natural History* 8.205) and is used in this sense by Sannazaro in 1.165 (passage 2).

82 *Zephyris*: the gentle west winds.

83 *carpit ... scindit ... tranat*: the three present tense verbs in this single line inject a powerful sense of movement into this flight of fantasy.

85–90 In this striking and layered simile Gabriel is likened to a swan descending to Mary. The scene is a clear allusion to Mercury's descent to Aeneas in the *Aeneid* (4.245–58), just as the earlier scene rewrites Jupiter's conversation with Mercury, and readers will be able to identify the many similarities in vocabulary and imagery:

illa fretus agit ventos et turbida tranat
nubila. Iamque volans apicem et latera ardua cernit
Atlantis duri caelum qui vertice fulcit,
...
Hic primum paribus nitens Cyllenius alis
constitit; hinc toto praeceps se corpore ad undas
misit avi similis, quae circum litora, circum
piscosos scopulos humilis volat aequora iuxta.
Haud aliter terras inter caelumque volabat
litus harenosum ad Libyae, ventosque secabat
materno veniens ab avo Cyllenia proles.

'Relying on this [wand], he [Mercury] drives the winds and skims the stormy clouds. And now in flight he descries the peak and steep sides of toiling Atlas, who props up heaven on his peak. . . . Here, poised on even wings, the Cyllenian first halted; hence with his whole frame he sped sheer down to the waves like a bird, which round the shores, round the fish-haunted cliffs, flies low near the waters. Even thus between earth and sky flew Cyllene's nursling to Libya's sandy shore, and cut the winds, coming from his mother's sire.' (The translation is taken from the Loeb edition: Virgil. *Eclogues. Georgics. Aeneid: Books 1–6*, trans. H. Rushton Fairclough; revised by G. P. Goold.)

Yet, in Virgil, Mercury is compared to a generic bird (*avi*), not specifically a swan. It may be that Sannazaro also had in mind the following passages: Virg. *Aen*. 7.699, where the Latin army are compared to white swans (*nivei . . . cycni*) singing as they fly back from the river; *Aen*. 5.213–17, which describes the flight of a dove whose wings are swift but scarcely move, like Mnestheus in the rowing race; and *Aen*. 9.563 with the phrase *candenti corpore cycnum* ('swan of gleaming white body'). While Sannazaro certainly took the elements of his simile from Virgil, and skilfully amalgamated aspects of Virgilian diction and rhythm, that debt does not account for the peculiar power of his own simile. Indeed, it is in several respects quite different to Virgil's – for example, in the use of *implumis segnisque* to conjure a pronounced feeling of impatience, even as Gabriel speeds on. The epithet *placidi* (of *Caystri*) is likewise eye-catching and perhaps points to the peaceful nature of the woman whom Gabriel is about to reach, Mary, who, in line 156, is described as speaking *placido . . . ore* (passage 2).

85 *maeandria*: the Maeander was a river that flowed between Lydia and Caria (both in modern Turkey), proverbial for its winding course. *ma*eand*ria* is perhaps a play on Mary's (*Maria*) name.

86 The Cayster was a river in Lydia, celebrated for its great number of swans. For this location in Virgil, see *Georgics* 1.384: *dulcibus in stagnis . . . Caystri* ('in Cayster's . . . sweet pools'). The region is associated in that passage and more generally with birds; see also Homer, *Iliad* 2.459–66, which has geese, cranes and swans gathering around the Cayster. The name might also signal Mary's *castitas* ('chastity'), another example of how Sannazaro uses a sequence of sound effects to endow the passage with aural pregnancy. Allusions to locations from classical literature rather than places Sannazaro or his readers had actually seen was typical of his poetry and many Renaissance writers.

Passage 2

155 *sedato pectore*: the phrase underscores the challenging situation Mary finds herself in: in Virg. *Aen.* 9.740, Turnus, when faced with the threats of Pandarus in battle, is said to smile *sedato pectore.*

157–62 Sannazaro deviates radically from the simpler formulation of Luke which (at 1:34) has: *Dixit autem Maria ad angelum: Quomodo fiet istud, quoniam virum non cognosco?* ('Then said Mary unto the angel, "How shall this be, seeing I know not a man?"', KJV). This strong anachronism imposes on Mary (with some one-upmanship) the hagiographical model of later consecrated virgins, who are often said to have resolved on chastity in their earliest youth. The perpetual virginity of Mary is Christian tradition and doctrine, not stated in Scripture, and Mary's vow of virginity is a patristic notion, and attested to in Augustine.

158 Sannazaro almost certainly had in mind Mantovano's *tactus non passa viriles* ('not bearing a man's touch') in his *Parthenice Mariana* 2.597, though in that work these words are spoken by Gabriel rather than Mary.

159 *nitenti*: the present participle is from the verb *nitor*, meaning 'to strive' (or 'be in labour'), rather than *niteo*, meaning 'to shine', as the initial 'i' of *nitenti* is long, as it is in *nitor* but not in *niteo*). It is qualifying ablative *alvo* rather than dative *cui*: this is a hypallage of sorts, since it is literally the womb, not the mother, who is labouring. The phrase represents a reference to Mary's own Immaculate Conception.

160 *inconcussum et ineluctabile*: the repetition of the prefix *in-* and the metrical weight of these two long words gives ballast to Mary's insistence on the inviolability of her oath.

161–2 *nec* . . . *foedera rumpam*: a phrase highly reminiscent of Virgil's *foedera rumpant* (*Aen.* 8.540), albeit here with a shift. Whereas Aeneas, following a sign from the gods, dares the Laurentines to call for battle and 'break their covenant', Mary uses the term in the context of her inviolable virginity.

163 *rere*: an alternative form of *reris*, a second person singular present active indicative of the deponent verb *reor*. The phrase *quod* . . . *minime* . . . *rere* is drawn from Virgil, *Aen.* 6.97, spoken, not coincidentally, by the Sibyl.

per aures: this phenomenon of 'aural penetration' was one commonly featured in art works of the time. It forms an appropriate connection between the genesis of Christ and Christ as the Word of God – see note on 1.190 (passage 3).

164 *Spiritus*: Gabriel informs Mary that the Holy Spirit will flow into her womb. In passage 3 we are told it is God (*Deus*). The combination of the two divine names to produce the baby Christ neatly evokes the Trinity. Cf. Luke 1:35: . . . *Spiritus Sanctus superveniet in te, et virtus altissimi obumbrabit tibi. Ideoque et quod nascetur ex te sanctum, vocabitur Filius Dei* ('The Holy Ghost shall come upon thee, and the power of the Highest shall overshadow thee: therefore also that holy thing which shall be born of thee shall be called the Son of God', KJV).

165 *implebit*: see note on 1.79 (passage 1).

Passage 3

185 *penates*: Sannazaro regularly uses this term which for a Roman denoted the gods of the household. It is possible that there is a play on the noun *penis* in *penates* at this conception moment.

187 Sannazaro possibly had in mind the story of Semele and Jupiter in Ovid's *Metamorphoses* (3.253–315), where Semele cannot endure the heat and light of Jupiter, although in that account, unlike here, Semele does not survive; see, for example, 3.308–9, *corpus mortale tumultus | non tulit aetherios* ('her mortal body bore not the onrush of heavenly power'), and 3.310–11, *inperfectus adhuc infans genetricis ab alvo | eripitur* ('The baby [Bacchus] still not wholly formed is snatched from the mother's womb'). The echoes are uncomfortable insofar as Jupiter's behaviour is scandalous rather than holy.

188 *mirabile dictu* is a famous phrase, used regularly by Virgil to mark a particularly magical or supernatural force: see *Geo.* 2.30; 4.554; *Aen.* 1.439; 2.174, 2.680; 3.26; 4.182; 7.64 (usually, as here in Sannazaro, at the ends of lines). *mirabile* may also be playing on Mary's name. The scene that unfolds is clothed in mystical language that conveys a liturgical and lyric solemnity (Fantazzi 1997: 243).

190 *verbo*: Sannazaro has in mind the Christian *logos* ('Word'), a name or title of Christ derived from the prologue to John's Gospel (1:1) and also referred to in the Book of Revelation (19:13).

191 *complens*: Sannazaro repeats the verb he has just used in line 186 (*complerat*), so that the first use foreshadows the second. This translation renders the verbs differently for impact, but 'fill' or 'penetrate' would suffice in both places.

192 *deus ille, deus*: Sannazaro is here varying Lucretius' words on the divinity of Epicurus (*De rerum natura* 5.8, *deus ille fuit, deus*), words that Virgil also reshapes at *Ecl.* 5.64: *deus, deus ille, Menalca.*

190–3 The numerous repetitions, including most obviously *vigor* (three times), but also *Deus* (twice) and the *-ens* endings, lend the necessary weight to these lines depicting the moment of divine conception. The threefold *vigor* might also point to the Trinity. While the narrative necessarily preserves Mary's virginity intact – the fact is explicitly stated –, the presentation of this scene, while not carnal, does contain a sexual charge. The verb *misceo*, in particular, could in classical literature denote sexual intercourse.

193 *tacta*: in 1.75 (passage 1) God had referred to Mary's womb as *intacta.*

194 *natura*: all of nature bears witness to this supernatural event, whose repercussions are felt to the ends of the earth. Sannazaro introduces an interesting shift in perspective: normally humans investigate the causes of nature; here even nature herself wants to understand causes.

198–200 *laevum … testatus*: a fine example of the fusion of Christian and classical coordinates, with the Christian juxtaposition of Father and Son (line 200) and the classical apparatus of divine signs and the depiction of the Father as the 'thunderer': see also Virg. *Aen.* 9.630–1: *audiit et caeli genitor de parte serena | intonuit laevum* ('The Begetter heard and from a clear space of sky thundered on the left'). In such contexts, the left was associated with auspicious omens.

With *rerum cui summa potestas*, Sannazaro subtly varies Virgil's *rerum cui prima potestas* ('whose power over [the nature] of things is foremost', *Aen.* 10.100), perhaps as a means to convey the superiority of the Christian God over Jupiter. Sannazaro evidently also had in mind various late antique Christian sources, the phrase *rerum cui summa potestas* occurring in Proba, *Cento* 64 and Prudentius, *Hamartigenia* 20, for example.

202 Tethys was a sea goddess and the wife of Oceanus; Amphitrite is another goddess of the sea and consort of Neptune.

3

The Abbot and the Learned Woman

Desiderius Erasmus (1466–1536), *Colloquia* (*Abbatis et Eruditae*)

Astrid Khoo

Introduction

The *Colloquia* of Desiderius Erasmus (1466–1536) were first published, in twelve editions between 1518 and 1533, as pedagogical resources exemplifying conversational *formulae* in realistic scenarios. By providing his pupils with these Latin phrases and constructions, Erasmus equipped them with useful templates that could be altered for use in conversation and letter writing. Despite this schoolroom origin, however, they are now rightfully perceived as literary texts with artistic merit. While fundamentally comic in tone, they centre upon issues that Erasmus and his contemporaries considered significant, some of which continue to dominate popular discourse today: education (of both boys and girls), marriage and adultery, motherhood, old age, luxury and the injustices of the Church.

These topics were as much a part of Erasmus' life as of his work. He was the illegitimate son of a priest, Roger Gerard, and the laywoman Margareta Rutgers. Erasmus and his elder brother Pieter were sent to the Latin school attached to the cathedral of St Lebuin in Deventer (Netherlands), over which the humanist pedagogue Alexander Hegius (d. 1498) presided. After their parents succumbed to the plague in 1483, both boys entered religious life, Erasmus as a canon regular of St Augustine (1488; ordination 1492). However, Erasmus soon obtained a post as secretary to Henry, Bishop of Cambrai, under whose patronage he studied and taught at, among others, the University of Paris (1495–9; 1500–6), the University of Turin (1506) and Queen's College, Cambridge (1510–15). During the Reformation he took a middle course, criticizing both the abuses of the Church and Luther's theology, which he condemned as reactionary in the *Hyperaspistes* of 1526. The famed eloquence and learning with which he articulated his views made him a coveted guest of Europe's bishops and princes; at the time of his death from dysentery in 1536, he was in the process of relocating to Brabant at the invitation of Mary of Hungary, Regent of the Netherlands.

The Erasmian corpus is characterized by quantity and variety. Erasmus was the first to edit and publish the Greek New Testament (1516). In addition, he produced numerous editions of both pagan and patristic texts, including Seneca the Younger (1515), St Jerome (1516), St Hilary (1522), St Irenaeus (1526), St John Chrysostom (1527) and Origen (1536). He also published a collection of St Augustine's works (1528–9), which enjoyed such great popularity that it was reprinted ten times. Notable among Erasmus' original writings are his *Letters*, the satirical *Praise of Folly* (1511) and the *Ciceronianus* (1528). The *Colloquia* belong to a wider category of didactic works, which include not only the *Adages* (1500), but also 'mirrors' for young men, such as the *Handbook of a Christian Knight* (1503) and *The Education of a Christian Prince* (1516; published 1532).

The *Colloquia* are, however, distinguished from these other works by their dialogic format. Dialogues have a long history in Latin pedagogy. Roman youth learned oratory by practising, under a teacher's guidance, declamatory exercises such as those collected by Seneca the Elder, Ps.-Quintilian and Calpurnius Flaccus. Erasmus' *Colloquia* are, however, closer in form and intent to late antique manuals such as the *Hermeneumata*, which focused on equipping Greek-speaking students with basic Latin phrases for communicating with their teachers and fellow pupils. These didactic tools appealed to humanist educators who aimed to revive classical Latin in day-to-day interactions. Accordingly, Erasmus' *Colloquia* are but one of many works in this genre, which includes Mathurin Cordier's (1479–1564) *Colloquia Scholastica* and Giovanni Pontano's (1542–1626) *Progymnasmata*.

Writing colloquies might, moreover, have been politically expedient for Erasmus, since they allowed him to ascribe views to fictional characters, thus distancing himself from controversial perspectives. Furthermore, dialogues are both entertaining and accessible; Erasmus himself learned to read Greek by translating 'eighteen of the shorter dialogues' by the second-century CE satirist Lucian, who wrote in a famously easy and humorous style (Allen 1: 8, *CWE* 9: 301). These generic characteristics are displayed in full within the *Abbatis et Eruditae*, which stands out among Erasmus' ninety-five colloquies for its audacity, humour and simplicity.

As its title indicates, the colloquy's two main characters are an abbot, Antronius, and a learned woman, Magdalia, who argue over the central theme: what does it mean to live well? The abbot, a boldly drawn stereotype of the corrupt clergyman, advocates for the worldly pleasures of drinking and hunting. By contrast, Magdalia, who comes across almost as a caricatural 'bluestocking', emphasizes the importance of acquiring wisdom. A major sticking point between Antronius and Magdalia is women's education, of which the former naturally disapproves, but which the latter embodies. While many women were schooled in reading and writing for the purpose of domestic administration, teaching them not only Latin but also the art of disputation – which Magdalia has evidently mastered – was a radical new practice in Erasmus' day, restricted largely to princesses such as Elizabeth and Mary Tudor, or to the daughters of learned humanists such as Thomas More. For the reader, therefore, the excitement of this dialogue lies not only in the intellectual sparring between Antronius and Magdalia, but also in the sense that a great door is swinging open for the very first time, revealing behind it the possibility of intellectual equality between women and men. This remained just that – a remote 'possibility' – in Erasmus' age, as indicated by Antronius' disdain for Magdalia and her ilk, but has since solidified, throughout many parts of the world, into a welcome reality.

Bibliography

Allen = Allen, P. S., H. M. Allen and H. W. Garrod (eds) (1906–58), *Opus Epistolarum Des. Erasmi Roterodami.* 12 vols, Oxford.
ASD = (1969–), *Opera Omnia Desiderii Erasmi Roterodami*, Amsterdam.
CWE = (1975–), *Collected Works of Erasmus*, Toronto.

Albala, K. (2002), *Eating Right in the Renaissance*, Berkeley / Los Angeles.
Burke, P. (1989), 'The Renaissance Dialogue', *Renaissance Studies*, 3: 1–12.
Huizinga, J. (1924), *Erasmus* [trans. F. Hopman], New York / London.
Massey, W. (1755), *Corruptae Latinitatis index*, London.
Saetveit Miles, L. (2014), 'The Origins and Development of the Virgin Mary's Book at the Annunciation', *Speculum*, 89: 632–69.
Tracy, J. D. (1972), *Erasmus: The Growth of a Mind*, Geneva.
Tunberg, T. (2012), 'The Way Many Aspired to the Eloquence of the Few: The Neo-Latin Colloquium', in N. van Deusen and L. M. Koff (eds), *Mobs: An Interdisciplinary Inquiry*, 189–202, Leiden.
Warnicke, R. M. (1983), *Women of the English Renaissance and Reformation*, Westport / London.
Watkins, R. N., ed. and trans. (1978), *Humanism and Liberty: Writings on Freedom from Fifteenth-Century Florence*, Columbia SC.

Source of the Latin text

The text is a revised version of the *ASD* edition, adjusted according to the conventions of classical Latin orthography: L. E. Halkin, F. Bierlaire and R. Hoven (eds) (1972), *Opera omnia Desiderii Erasmi Roterodami, I.3: Colloquia*, Amsterdam: 403–8.

I refer throughout to the following English editions:

Thompson, C. R., ed. and trans. (1996), 'The Abbot and the Learned Lady', in E. Rummel (ed.), *Erasmus on Women*, 174–86, Toronto / Buffalo / London.

Thompson, C. R., ed. and trans. (1997), *Colloquies, I*. 499–519, Toronto / Buffalo / London (Collected Works of Erasmus 39).

Latin text

ANTRONIVS, MAGDALIA[1]

ANTRONIVS. Quam hic ego supellectilem video?

MAGDALIA. An non elegantem?

A. Nescio quam elegantem, certe parum decoram et puellae et matronae.

M. Quamobrem?

A. Quia librorum plena sunt omnia.

M. Tu tantus natu,[2] tum abbas et aulicus, nunquam vidisti libros in aedibus heroinarum?[3]

A. Vidi, sed Gallice scriptos, hic video Graecos et Latinos.

M. An soli Gallice scripti libri docent sapientiam?

A. Sed decet hoc heroinas, ut habeant quo delectent otium.[4]

M. An solis heroinis licet sapere ac suaviter vivere?

A. Male connectis sapere et suaviter vivere, non est muliebre sapere, heroinarum est suaviter vivere.

M. Nonne omnium est bene vivere?

A. Opinor.

M. Qui potest autem suaviter vivere, qui non vivat bene?[5]

A. Immo qui potest suaviter vivere, qui vivat bene?

M. Ergo tu probas eos qui vivunt male, modo suaviter.

A. Arbitror illos bene vivere qui vivunt suaviter.

M. Sed ista suavitas, unde proficiscitur, e rebus extrariis, an ex animo?[6]

A. E rebus extrariis.

M. O subtilem abbatem, sed crassum philosophum. Dic mihi, quibus rebus tu metiris suavitatem?

A. Somno, conviviis, libertate faciendi quae velis,[7] pecunia, honoribus.

M. Verum si istis rebus Deus addiderit sapientiam, num vives suaviter?

A. Quid appellas sapientiam?

M. Hoc est, si intelligeres hominem non esse felicem, nisi bonis animi; opes, honores, genus neque feliciorem reddere neque meliorem.

A. Valeat ista quidem sapientia.[8]

English translation

ANTRONIUS, MAGDALIA[1]

ANTRONIUS. What equipment do I see here?
MAGDALIA. Isn't it elegant?
A. I don't know how 'elegant' it is, but certainly it poorly befits both a young maiden and a married woman.
M. Why so?
A. Because everything is full of books.
M. Have you, at such an age,[2] and an abbot as well as a courtier, never seen books in court ladies'[3] houses?
A. I have seen them, but only ones written in French; here I see Greek and Latin books.
M. Are books written in French the only ones which teach wisdom?
A. But it befits court ladies to have [books] which spice up their spare time.[4]
M. Are court ladies the only ones allowed to acquire wisdom and live pleasantly?
A. You're mistaken in conflating the acquisition of wisdom with living pleasantly. It's not womanly to acquire wisdom, but a court lady's business is to live pleasantly.
M. Surely it's everyone's business to live well?
A. I think it is.
M. But who can live pleasantly without living well?[5]
A. On the contrary: who can live pleasantly if he lives well?
M. So you approve of those who live badly as long as [they live] pleasantly.
A. I deem those who live pleasantly to be living well.
M. But from where does this pleasure originate: from external things, or from the mind?[6]
A. From external things.
M. Oh, [you] sagacious abbot but thick-headed philosopher! Tell me, by what things do you measure pleasure?
A. By sleep, parties, the freedom to do what you wish,[7] money, accolades.
M. But if God should add wisdom to these things, you wouldn't live pleasantly, would you?
A. What do you term 'wisdom'?
M. It's this: if you understand that a man is not happy unless via the goods of his mind, [and if you understand] that wealth, accolades and good birth make him neither happier nor better.
A. Away with that 'wisdom' indeed![8]

M. Quid si mihi suavius sit legere bonum auctorem, quam tibi venari, potare aut ludere aleam, non videbor tibi suaviter vivere?
A. Ego non viverem.
M. Non quaero, quid tibi sit suavissimum, sed quid deberet esse suave.
A. Ego nolim meos monachos frequentes esse in libris.
M. At meus maritus hoc maxime probat.[9] Sed quamobrem tandem non probas hoc in monachis tuis?
A. Quoniam experior illos minus morigeros. Responsant ex decretis, ex decretalibus, ex Petro, ex Paulo.[10]
M. Imperas igitur quae pugnant cum Petro et Paulo?
A. Quid illi doceant, nescio. Sed tamen non amo monachum responsatorem,[11] neque velim quenquam meorum plus sapere, quam ego sapiam.
M. Istud ita vitari possit, si tu des operam, ut quam plurimum sapias.
A. Non est otium.
M. Qui sic?
A. Quia non vacat.
M. Non vacat sapere?
A. Non.
M. Quid obstat?
A. Prolixae preces, cura rei domesticae, venatus, equi, cultus aulae.
M. Itane ista tibi sunt potiora sapientia?
A. Nobis sic usu venit.
M. Iam illud mihi dicito, si quis Iupiter hanc potestatem tibi daret, ut posses et monachos tuos et teipsum vertere in quodcunque animal velles, an illos in porcos verteres, teipsum in equum?
A. Nequaquam.
M. Atqui sic vitares, ne quis plus te uno saperet.
A. Mea non magni referret, quod genus animantis essent monachi, modo ipse essem homo.
M. An hominem esse censes, qui nec sapiat nec velit sapere?
A. Mihi sapio.[12]
M. Et sibi sapiunt sues.
A. Videre[13] mihi sophistria[14] quaepiam, ita argutaris.
M. Non dicam quid tu mihi videaris. Sed cur haec displicet supellex?
A. Quia fusus et colus sunt arma muliebra.

M. What if it's more pleasant for me to read a good author than for you to hunt, drink or play dice? Would I not seem to you to be living pleasantly?
A. I wouldn't live [that way].
M. I'm not asking what is most pleasant to you, but what should be pleasant.
A. I wouldn't want my monks to busy themselves with books.
M. But my husband strongly approves of this.[9] Yet why in the world don't you approve of this in your monks?
A. Because I find that they are less obedient. They answer back [by quoting] from decrees, from decretals, from Peter, from Paul.[10]
M. So you command things which conflict with Peter and Paul?
A. I don't know what those men teach, but, in any case, I don't like a monk who answers back,[11] nor do I want any of my [monks] to acquire more wisdom than I have.
M. That can be avoided if you take care to acquire as much wisdom as possible.
A. I don't have the leisure.
M. How so?
A. Because there's no free time.
M. No free time to acquire wisdom?
A. No.
M. What's stopping you?
A. Extended prayers, housekeeping, hunts, horses, the court lifestyle.
M. Are these things more important to you than wisdom, then?
A. That's just how it has come to be for us through force of habit.
M. Now tell me this: if some Jupiter gave you the power to turn both your monks and yourself into whatever animal you wished, would you then turn them into pigs and yourself into a horse?
A. Certainly not.
M. But in so doing you would avoid anyone knowing more than you on your own.
A. I wouldn't really care what kind of creature the monks should become, as long as I myself were a human being.
M. Do you think someone who neither is wise nor wants to acquire wisdom is 'human'?
A. I have wisdom enough for myself.[12]
M. And pigs have wisdom enough for themselves.
A. You seem[13] to me to be some kind of sophistress,[14] the way you argue.
M. I shan't mention what you seem to me to be. But why does this furniture displease [you]?
A. Because a distaff and spindle are a woman's [proper] implements.

M. Nonne matronae est administrare rem domesticam, erudire liberos?
A. Est.
M. An rem tantam existimas administrari posse sine sapientia?
A. Non arbitror.
M. At hanc sapientiam docent me libri.
A. Ego domi habeo sexaginta duos monachos, tamen nullum librum reperies in meo cubiculo.
M. Bene itaque prospectum est monachis illis.
A. Feram libros, non fero Latinos.
M. Quapropter?
A. Quia non convenit ea lingua feminis.
M. Expecto causam.
A. Quia parum facit ad tuendam illarum pudicitiam.
M. Ergo nugacissimis fabulis pleni libri Gallice scripti faciunt ad pudicitiam?[15]
A. Aliud est.
M. Dic istud quicquid est, aperte.
A. Tutiores sunt a sacerdotibus, si nesciant Latine.[16]
M. Immo isthinc minimum est periculi vestra opera, quandoquidem hoc agitis sedulo, ne sciatis Latine.
A. Vulgus ita sentit, quia rarum et insolitum feminam scire Latine.
M. Quid mihi citas vulgum, pessimum bene gerendae rei autorem? Quid mihi consuetudinem, omnium malarum rerum magistram? Optimis assuescendum. Ita fiet solitum, quod erat insolitum; et suave fiet, quod erat insuave; fiet decorum, quod videbatur indecorum.
A. Audio.
M. Nonne decorum est feminam in Germania natam discere Gallice?
A. Maxime.
M. Quamobrem?
A. Ut loquatur cum his qui sciunt Gallice.
M. Et mihi putas indecorum, si discam Latine, ut cotidie confabuler cum tot autoribus, tam facundis, tam eruditis, tam sapientibus, tam fidis consultoribus?
A. Libri adimunt multum cerebri feminis, quum alioqui parum illis supersit.
M. Quantum vobis supersit, nescio; certe mihi quantulumcunque est, malim in bonis studiis consumere, quam in precibus sine mente dictis, in pernoctibus conviviis, in exhauriendis capacibus pateris.
A. Librorum familiaritas parit insaniam.

M. Isn't it a married woman's business to take care of the household [and] instruct children?
A. [Yes,] it is.
M. Do you think that so great a matter can be taken care of without wisdom?
A. I don't suppose so.
M. But books teach me this wisdom.
A. I have sixty-two monks at home, and yet you'll find no book in my bedroom.
M. Those monks are well provided for, then.
A. I could tolerate books, but I don't tolerate Latin ones.
M. Why?
A. Because that language doesn't suit women.
M. I'm waiting for your rationale.
A. Because it does little to protect their chastity.
M. So books written in French full of the most worthless stories foster chastity?[15]
A. There's something else.
M. Tell me whatever it is – [and] clearly.
A. They are safer from priests if they don't know Latin.[16]
M. But then there's no danger at all in that respect thanks to your efforts, since you work so hard not to know any Latin.
A. The public agree [with me] that it's a rare and unusual thing for a woman to know Latin.
M. Why cite the public to me, the worst authority on good behaviour? Why [cite] habit to me, the teacher of all evils? One should get used to the best [principles]; then what was unusual will become usual, what was unpleasant will become pleasant, [and] what seemed unseemly will become seemly.
A. I'm listening.
M. Is it seemly for a woman born in Germany to learn French?
A. Of course.
M. Why?
A. So that she might speak to those who know French.
M. And you think it unseemly for me if I learn Latin, in order to converse every day with so many authors, [who are] so eloquent, so learned, so wise, [and] such trustworthy advisors?
A. Books sap up much of the female brain, of which not much exists in the first place.
M. I don't know how much of yours remains; at any rate I prefer to use up however little I have on useful studies rather than in prayers recited mindlessly, all-night parties, [and] draining deep flagons.
A. Friendship with books drives one crazy.

M. An non colloquia combibonum, scurrarum et sannionum tibi pariunt insaniam?
A. Immo depellunt taedium.
M. Qui fiat igitur ut tam amoeni confabulones[17] mihi pariant insaniam?
A. Sic aiunt.
M. At aliud ipsa loquitur res. Quanto plures videmus, quibus immodica potatio et intempestiva convivia, quibus temulenta pervigilia, quibus impotentes affectus pepererunt insaniam?
A. Ego sane nollem uxorem doctam.[18]
M. At ego mihi gratulor, cui contigerit maritus tui dissimilis. Nam et illum mihi et me illi cariorem reddit eruditio.
A. Immensis laboribus comparatur eruditio, ac post moriendum est.
M. Dic mihi, vir egregie, si cras tibi moriendum esset, utrum malles mori stultior an sapientior?
A. Si citra laborem contingeret sapientia.
M. Si nihil homini citra laborem contingit in hac vita, et tamen quicquid paratum est, quantisvis laboribus comparatum est, hic relinquendum est, cur pigeat nos in re omnium pretiosissima sumere laboris aliquid, cuius fructus nos in alteram quoque vitam comitatur?
A. Frequenter audivi vulgo dici feminam sapientem bis stultam esse.
M. Istuc quidem dici solet, sed a stultis. Femina quae vere sapit, non videtur sibi sapere. Contra quae cum nihil sapiat, sibi videtur sapere, ea demum bis stulta est.
A. Nescio quomodo fit, ut quemadmodum clitellae non conveniunt bovi,[19] ita nec litterae mulieri.
M. Atqui negare non potes, quin magis quadrent clitellae bovi, quam mitra asino aut sui. Quid sentis de Virgine matre?
A. Optime.
M. Nonne versabatur in libris?[20]
A. Versabatur, at non in istis.
M. Quid igitur legebat?
A. Horas canonicas.
M. Ad quem usum?
A. Ordinis Benedictini.[21]
M. Sit ita sane. Quid Paula et Eustochium,[22] nonne versabantur in sacris libris?
A. Verum istuc nunc rarum est.

M. But conversations with drinking-buddies, slackers and buffoons don't drive you crazy?
A. On the contrary! They repel boredom.
M. How might it happen, therefore, that such pleasant interlocutors[17] could drive me crazy?
A. That's what people say.
M. But reality itself tells a different story. How many more people do we see who have gone crazy through unrestrained drinking and overfrequent parties, [not to mention] drunken all-nighters and uncontrolled desires?
A. I for sure wouldn't want an educated wife.[18]
M. But I congratulate myself, since I have found a husband [very] different from you. For learning makes him dearer to me and me dearer to him.
A. Learning is acquired through intense drudgery, and after that we must die.
M. Tell me, my good man, if you were to die tomorrow, would you prefer to die stupider or wiser?
A. If wisdom could be obtained without drudgery –
M. Since man obtains nothing in this life without drudgery, and yet whatever has been obtained, no matter through how much drudgery it has been collected, must be left behind here, why do we resent putting in some effort towards the most precious of all things, whose benefits accompany us into the next life also?
A. I have often heard it said publicly that a wise woman is twice foolish.
M. That's indeed often said, but by fools. A woman who has truly acquired wisdom does not seem to herself wise. Conversely, she who thinks that she has acquired wisdom though she has none is indeed twice foolish.
A. Somehow it is the case that, just as packsaddles don't suit a cow,[19] so, too, does literary learning not suit a woman.
M. Yet you cannot deny, that packsaddles suit a cow more than a mitre suits a donkey or a pig. What do you think of the Virgin Mother?
A. [I think] the best [of her].
M. Did she not occupy herself with books?[20]
A. She did, but not in those [books].
M. What was she reading, then?
A. The canonical orders.
M. According to which practice?
A. That of the Benedictine Order.[21]
M. A likely theory. What about Paula and Eustochium,[22] surely they occupied themselves with the Holy Scriptures?
A. But that's a rare thing these days.

M. Sic olim rara avis erat abbas indoctus, nunc nihil vulgatius. Olim principes et Caesares eruditione non minus quam imperio praeminebant. Neque tamen usque adeo rarum est, quam tu putas, sunt in Hispania, sunt in Italia non paucae mulieres adprime nobiles, quae cum quovis viro queant contendere, sunt in Anglia Moricae, sunt in Germania Bilibaldicae et Blaurericae.[23] Quod nisi caveritis vos, res eo tandem evadet, ut nos praesideamus in scholis theologicis, ut contionemur in templis. Occupabimus mitras vestras.[24]

A. Ista Deus avertat.

M. Immo vestrum erit hoc avertere. Quod si pergetis, ut coepistis, citius anseres concionaturi sint, quam vos mutos pastores ferant. Videtis iam inverti mundi scenam. Aut deponenda est persona, aut agendae sunt suae cuique partes.

A. Unde incidi in hanc feminam? Si quando vises nos, ego te suavius accipiam.

M. Quibus modis?

A. Saltabimus, bibemus affatim, venabimur, ludemus, ridebimus.

M. Mihi quidem iam nunc ridere libet.

M. So, too, an uneducated abbot was, once upon a time, a rare bird; now there's nothing more common. Once upon a time princes and emperors excelled no less in learning than in power. However, even now this is not as rare as you think: there are in Spain and Italy not a few women of the most noble class, who could compete with any man. There are the More daughters in England, and in Germany the Pirckheimer and Blarer girls.[23] Unless you are careful, the final result will be that we lead the theological schools and preach in churches. We will take over your mitres.[24]

A. God forbid.

M. On the contrary it's your responsibility to forbid this. For if you continue just as you have begun, geese will sooner preach than tolerate you speechless priests. You see now that the world's stage is turned upside down. Each person must either shed his mask or play his role.

A. How did I stumble upon this woman? If you visit us some time, I will welcome you more pleasantly.

M. In what ways?

A. We shall dance, drink to bursting point, hunt, play, [and] laugh.

M. Indeed, even now I wish to laugh.

Commentary

1 The dialogue was first published as *Antronius, Magdalia* in the March 1524 edition of the *Colloquia*. It was accompanied by three other new dialogues, which share themes with it, in that they either satirize the Church (*Inquisition on Faith*, *The Rich Beggars*) or discuss the good life (*The Old Men's Dialogue*). See *CWE* 39: 505 for the negative connotations of the name 'Antronius'.

2 This collocation combining the adjective *tantus* ('so great, so much, such') with the ablative of *natus* ('birth, age') is associated with mockery: cf. e.g. Plaut. *Bacch.* 124 *qui tantus natu deorum nescis nomina* ('you, who, at such an age, [still] don't know the names of the gods').

3 In classical verse *heroina* is used to mean 'demi-goddess' or 'heroine' in the mythical sense (Propertius 1.19.14), but by Erasmus' time it had taken on the specialized meaning of 'court lady', probably deriving from its use as a compliment to designate particularly attractive or accomplished women.

4 Sixteenth-century European noblewomen were indeed expected to master vernacular languages instead of Greek (which was unusual even for male scholars) and Latin: Margaret, Countess of Richmond, the mother of Henry VII, 'learned to read French ... and to write English' but only 'enough Latin to follow the service' (Warnicke 1983: 11). Scholars generally identify Magdalia as another Margaret: Margaret More Roper, one of Sir Thomas More's four daughters. Erasmus enjoyed a close friendship with More himself and kept up a correspondence with the More girls in Latin (Allen 1233: 74; *CWE* 2: 81).

5 This statement paraphrases Plato, *Protagoras* 351b: τί δ' εἰ ἡδέως βιοὺς τὸν βίον τελευτήσειεν; οὐκ εὖ ἄν σοι δοκεῖ οὕτως βεβιωκέναι; ('If a man lived pleasantly and so ended his life, would you not consider he had thus also lived well?'). Magdalia's argument more generally corresponds to that of Socrates in Plato's *Republic* 349b–54a – i.e. living pleasurably is equivalent to living virtuously – and is delivered to Antronius via Socratic questioning.

6 The use of *proficisci* to mean 'originate from' is attested in classical Latin, but always with the preposition *a/ab* instead of *e/ex* (e.g. Cic. *De or.* 2.14.58; *Fin.* 5.8.23; Nep. *Att.* 9.4). However, as Erasmus makes clear in his *Ciceronianus*, he was not among those who 'worshipped the divine, inimitable Ciceronian diction' (*ASD* I–2: 622; *CWE* 28: 364).

7 Personal freedom may seem out of place in a list of vanities, but by squandering his *libertas* in hunts and parties, Antronius perverts the Renaissance ideal of personal liberty. The residents of François Rabelais'

abbey at Thélème are allowed full freedom, as encapsulated in their motto *fais ce que voudras* ('do what you like'), but make use of that privilege 'virtuously' by reading, writing, singing and learning languages (*Gargantua* 54). Antronius' *libertas* also clashes with contemporary conceptualizations of political liberty, which was closely tied to productive participation in communal institutions. Alamanno Rinuccini in his 1479 *Dialogue on Liberty* defines that concept as the free debate of civil matters in public meetings (Watkins 1978: 197–207).

8 The incorporation of *valere* ('to be well') into the colloquial formula 'away with . . .' (cf. e.g. Hor. *Ep.* 2.1.180) ultimately derives from the use of that verb to say 'farewell'.

9 Despite advocating for women's education, Erasmus believed wives should defer to their husbands in marriage: 'A wife who makes war on her husband is making war on God' (*ASD* V–6: 194; *CWE* 69: 368). Accordingly, Magdalia emphasizes that her husband approves of her studies.

10 The 'Peter' and 'Paul' mentioned here are not the Apostles – even though the parallel is intentional – but the legal commentators Baldo degli Ubaldi and Paulo de Castro. Antronius fears that his monks will read these author's works, along with Gratian's *Decretum* and Gregory IX's *Decretales* (Tunberg 2012: 199–200).

11 *responsator* is a rare word, first used by a late-fourth-century commentator on St Paul's epistles, whom seventeenth-century scholars termed Ambrosiaster in reference to the long-standing misattribution of his work to St Ambrose, as discussed by Erasmus in his 1527 edition of the latter's writings. Ambrosiaster employed *responsator* as a descriptor of what good servants ought *not* to be, just as Antronius in this dialogue specifies that he does *not* want a *monachum responsatorem*. Ambrosiaster, *Tit.* 2.1: *servos dominis suis subditos esse in omnibus, optimos, non responsatores, non fraudantes* ('servants subject to their masters in all things, the best [servants], neither back-talkers nor deceivers').

12 *mihi* (and *sibi* below) is a dative of advantage.

13 *videre* is a shortened form of *videris*, the second person singular present passive indicative form of *video, -ere* ('to see').

14 The term 'sophistress' is no compliment and not only highlights Antronius' uncharitable attitude towards Magdalia, but also reveals some reticence, on Erasmus' part, to fully endorse Magdalia's world view; his Folly foolishly chooses the title of 'sophist' rather than that of 'wise man' (cf. *ASD* IV–3: 72; *CWE* 27: 87).

15 *facere* is paired with *ad* to denote a process of 'making', i.e. 'fostering, building towards, cultivating, benefiting' (cf. *non multum faciunt ad vitam communem*, '[these writings] do not foster communal living', *ASD* I–2: 233; *CWE* 25: 25).

16 Antronius' cynical view of clergymen, though ironic given that he is himself a priest, reflects the broader current of anticlericalism in humanist rhetoric. Erasmus was particularly opposed to the rigid hierarchy of the Church, which led not only to abuses of power and privilege such as Antronius' luxurious lifestyle, but also to what he saw as the unjustified elevation of religious over lay vocations (see e.g. *ASD* IV–3: 159–68; *CWE* 27: 131–6).

17 The noun *confabulo*, *-onis* ('interlocutor') is an Erasmian formation; an early modern lexicographer, William Massey, complained that 'it has the stamp of barbarism upon it. It ought not to be given to young scholars' (Massey 1755: 13). Here, Magdalia utilizes *confabulones* in referring to her books, thereby differentiating her lifestyle from that of Antronius, who has just employed the similarly structured, but classical, compound *combibonum* to designate his 'drinking-buddies'.

18 Antronius speaks hypothetically, as indicated by the counterfactual imperfect subjunctive *nollem*. Erasmus' negative opinion of clerical celibacy may be in play here: cf. *ASD* I–2: 400–28; *CWE* 25: 129–45.

19 Erasmus likely borrowed this incongruous image of *clitellae* ('packsaddles', meant for horses) and *bovi* ('cow') from Cicero, who himself quoted the metaphor from a now-lost comedy (Cic. *Att.* 108.3: *clitellae bovi sunt impositae; plane non est nostrum onus*, 'packsaddles have been placed upon the ox; that is clearly not the burden for me').

20 The trope of the Virgin Mary as a reader stems from her characterization as prudent and learned. This depiction goes back to the early medieval period: in the fourth century CE Ambrose noted that Mary was 'most studious in reading' (*De virginibus ad Marcellinam* 2.2.7), and the Carolingian-era *Gospel of Pseudo-Matthew* emphasizes that she was 'learned in the wisdom of the law of God' (6.2). However, it was only in the twelfth century, when the roles of anchoresses and other female religious positions were being progressively defined, that the image of Mary as reader gained popularity in art and literature – especially in depictions of the Annunciation – and served as a model of spiritual learning for women (Saetveit Miles 2014: 632–69).

21 Antronius here demonstrates the consequences of ignorance in clergymen by uttering two anachronisms in quick succession: the Virgin Mary could

evidently not have read the canonical hours and especially not those associated with the sixth-century Benedictine rule. Erasmus' target is not so much the Benedictines, to whom Antronius ostensibly belongs, as misplaced pride for one's own order and rivalries between orders in general, which Peace identifies as a major source of social conflict in the *Querela Pacis*: 'There are as many factions as communities, Dominicans wrangling with Franciscans, Benedictines with Bernardines' (*ASD* IV-2: 67; *CWE* 27: 298).

22 The saints Paula and her daughter Eustochium studied scripture with St Jerome. In his own analysis of this colloquy (which he refers to using the title *Erudita Puella*) Erasmus notes that he created the character of Magdalia in an attempt to 'renew the ancient example' of Paula, Eustochium and Marcella, another of Jerome's students (*ASD* I-3: 746; *CWE* 39–40: 1102).

23 On these real-world women and their scholarly fathers (Thomas More, Willibald Pirckheimer, Ambrosius and Thomas Blarer), with whom Erasmus was personally acquainted, see *CWE* 39: 516–17.

24 Nowhere in his writings does Erasmus advocate for the ordination of women, and Magdalia's pronouncement should not be read as a realistic threat, but as a hyperbolic indictment of Antronius and his ilk, as well as a reflection on how their indolence might feed the fires of reform within the Church.

4

Christopher Columbus' First Voyage

Pietro Bembo (1470–1547), *Rerum Venetarum Historiae Libri*, Extracts from 6.1–3

Gareth Williams

Introduction

In 1530 the eminent Venetian humanist Pietro Bembo (1470–1547, cardinal from 1539) succeeded Andrea Navagero as official historian of the Venetian Republic. By 1547 he had completed his twelve-book *History of Venice*, spanning the period from 1487 to 1513, in both its original Latin version and his subsequent Italian vernacular translation of that original. After his death in that year, both versions were subjected to censorship by the ever-watchful Venetian authorities, and the modified Latin text was published only in 1551 in Venice under the title *Rerum Venetarum historiae libri XII*. Book 6, on 1501–4, begins with a digression that ranges far from the Republic but still vitally concerns it: in describing Columbus' voyages to the New World and those of the Portuguese to the East, Bembo recounts developments that not only jeopardized the Venetian economy by opening up rival trade routes, but also redrew the geopolitical map through the new Iberian ascendancy. In lamenting this 'unforeseen misfortune' (6.1) for Venice, Bembo writes as 'a loyal factotum of the Republic' (McCarthy-King 2012: 33); but he combines this Venice-centred perspective with open admiration for what such pioneers as Columbus and Magellan achieved (cf. 6.13). These different tendencies – dismay in tension with wonder – permeate Bembo's account of Columbus and reflect the larger picture of mixed Venetian reaction to the voyages of discovery.

Though profoundly affected by the strategic and economic consequences of these voyages, Venice remained a central locus of knowledge, inquiry and introspection about the rapidly expanding world. Various factors drove this phenomenon: Venice's mercantile importance ensured a steady influx of traders, diplomats and visitors who fed curiosity about the wider world; the city's prominence in the nascent history of printing made it a major centre for the dissemination of the travel anthology, a genre that was itself given major impetus by the voyages of discovery; and the French invasion of 1494 initiated the so-called Italian Wars that lasted down to 1559, a period of turbulence that – like the Iberian discoveries – led to much introspection and unease about Venice's place in the emerging world order.

This anxiety of engagement with the voyages of discovery at Venice is further illustrated by the sources on which Bembo drew for his account of Columbus. By his death in 1529 Navagero had made little tangible progress with his history of Venice, but he had apparently completed an Italian translation of part of Peter Martyr's Latin *Decades of the New World* (*De orbe novo decades*, first published in 1511) and also of Gonzalo Fernández de Oviedo's Spanish *Summary of the Natural History of the Indies* (*Sumario de la natural historia de las Indias*) of 1526. The two translations were subsequently included in the anonymous 1534 Italian vernacular compilation entitled *Summary of the General History of the West Indies* (*Summario de la general historia de l'Indie occidentali*), commonly attributed to the distinguished Venetian geographer Giovanni Battista Ramusio. The content of this summary was later absorbed into Ramusio's famous three-volume *Navigations and Travels* (*Navigationi e viaggi*) published in 1550–9. Bembo's close association with both Navagero and Ramusio clearly influenced his portrayal of Columbus. Further, while his debt to Peter Martyr is evident in points of verbal detail in *History of Venice* 6, in a letter to Oviedo of 20 April 1538 Bembo also claims the latter as his source: after the publication of Oviedo's *Summary* in 1526, the first edition of part 1 of his massive *General and Natural History of the Indies* (*Historia general y natural de las Indias*) was published in 1535 in Seville. In his *Navigations and Travels* in particular Ramusio casts Spain and Portugal as arriviste rivals to Venice's already long-established cosmopolitanism and Columbus as an Italian hero: even as the Iberian peninsula encroached on Italian power and prestige, Ramusio's pen sought to vindicate Venice's place in the world – a tendency no less visible in Bembo's favourable treatment of Columbus as by implication 'one of our own'.

By inserting Columbus into his *History of Venice*, then, and even at the cost of registering how Venetian interests were damaged by the voyages of discovery, Bembo writes the Republic into the grand narrative of this age of exploration: Columbus is viewed from a Venetian perspective, in an account that heavily relies on the intermediary Venetian authority of Navagero and Ramusio, while also reflecting the Republic's prominence as a disseminator (in both the printed word and cartography) of knowledge about the expanding world. The classical purity and formalism of Bembo's Latinity further underscore this patriotic agenda by describing Columbus' achievement in the New World in all the finery of Old World linguistic culture: even as horizons were beginning to expand overseas, the chapters below show how the novelty of the exotic and different is reassuringly absorbed and articulated by the time-honoured modulations of Eurocentric Latinity – albeit modulations that are given a particular Venetian stamp through Bembo's fame as a Latin stylist in his own day. In sum, Bembo's Columbus rides the waves, but on a familiar Latinate wavelength.

Bibliography

Cachey, T. J. (2002), 'Italy and the Invention of America', *The New Centennial Review*, 2.1: 17–31.

Carrillo, J., D. Avalle-Arce and A. Pagden (2000), *Oviedo on Columbus*, Turnhout (Repertorium Columbianum Volume IX).

Cro, S. (1992), 'Italian Humanism and the Myth of the Noble Savage', *Annali d'Italianistica*, 10: 48–68.

Eatough, G., ed. (1998), *Selections from Peter Martyr*, Turnhout (Repertorium Columbianum Volume V).

Headley, J. M. (1997), 'The Sixteenth-Century Venetian Celebration of the Earth's Total Habitability: The Issue of the Fully Habitable World for Renaissance Europe', *Journal of World History*, 8.1: 1–27.

Horodowich, L. (2018), *The Venetian Discovery of America: Geographic Imagination and Print Culture in the Age of Encounters*, Cambridge.

Kidd, I. G. (1988), *Posidonius. Volume II: the Commentary*, 2 vols, Cambridge (Cambridge Classical Texts and Commentaries 14A/B).

Kidd, I. G. (1999), *Posidonius. Volume III: the Translation of the Fragments*, Cambridge (Cambridge Classical Texts and Commentaries 36).

McCarthy-King, E. (2012), 'The Voyage of Columbus as a "non pensato male": The Search for Boundaries, Grammar, and Authority in the Aftermath of the New World Discoveries', in A. Moudarres and C. Purdy Moudarres (eds), *New Worlds and the Italian Renaissance: Contributions to the History of European Intellectual Culture*, 25–44, Leiden.

Moody, E. A. (1941), 'John Buridan on the Habitability of the Earth', *Speculum*, 16.4: 415–25.

Perocco, D. (1990), '"Un male non pensato": Pietro Bembo e la scoperta dell'America', in A. C. Aricò (ed.), *L'impatto della scoperta dell'America nella cultura veneziana*, 279–93, Rome.

Ulery, R. W., ed. (2008), *Pietro Bembo: History of Venice. Volume 2: Books V–VIII*, Cambridge MA / London (The I Tatti Renaissance Library 32).

Weinstein, D. (1960), *Ambassador from Venice: Pietro Pasqualigo in Lisbon, 1501*, Minneapolis.

Source of the Latin text

Text, translation and notes are available in Ulery 2008; the Latin extracts follow that edition.

Latin text

6.1 Talibus iactatae incommodis[1] civitati malum etiam inopinatum ab longinquis gentibus et regionibus extitit. Petri enim Pascalici, apud Emanuelem Lusitaniae regem legati, litteris patres certiores facti sunt[2] regem illum per Mauritaniae Getuliaeque[3] oceanum convehendis ex Arabia Indiaque mercibus itinera, suis temptata saepe navibus, demum explorata compertaque[4] habuisse, navesque aliquot eo missas pipere et cinnamis eiusmodique rebus onustas Olysipponem revertisse; itaque futurum ut,[5] eius rei facultate Hispanis hominibus tradita, nostri in posterum cives parcius angustiusque mercarentur, magnique illi proventus, qui urbem opulentam reddidissent toti paene terrarum orbi rebus Indicis tradendis, civitatem deficerent. Eo nuntio patres accepto non parvam animi aegritudinem contraxerunt, quam tamen compendiis[6] aliorum populorum solabantur. Simul et illud cogitabant: amabile profecto esse novas regiones alterumque prope acquiri orbem, gentesque abditas atque sepositas celebrari. Ac postea quam hunc ad locum meorum me commentariorum[7] cursus perduxit, non alienum esse arbitror, quod eius rei, omnium quas ulla aetas umquam ab hominibus effectas vidit maximae atque pulcherrimae, fuerit initium, tum quae terrarum portio post id quaeve gentes et quibus moribus sint repertae, quantum suscepti operis ratio permittet, breviter dicere.

6.2 Erat Columbus[8] homo Ligur ingenio peracri, qui multas emensus regiones, multum maris et oceani[9] perlustraverat. Is, ut est humanus animus novarum rerum appetens, Ferdinando et Isabellae,[10] Hispaniae regibus, proponit edocetque illud, quod omnis fere antiquitas credidit – quinque esse caeli partes,[11] quarum media caloribus, extremae duae frigoribus sic afficiantur, ut quae sub illis sint totidem terrae plagae incoli ab hominibus non possint, duae tantum inter eas sub eisdem positae caeli partibus possint – inanem esse antiquorum hominum fabulam, et nullis veris rationibus fultam et confirmatam descriptionem; improvidum prope necesse esse haberi Deum,[12] si ita mundum sit fabricatus, ut longe maior terrarum pars propter nimiam intemperiem hominibus vacua nullum ex sese usum praebeat; globum esse terrae hunc eiusmodi, ut commeandi per omnes eius partes facultas hominibus ne desit . . . Hac oratione apud reges habita, petit ut

English translation

6.1 Disturbed by setbacks of this kind,[1] the state also encountered an unforeseen misfortune from far-off peoples and regions. For the senators were apprised by a letter of Pietro Pasqualigo, ambassador at the court of Manuel, King of Portugal,[2] that that king had often, with his own ships, tried to find routes for transporting goods from Arabia and India through the seas off Mauritania and Gaetulia,[3] and that he had finally discovered and verified[4] those routes; and that several ships that had been sent there had returned to Lisbon laden with pepper and cinnamon and other such commodities; and so, since the Spanish peoples had been handed this capability, our citizens would[5] inevitably trade in time to come on a smaller, more limited scale; and those great revenues that had made the city rich by delivering Indian goods to almost the entire world would be lost to the state. The senators were caused considerable anguish when they received this report – [anguish] for which they found solace, however, in the shorter routes[6] to other peoples. At the same time they also reflected on this – that it was certainly desirable for new regions to be acquired, and almost another world, and for hidden and remote peoples to become known. And now that the course of my narrative[7] has led me to this topic, it is not inappropriate, I think, briefly to tell, insofar as the plan of my undertaking will allow, of the beginning of this activity – the greatest and most glorious of all the achievements that any generation has ever seen accomplished by humankind; [and] then [to tell of] what part of the world was discovered thereafter and what peoples and their customs.

6.2 Columbus[8] was a Ligurian of very sharp intellect who had travelled through a good many regions and ranged over much of the sea and ocean.[9] In keeping with the human mind's appetite for new discoveries, he made a representation before the Spanish sovereigns, Ferdinand and Isabella,[10] fully explaining that what was almost universally believed in the ancient past – that there are five regions of the heavens,[11] of which the middle one experiences such heat, the two outermost ones such cold, that the equivalent stretches of the earth beneath them are uninhabitable by humans, [and] that only the two intermediate stretches set under the corresponding regions of the heavens are habitable – was an empty fiction of the ancients, and an account based on and bolstered by no true grounds of reasoning. It would [he explained] be all but necessary for God[12] to be regarded as improvident if he shaped the world in such a way that by far the earth's greater part is devoid of humankind because of the climatic extremes and offers no utility from itself; [he added that] this terrestrial sphere was of such a kind so that humans had no shortage of opportunity to travel through all its parts ... After making this speech before the sovereigns, he asked

sibi liceat eorum opibus novas insulas, nova litora quaerere; spem se habere non defore inceptis fortunam, dicionemque ipsorum magnopere iri auctum, si rem susceperint, confirmat.

6.3 Ab regibus nova spe allectis sententia Columbi, quam quidem totum septennium[13] reiecerant, ad extremum comprobata (quam tamen multo antea Posidonii philosophi, Panaetii discipuli,[14] primum, deinde etiam Avicennae medici[15] fuisse video, magni et praeclari viri), anno ab urbe condita millesimo septuagesimo primo[16] tribus cum navibus Columbus ad insulas Fortunatas, de quibus superioribus libris sermonem habuimus,[17] quas Canarias appellant, profectus, atque ab iis tres et triginta totos dies occidentem secutus solem, sex numero insulas reperit, quarum sunt duae ingentis magnitudinis; quibus in insulis lusciniae Novembri mense canerent,[18] homines nudi, ingenio miti, lintribus ex uno ligno factis uterentur[19] ... Aurum,[20] quod in fluminum arenis legunt, habent; ferrum non habent. Itaque praeduris atque acutis lapidibus et ad lintres cavandos et ad reliquam materiam in usum domesticum formandum aurumque molliendum pro ferro utuntur. Sed aurum cultus tantummodo gratia molliunt, idque auribus et naribus perforatis pendulum gerunt; neque enim nummos noverunt neque stipis ullo genere utuntur. Harum duarum insularum unius cum rege amicitia foedereque inito,[21] Columbus, duo de quadraginta ex suis apud illum relictis, qui mores et sermonem gentis addiscerent seque brevi rediturum exspectarent, decem ex insularibus secum ducens in Hispaniam rediit. Haec illorum itinerum origo institutaeque ad incognitas orbis terrarum oras navigationis initium[22] hoc fuit.

to be given licence to seek out, with their support, new islands [and] new shores; he affirmed his expectation that the undertaking would have no lack of success and that their dominion would be greatly increased if they ventured upon the enterprise.

6.3 After spurning Columbus' idea for the entirety of seven years,[13] the sovereigns were drawn by fresh hope and ultimately approved it (I see, however, that, far earlier, it had been [the idea] first of the philosopher Posidonius, Panaetius' pupil,[14] and then also of the physician Avicenna,[15] a man of great distinction). In the year 1071 from the city's foundation,[16] Columbus set forth with three ships for the Fortunate Isles (I have spoken of them in previous books),[17] which they call 'Canaries', and heading towards the setting sun from there for thirty-three days in all, he discovered islands [that were] six in number, two of them of vast size; on these islands nightingales would sing in November[18] [and] naked people of a gentle nature would use small boats crafted from a single tree trunk[19] . . . They have gold,[20] which they collect in the sands of rivers; iron they do not have, and so instead of iron they use very hard and sharp stones both to carve out the small boats and for shaping the remaining wood for domestic purposes, and for fashioning gold. But they fashion gold only for adornment, wearing it hanging down from their pierced ears and nostrils; for they know nothing of coinage, and use no money of any kind. After entering into terms of friendship with the king of one of these two islands,[21] Columbus left thirty-eight of his own men with him, to learn the ways and language of the people and to await his return after a short time; taking with him ten of the islanders, he went back to Spain. This was how those journeys came into being, and such was the beginning[22] of the sea-travel that was started on to the unknown margins of the world.

Commentary

6.1

1 *incommodis*: the loss to the Turks of Navarino (modern Pylos) and Durazzo (modern Durrës in Albania), as recounted in book 5.59–61.

2 *Petri enim Pascalici . . . facti sunt*: after the first of the Portuguese spice ships returned to Lisbon on 23 June 1501, Pasqualigo (1472–1515) composed or forwarded the first official report of that event on 27 June; Bembo presumably refers to that particular report. Venetian policy had originally been to court Portuguese support for the campaign against the Turks, but news of the Portuguese voyages gave a secondary thrust to Pasqualigo's diplomatic agenda; for 'if the Venetians were successful in diverting the King from his Eastern designs to the Mediterranean they would have done something to solve both their problems together' (Weinstein 1960: 24).

3 *Mauritaniae Getuliaeque*: ancient Roman names for territories in North Africa, but here in effect 'West Africa'.

4 *temptata . . . explorata compertaque*: see *OLD* s.v. *habeo* 27a for these perfect participles in relation to *habuisse* (lit. 'the king had had the routes [*itinera*] discovered and verified').

5 *futurum* is elliptical for *futurum esse*, and *ut* is consecutive; the indirect discourse introduced by *patres certiores facti sunt regem . . .* continues.

6 *compendiis*: for 'short cut' see *OLD* s.v. 3a, but also with a hint of trade profits (cf. *OLD* s.v. 1).

7 *commentariorum*: of a historical record in particular see *OLD* s.v. 1b.

6.2

8 *Columbus*: beyond Oviedo as a declared source (see Introduction), there are striking verbal overlaps with Peter Martyr (see 1.1.2 in Eatough 1998: 129, based on the 1516 printed text): e.g. *homo Ligur* Bembo ~ *ligur vir* Martyr; *Ferdinando et Isabellae, Hispaniae regibus, proponit edocetque* Bembo ~ [*F*]*ernando et* [*H*]*elisabethae regibus catholicis proposuit et suasit* Martyr.

9 *maris et oceani*: presumably the Mediterranean and the Atlantic (cf. *OLD* s.v. *Oceanus* 2a).

10 *Ferdinando et Isabellae*: through their marriage and joint sovereignty, Isabella I of Castile (1451–1504) and Ferdinand II of Aragon (1452–1516) laid the foundation for a newly unified Spain.

11 *quinque . . . caeli partes*: the five-zone theory extends back at least to the Presocratic philosopher Parmenides (cf. Strabo, *Geography* 2.2.2) and is amply attested and sometimes contested in later classical sources (e.g. Cicero, *De re republica* 6.21; Seneca, *Naturales quaestiones* 5.17.2; Manilius 1.566–602); see Headley 1997: esp. 5–6.

12 *Deum*: after the debunking of ancient pagan belief, Bembo's 'corrective' assertion of the earth's full habitability pointedly invokes the beneficence of the Christian God, albeit through the filter of 'the Platonic argument of a divine plenitude' as notably exemplified in Ramusio's *Navigations and Travels* (see Headley 1997: esp. 14–18). The content of Columbus' speech as reported by Bembo is nowhere corroborated in the larger textual record. Bembo has crafted Columbus as one steeped in classical knowledge but as no captive to received wisdom, especially in the face of an enlightened divine logic that he piously and progressively espouses (further, Perocco 1990: 291–2).

6.3

13 *septennium*: corroborated by Oviedo in his *General and Natural History of the Indies* (3.5.3 in Carrillo et al. 2000: 46 and 111).

14 *Posidonii philosophi, Panaetii discipuli*: a pupil of the second-century BCE Stoic philosopher Panaetius of Rhodes, Posidonius of Apamea (*c.* 135–*c.* 51 BCE) held a five-zone theory of the earth, hypothesizing that the torrid, equatorial zone between the two tropics was habitable (further, Kidd 1988: 230–1 and 750–2 on frr. 49 and 210, and 1999: 111 and 275–6). Posidonius' writings were lost but accessible for Bembo through intermediary sources such as Strabo (see note on 6.2 *quinque . . . caeli partes*).

15 *Avicennae medici*: the Arab philosopher-physician and polymath Ibn Sina (980–1037) reportedly held that the most temperate climate exists at the (therefore habitable) equator: for sources see Moody 1941: 419.

16 *anno . . . primo*: Bembo emulates the ancient Roman convention of dating the given year from that of Rome's foundation (*ab urbe condita*). Venice was by legend founded at the stroke of noon on 25 March 421. By so dating Columbus' voyage, Bembo contextualizes it in relation to another (still more?) momentous historical event.

17 *de quibus ... habuimus*: in book 4.3. The elder Pliny's account of the Fortunate Isles in his *Natural History* (6.202–5) is the first attestation of the name *Canaria*. Pliny states that one of the islands is so called because of its 'multitude of dogs (*canum*) of vast size'.

18 *sex ... canerent*: Bembo appears to follow Peter Martyr 1.1.5 (Eatough 1998: 131), who names the two large islands as Hispaniola (Haiti/Dominican Republic) and Juana (Cuba); with *lusciniae* Bembo varies Martyr's *philomela* for 'nightingale'.

19 *canerent... uterentur*: subjunctives in virtual *oratio obliqua* (Bembo does not himself vouch for the phenomena he reports).

20 *Aurum*: Bembo subscribes to the larger Renaissance discourse of a utopian Golden Age of innocence in the Americas – a discourse often implying by contrast a deep European decadence (see Cro 1992).

21 *cum rege amicitia foedereque inito*: the king is named as Guacanagari by Peter Martyr and Oviedo; Bembo appears to adapt Martyr's *icto singularis amicitiae foedere* (1.1.12 in Eatough 1998: 134), thereby reproducing Martyr's 'very formal language borrowed from the world of Roman Imperialism' (Eatough 1998: 241).

22 *initium*: in a neat symmetry of literal and narratival journeys, Columbus returns to Spain, and Bembo completes his own circuit by referring back to *eius rei... initium* at the end of 6.1; *initium* here also puns neatly on *itinerum origo*.

5

Morbid Measures and Contaminated Airs: The Poetics of Pox

Girolamo Fracastoro (1476/8–1553), *Syphilis sive de Morbo Gallico*, Extracts

Gareth Williams

Introduction

The eminent Veronese physician, poet and polymath Girolamo Fracastoro (1476/8–1553) may have embarked on his 1,346-line *Syphilis* as early as 1510, but it was published only in 1530. He was trained medically at the University of Padua, where he taught from 1502, counting Copernicus among his associates. Having returned to Verona by the end of the decade, he practised as a physician there and devoted himself to his studies. A measure of his eminence is that in 1545 he was named by Pope Paul III as doctor of the Council of Trent.

The disease 'syphilis' takes its name from Fracastoro's famous poem. The 1530 edition was in three books that are broadly Virgilian in their didactic mission and feel. But the *Georgics* vies with the many other classical traces (Lucretius' *On the nature of things* prominent among them: Goddard 1993, and see further below) that are symptomatic of the poem's own allusive contagiousness. Book 1, dedicated to the distinguished Venetian humanist Pietro Bembo (1470–1547; see Text 4), first explores the causes of the disease, which Fracastoro posits to be airborne and generated in the putrid atmosphere (1.119–29); he then describes symptoms and effects in a passage (1.307–469) from which the first extract is drawn. Early in book 2 Fracastoro lauds Pope Leo X, whom Bembo served as Papal secretary down to Leo's death in 1521: Leo's exploits as a healing presence who ushers in a new age of peace and prosperity (2.43–60) set a suitably positive tone for Fracastoro's ensuing discourse on remedial treatments for syphilis. Book 3, sampled in three further excerpts, voyages to America with Christopher Columbus: two myths explain why both the Spaniards (3.151–99) and the Amerindians (3.288–379) are stricken with syphilis; but the book's central topic is the curative properties of the guaiacum tree, native to the Caribbean: imported to Europe, by the 1520s it was widely applied in decocted form to treat the disease, but with no significant effectiveness.

In 1525 Fracastoro sent Bembo a version of his *Syphilis* in two books. In a letter of 26 November 1525 Bembo duly praised the poem, but in an accompanying document (Pellegrini 1955: 38–61) he proposed 111 adjustments. Many of those suggestions were heeded by Fracastoro; but more significant is his resistance to Bembo's later protestations, in a letter of 5 January 1526, against extending the poem beyond two books. What was gained by the addition of a third book despite Bembo's urging to the contrary?

One major advantage was that Fracastoro acquired a certain room for manoeuvre and equivocation in addressing issues of deep controversy in his own day. The problem of syphilis' place of origin was paramount. Was it imported to the Old World from the New? Or did it already exist in Europe before it erupted in Italy during the French invasion under Charles VIII in 1494, then spreading throughout the continent after the disbanding and dispersal of Charles's army a year later? In book 1 Fracastoro directly contemplates the American theory (1.32–52), only to reject it out of hand (1.53–79): the disease could not have spread so widely in so short a time if brought to Europe only in the 1490s; and how to explain its simultaneous outbreak in such disparate parts of the continent if it were imported via a single entry point? Yet after he dismisses the American theory in book 1, his coverage of the guaiacum cure in book 3 requires him to show syphilis erupting as a heaven-sent punishment in the New World: in a diverting aetiological story, Fracastoro has it that a shepherd named Syphilus (Fracastoro's invention) was its first sufferer because of his hubristic worship of his king – the fictional Alcithoos – as a god on earth (3.310–34). For all his efforts to assert that the pestilence was simultaneously erupting in many loci across Europe (3.384–6) and that it was therefore not American by origin, Fracastoro's extended stay in the New World galvanizes our attention on the very locus from which he seeks to dislodge us in book 1. This turning to Columbus is perhaps motivated in part by Fracastoro's self-identification with that adventurer: the first to offer a poetic account of Columbus' discovery, he embarks on his own voyage of discovery in exploring syphilis and 'tell[ing] of things never seen before in our forebears' time, or ever spoken by anyone' (3.11–12). Just as Columbus charts the new territories, bringing them to order by cruel force and by 'the imposition of our laws and our names' (3.22), so in his different way Fracastoro brings the New Scourge to order by explaining it, by asserting remedies for it and also by taming it through the classificatory power of nomenclature: by derivation from Syphilus, Fracastoro's syphilis is 'processed' via the assured protocols of classical aetiology – a central example of how the poetic medium itself, by its recourse to mythopoeia, goes beyond technical exegesis to treat the disease through strategies of calming, even charming, textual sedation.

In the balance of books 1 and 3, then, Fracastoro denies the American theory of syphilis' origin and yet still allows for its emergence in the New World. By incorporating the American dimension, the poem may be seen to gesture to a theory of origin that it does not endorse – a technique of cautious equivocation at a moment when medical science was feeling its way in its rationalization and treatment of the new disease. At least two other factors inform this equivocal approach. First, in positing that syphilis is cyclical in its operation, re-emerging after long periods of dormancy (1.100–8), and that its emergence at any given time is occasioned by astral conjunction (1.219–55, esp. 250–4), Fracastoro appears reluctant – at least in book 1 – to explain the disease as a divine punishment; in claiming that it is airborne, he also discounts its transmission through sexual contact. One of the advantages of a theory of airborne transmission, with no overt stress on divine vengeance, was tactful circumspection: the widespread occurrence in Fracastoro's day of syphilis among the aristocracy and senior clergy became explicable without any intimation of moral judgment.

Secondly, Fracastoro's own thinking on syphilis developed over time: after his *Syphilis* was published in 1530, he composed a separate tract on the disease *c.* 1533 (first published in Pellegrini 1939), and syphilis again figures prominently (2.11–12; 3.10) in his three-book prose treatise of 1546, *De contagione et contagiosis morbis et curatione* ('*On contagion and contagious diseases and their treatment*'). After dismissing the American theory of syphilis' origin in his *Syphilis*, Fracastoro is less sure on this point in *On contagion*. Similarly, his insistence on the airborne transmission of the disease in the poem is later modified by his openness to secondary transmission through direct physical contact. His 'seed' theory of syphilis' spread – in his poem he redirects the Lucretian language of atomic *semina* to posit a separate order of living entities, the seeds of disease – also later underwent shifts of terminology (he was the first to use the term *seminaria* of the infective agents) and of theoretical elaboration: so, e.g., he pioneered the use of *fomes* (lit. 'tinder') for the medium (such as clothing) by which the disease was passed on. Given these and other such modifications, Fracastoro's analysis of the disease in his *Syphilis* is best viewed as developmental and progressive, rather than as a fixed and final position. Moreover, despite Fracastoro's visionary stress on airborne transmission, there was much in his thought that was traditional, conventional and uncontroversial: so, for example, there were significant ancient precedents for his conception of seeds of disease; he accepted traditional humoral theory; and many earlier physicians had already discussed plague in terms of contagion (see Nutton 1983 and 1990). Hence it is an oversimplification to hail Fracastoro as a clairvoyant trailblazer in the modern history of bacteriology. Yet this qualification in no way detracts from his eminence as a deeply learned and distinctive medical theorist, and as a poet of ingenious resourcefulness in his remarkable *Syphilis*.

Metre: dactylic hexameter

Bibliography

Arrizabalaga, J., J. Henderson and R. French (1997), *The Great Pox: The French Disease in Renaissance Europe*, New Haven / London.

Cairns, F. (1994), 'Fracastoro's *Syphilis*, the Argonautic Tradition, and the Aetiology of Syphilis', *Humanistica Lovaniensia*, 43: 246–61.

Cohen, J. M., ed. (1969), *The Four Voyages of Christopher Columbus*, London.

Eatough, G., ed. (1984), *Fracastoro's Syphilis*, Liverpool.

Gardner, J., ed. (2013), *Girolamo Fracastoro: Latin Poetry*, Cambridge MA / London (The I Tatti Renaissance Library 57).

Goddard, C. (1993), 'Lucretius and Lucretian Science in the Works of Fracastoro', *Res Publica Litterarum*, 16: 185–92.

Hendrickson, G. L. (1934), 'The *Syphilis* of Girolamo Fracastoro, with Some Observations on the Origin and History of the Word "Syphilis"', *Bulletin of the Institute of the History of Medicine*, 2.9: 515–46.

Munger, R. S. (1949), 'Guaiacum, the Holy Wood from the New World,' *Journal of the History of Medicine and Allied Sciences*, 4.2: 196–229.

Nutton, V. (1983), 'The Seeds of Disease: An Explanation of Contagion and Infection from the Greeks to the Renaissance', *Medical History*, 27: 1–34.

Nutton, V. (1990), 'The Reception of Fracastoro's Theory of Contagion: The Seed that Fell Among Thorns?', *Osiris*, 2nd ser., 6: 196–234.

Pellegrini, F., ed. (1939), *Trattato inedito in prosa di Gerolamo Fracastoro sulla sifilide. Codice CCLXXV-I, Biblioteca Capitolare di Verona*, Verona.

Pellegrini, F., ed. (1955), *Scritti inediti di Girolamo Fracastoro, con introduzione, commenti e note*, Verona.

Renwick, W. R. (1928), *Hieronymus Fracastorius and his Poetical and Prose Works on Syphilis*, Toronto.

Spitzer, L. (1955), 'The Etymology of the Term "Syphilis"', *Bulletin of the History of Medicine*, 29.3: 269–73.

Source of the Latin text

Texts, translations and notes are available in Eatough 1984 and Gardner 2013. The Latin extracts given below follow Gardner 2013 with minor adaptations.

Latin text

Passage 1: 1.332–59. The gruesome symptoms of syphilis

Tum manifesta magis vitii se prodere signa.
Nam, simul ac purae fugiens lux alma diei
cesserat, et noctis tristes induxerat umbras,
innatusque calor noctu petere intima suetus
liquerat extremum corpus, nec membra fovebat
obsita mole pigra humorum, tum vellier artus
brachiaque scapulaeque gravi suraeque dolore.
Quippe, ubi per cunctas ierant contagia venas,
humoresque ipsos et nutrimenta futura
polluerant, natura, malum secernere sueta,
infectam partem pellebat corpore ab omni
exterius. Verum crasso quia corpore tarda
haec erat et lentore tenax, multa inter eundum
haerebat membris exsanguibus atque lacertis.
Inde graves dabat articulis extenta dolores.
Parte tamen leviore magisque erumpere nata,
summa cutis pulsa et membrorum extrema petebat.
Protinus informes totum per corpus achores
rumpebant, faciemque horrendam et pectora foede
turpabant: species morbi nova, pustula summae
glandis ad effigiem et pituita marcida pingui,
tempore quae multo non post adaperta dehiscens
mucosa multum sanie taboque fluebat.
Quin etiam erodens alte et se funditus abdens,
corpora pascebat misere. Nam saepius ipsi
carne sua exutos artus squallentiaque ossa
vidimus, et foedo rosa ora dehiscere hiatu,
ora atque exiles reddentia guttura voces.

English translation

Passage 1: 1.332–59. The gruesome symptoms of syphilis

Then symptoms of the blight revealed themselves more plainly.
For as soon as the nurturing light of clear day had passed away
in flight, ushering in the gloomy shadows of night,
and the inherent heat that usually, at night, makes for the [body's]
inmost depths had deserted its outmost parts and no longer warmed
the limbs that were filled with a sluggish mass of the humours,
then the joints were tormented by an intense pain, as were the arms,
and the shoulders, and the calves. The reason for this is that, when the infection
had run through all the veins, contaminating the humours themselves
and the fuel-sources that are meant to sustain us, nature – accustomed
to reject what does harm – set about expelling the infected component
outwards from the entire body; but because this [substance] was slow-
moving due to its thickness, and held fast in its viscosity, much of it
stayed put, in the course of its passage, in the bloodless limbs and sinews.
As it spread from there, it gave the joints intense pains.
But because its subtler element was more naturally disposed to burst forth,
in the process of its expulsion it made for the surface of the skin
and the limbs' extremities. Hideous sores would immediately break out
over the entire body and repulsively disfigure the horrifying face
and chest. The disease [then] showed a new complexion: pustules
shaped like the top of an acorn and rotten with thick pus, which
would not long after be split wide open and flow with a considerable
amount of phlegm-like blood and putrid discharge.
Moreover, when [the disease] ate deeply into the body and secreted itself
far within, it fed on it to grievous effect. For I myself have quite often
seen limbs stripped bare of their flesh and bones of barren filthiness,
while mouths that have been devoured gape open with a hideous
yawning, with the mouth and throat giving out [but] feeble sounds.

Passage 2: 3.1–29. Voyage to America

Sed iam me nemora alterius felicia mundi
externique vocant saltus: longe assonat aequor
Herculeas ultra metas, et litora longe
applaudunt semota. Mihi nunc magna deorum
munera et ignoto devecta ex orbe canenda
sancta arbos, quae sola modum requiemque dolori,
et finem dedit aerumnis. Age, diva, beatum,
Uranie, venerare nemus, crinesque revinctam
fronde nova iuvet in medica procedere palla
per Latium et sanctos populis ostendere ramos,
et iuvet haud umquam nostrorum aetate parentum
visa prius, nullive umquam memorata referre.
   Unde aliquis forsan, novitatis imagine mira
captus et heroas et grandia dicere facta
assuetus, canat auspiciis maioribus ausas
Oceani intacti tentare pericula puppes,
necnon et terras varias et flumina et urbes
et varias memoret gentes, et monstra reperta
dimensasque plagas, alioque orientia caelo
sidera, et insignem stellis maioribus Arcton,
nec taceat nova bella, omnemque illata per orbem
signa novum, et positas leges et nomina nostra;
et canat (auditum quod vix venientia credant
saecula) quodcumque Oceani complectitur aequor
ingens omne una obitum mensumque carina.
Felix, cui tantum dederit Deus. At mihi vires
arboris unius satis est usumque referre,
et quo inventa modo fuerit nostrasque sub auras
advena per tantum pelagi pervenerit aequor.

Passage 2: 3.1–29. Voyage to America

But now the fertile groves and foreign woodland-pastures
of another world summon me; the sea resounds far off,
beyond the Pillars of Hercules, and the distant shores add
their applause from afar. Now must I sing of the great gifts
of the gods and of the sacred tree, transported from an unknown world,
which alone has moderated and relieved the pain,
and brought an end to the afflictions. Come, goddess Urania,
honour [this] blessed grove; and with your hair bound up with a fresh
chaplet, may it please you to make your way through Latium
in your doctor's garb, revealing the sacred branches to the peoples;
and may it please you to tell of things never seen before
in our forebears' time or ever spoken by anyone.
   Hence, perhaps, someone captivated by the wondrous vision
of newness, and well used to telling of heroes and their epic exploits,
may sing of the ships that dared, under rather weighty omens,
to brave the perils of an untried ocean.
He may also tell of different lands and rivers and cities,
and of different peoples and the discovery of marvels;
of the open expanses they surveyed, and the constellations rising in
a different sky, and the Pole marked out by stars of a greater dimension.
Nor would he stay silent about fresh wars, and our standards carried
throughout the entirety of the new world, and the imposition of our laws
and our names. And he may sing (though future generations would scarcely
believe their ears) of how the vast entirety of the Ocean's expansive
embrace was traversed and surveyed by a single ship.
Blessed is he [the poet] on whom God bestows so much. But, for me,
enough it is to tell of the powers of a single tree,
the purpose it serves, and how it was discovered and brought,
a stranger, across so vast a stretch of sea [to live] in our air.

Passage 3: 3.288–309. Crime and punishment I: Syphilus transgresses

The scene is reminiscent of Aeneas' friendly encounter with Evander in Aeneid 8, where, soon after Aeneas' arrival in Italy, Evander explains to Aeneas his ritual sacrifice to Hercules. Columbus and his men observe a crowd of syphilitic Amerindians writhing in pain on a riverbank (3.232–9). A priest touches them with pure water and guaiacum before spilling the blood of a sacrificial bullock over a shepherd and singing a paean to the Sun (3.240–5). The tribal king subsequently tells Syphilus' blasphemous story (3.258–332) in aetiological explanation of the ritual: the ritual atones for the blasphemy that the outraged Sun punishes with syphilis (3.339–51). Syphilus himself was to be the first sacrificial victim when the new rite honouring the Sun was established; but he was spared, a bullock replacing the human victim (3.361–8).

Syphilus, ut fama est, ipsa haec ad flumina pastor
mille boves, niveas mille haec per pabula regi
Alcithoo pascebat oves. Et forte sub ipsum
solstitium urebat sitientes Sirius agros,
urebat nemora, et nullas pastoribus umbras
praebebant silvae, nullum dabat aura levamen.
Ille, gregem miseratus et acri concitus aestu,
sublimem in Solem vultus et lumina tollens,
'Nam quid, Sol, te', inquit, 'rerum patremque deumque
dicimus, et sacras vulgus rude ponimus aras,
mactatoque bove et pingui veneramur acerra,
si nostri nec cura tibi est, nec regia tangunt
armenta? An potius superos vos arbitrer uri
invidia? Mihi mille nivis candore iuvencae,
mille mihi pascuntur oves: vix est tibi Taurus
unus, vix Aries caelo (si vera feruntur)
unus, et armenti custos Canis arida tanti.
Demens quin potius regi divina facesso,
cui tot agri, tot sunt populi, cui lata ministrant
aequora, et est superis ac Sole potentia maior?
Ille dabit facilesque auras frigusque virentum
dulce feret nemorum armentis aestumque levabit.'

Passage 3: 3.288–309. Crime and punishment I: Syphilus transgresses

The story has it that Syphilus was a shepherd by these very waters;
for King Alcithoos, he used to bring a thousand cattle [and] a thousand
snow-white sheep to graze over these pastures. And it happened
that, just before the summer solstice, the dog star was scorching
the parched fields, scorching the groves, and the woods offered
the shepherds no shade, the breeze gave no relief.
He [Syphilus] felt sorry for his flock and, provoked by the relentless
heat, he lifted his face and eyes to the sun on high, saying:
'So why, Sun, do we call you father and god of the world,
and why do we, the ignorant multitude, set up sacred altars [for you]
and worship [you] with the sacrifice of oxen and with rich incense,
if you show no concern for us, and the royal flocks leave [you] unmoved?
Or should I rather imagine that you gods above are burning
with envy? A thousand heifers white as snow are brought to pasture
by me, [and] a thousand sheep; you scarcely have (if report is true!)
a single Bull, scarcely a single Ram in heaven,
and a shrivelled Dog to guard so great a herd.
Fool that I am, why not rather do worship to the King,
who has so many territories, so many subjects, who is served
by the wide seas, and who has greater power than the gods above
and the Sun? *He* will both grant my herds favourable breezes, and bring them
the agreeable coolness of verdant glades, and relieve the heat.'

Passage 4: 3.326–34. Crime and punishment II: Syphilis results

Protinus illuvies terris ignota profanis
exoritur. Primus, regi qui sanguine fuso
instituit divina sacrasque in montibus aras,
Syphilus ostendit turpes per corpus achores.
Insomnes primus noctes convulsaque membra
sensit, et a primo traxit cognomina morbus,
Syphilidemque ab eo labem dixere coloni.
Et mala iam vulgo cunctas diffusa per urbes
pestis erat, regi nec saeva pepercerat ipsi.

Passage 4: 3.326–34. Crime and punishment II: Syphilis results

Right away an unknown pollution arose [to inundate]
the offending regions. Syphilus, who had shed blood in establishing
divine rites for the king, and sacred altars in the mountains,
was the first to show ugly sores throughout his body.
He was the first to experience sleepless nights and tortured limbs,
and from [this] first [sufferer] the disease drew its name; and
from him the local inhabitants called the ruinous condition Syphilis.
And soon the evil pestilence had spread willy-nilly throughout
every city; nor, in its harshness, had it spared the king himself.

Commentary

The following annotations are often indebted to, but seek to build on, the relevant sections in Eatough 1984.

Passage 1

334 *tristes*: itself used of disease (2.291–2) and of the melancholy it induces (cf. 2.108–9; 3.238).

335 *noctu*: Fracastoro highlights this intensity of nocturnal pain in *On contagion* 2.11; cf. 2.12 for the body's natural heat lodged at the surface by day, but 'at night, [it] is accustomed to turn inward and to desert those members to which it is called out by Nature during the day' (tr. Renwick 1928: 15).

337 *obsita*: via *sero* ('sow'; cf. *OLD obsero*[2]), suitably used in connection with seed-carried disease.

humorum: the four humours: blood, yellow bile, black bile and phlegm.

vellier: archaic passive infinitive: here historic in force.

341 *polluerant*: only here in *Syph*., and hence emphatic, possibly also hinting at moral/sexual defilement (cf. *OLD* s.v. 3, 4).

344 *haec* takes up *infectam partem* in 342.

345 *membris . . . atque lacertis*: apparently corresponding to *nervis et lacertis* at *On contagion* 2.12: 'The substance which gave the pains was not fixed in the joints themselves, because it was too thick [*crassior*; cf. *crasso . . . corpore*, 343] to penetrate the joints, wherefore it remained for the most part over the nerves and sinews [*nervis et lacertis*]' (tr. Renwick 1928: 14, with minor adjustments).

348 *pulsa*: nominative feminine singular, taking up *infectam partem* (342), its lighter component making for the skin's surface (*summa* neuter accusative plural).

349–54 Cf. *On contagion* 2.11: 'these [pustules] at first appear small, then (*mox*) gradually they grow to the size of an acorn cup, and not dissimilar to those in boys, which are called "Achores"' (tr. Renwick 1928: 9). Like *mox* here, *species morbi nova* (351) surely refers forward to the secondary-stage, acorn-like pustule in 351–2, not back to the formative *achores* of 349.

349 *informes*: literally 'shapeless,' in contrast to the acorn shape of 352.

achores: this transliteration of a Greek medical term occurs only three times in *Syph*.; here; 2.245, and at 3.329 (passage 4, below), where such *achores* duly affect Syphilus in the manner described at 1.349–50.

350 *rumpebant*: the promise of *erumpere nata* (347) is fulfilled.

352 A horrible disfigurement of the healthful acorn in ancient pastoral (e.g. Virg. *Georg.* 1.8, 148, 305).

352–4 The gruesome effect is underscored by the chaotic massing of discharges (*pituita*, *sanies*, *tabum*), the harsh alliteration in *m* and *p*, and allusion to Virgilian atrocity in 354 (cf. *Aen.* 8.487, *sanie taboque fluentis*, of the savage Mezentius' victims).

355–9 The disease's deeper entrenchment in the body counters nature's best efforts to force it outwards (*exterius*) in 342–3.

356 *corpora pascebat*: after contaminating the body's *nutrimenta* (340), the disease itself perversely takes nourishment from the body it destroys.

356–7 Through sibilant alliteration the disease virtually crackles with sound, the aural effect then synaesthetically complementing *vidimus* in 358; this cacophony contrasts with the sufferer's feebleness of voice in 359.

357 *squallentia* . . . *ossa*: plausibly a reference to syphilitic bone lesions.

358 *rosa*: passive past participle from *rodo*, taking up *erodens* in 355. Resonant *o* conveys the yawning vacuity of the devoured mouth, *hi*- its laboured wheezing (Eatough 1984: 27). *ora* is itself anagrammatically devoured by *rosa*. *dehiscere* echoes *dehiscens* (353) as the face *itself* becomes a gaping wound.

Passage 2

1 *felicia* sets the tone for Fracastoro's treatment of guaiacum in book 3, connoting 'fertility' in the wood (*OLD* s.v. 1) and 'happiness' in its healing effects (*OLD* s.v. 3, 4).

3 *Herculeas* . . . *metas*: traditionally Mount Calpe (now Gibraltar) and, opposite it in Morocco, Mount Abyla.

6 *sancta arbos*: one name of many given to guaiacum by Old World Latin writers was *lignum sanctum* (Munger 1949: 202–3); but, in view of the Paradisiacal associations of the New World, Fracastoro perhaps gently alludes to the tree of life and the tree of the knowledge of good and evil in the Garden of Eden (Genesis 2.11; see further Eatough 1984: 170).

8 *Uranie*: the muse of astronomy, invoked early in *Syph.* (1.26) because Fracastoro relates syphilis' outbreak to astral influence (cf. 1.250–4); at 1.213 she is cast as the guiding inspiration for the eminent humanist Giovanni

Gioviano Pontano (1426–1503), author of the five-book astronomical didactic poem *Urania*. The vocative in *-e* is a Greek form.

9 *procedere*: beyond denoting stately progression, the verb also plays lightly on Uranie's astronomical credentials (cf. *OLD* s.v. 5b, of constellations, etc., 'coming into view').

11–12 Given Fracastoro's stress on guaiacum as a *novel* cure from the *New* World (*ignoto*, 5; *nova*, 9), his reapplication of the familiar classical claim to poetic novelty (e.g. Manilius 1.6, *sacra . . . nulli memorata priorum*, 'sacred (poetic) offerings ... never mentioned by anyone before', directly echoed here) gives the trope fresh nuance.

nulli: dative of agent with *memorata*.

13–29 Through the familiar classical *recusatio* Fracastoro rejects the daunting task of recounting the epic voyages of Columbus and others, but with a hint of irony in his humble focus on 'the powers of a single tree' (26–7): *unius* (27) has shades of the outstanding epic 'one' (cf. P. Hardie, *The Epic Successors of Vergil*, Cambridge 1993: 3–10), and *advena* (29) is reminiscent of Aeneas' arrival in Italy as a stranger (28–9). After *Syph.*, the first dedicated Latin epic on Columbus, by Lorenzo Gambara, appeared in 1581, the second, by Julius Caesar Stella, in 1585.

14–18 Allusions to Catullus 64 liken exploration of the New World to the Argonautic voyage, but Aeneas, not Jason, is Fracastoro's preferred model for Columbus. Jason returned from Colchis with the Golden Fleece, but while the New World, too, yielded gold, the Argonautic analogy also prompts reflection on syphilis as (at least by one theory of origin) a secondary import (Cairns 1994).

18 *monstra:* see S. Greenblatt, *Marvelous Possessions: The Wonder of the New World*, Chicago 1991: esp. 53 on Columbus' 'highly self-conscious interest in the marvelous'.

19–20 *alioque* ... *caelo*: European explorations reaching the southern hemisphere; *Arcton* (20) here as southern pole, the polar emphasis overriding its usual northern designation.

21 *nova bella*: the warrings of the conquistadors (cf. 3.183).

22 *nomina*: for Columbus' frequent refrain of 'which I have named X' (*vel sim.*), see Cohen 1969: 62, 68, 69, 72, 120, etc.

25 *una*: with shades of the epic 'one,' as in *unius* (27: see on 13–29). In Columbus' first voyage with three ships, one was lost, and the two returning

craft became separated (see Cohen 1969: 101–2); of Magellan's five ships, only one completed the circumnavigation, returning to Spain (after his death) in September 1522.

28 *auras*: ironic if these breezes are suspected of carrying the airborne disease (cf. 1.119–26).

Passage 3

288 *Syphilus*: the origin of the term *syphilis* (and by extension *Syphilus*) remains uncertain, but derivation from Latin *sus* + Greek φίλος (= 'swine-lover') or from Greek σύν + φίλος (= 'he who makes love') is far-fetched; that from Greek σίφηλις (a skin disease mentioned in *On contagion*) is suggestive (Hendrickson 1934), but less plausible than Fracastoro's formation of a neologism from ἐρυσίπελας / Latin *erysipelas* (Spitzer 1955). Despite the different prosody, Fracastoro's *Sȳphilus* may also play on Ovid's *Sĭpylus* (*Met.* 6.231), one of Niobe's sons killed because of her blasphemy (hence a suggestive link with Syphilus' blasphemy).

288 *haec ad flumina*: the riverbank of 3.235 (see introduction to passage 3).

290 *Alcithoo*: the name is seemingly Fracastoro's invention, but perhaps related via blasphemy to Ovid's Alcithoe, who rejects Bacchus and is punished accordingly (*Met.* 4.1–4, 388–415). Syphilus' repudiation of the Sun in favour of his worshipful devotion to a mortal king is suggestively allegorical in implication, hinting at Henry VIII and his separation of the Church of England from Rome in 1534 (see Eatough 1984: 25).

291–2 *urebat* . . . *nemora*: the echo of Virg. *Aen.* 3.141–2 (where Sirius, the Dog Star, searing as a plague 'from a tainted expanse of the sky' [138], afflicts Aeneas' men on Crete) is neatly proleptic in implication, anticipating the airborne plague unleashed in *Syph.*

293 *nullum* . . . *levamen*: another proleptic irony; no breeze-borne relief here, and still less when the air is laden with syphilis (so *aura* at, e.g., 1.100, 248, 252).

294 brings at least partial mitigation of Syphilus' blasphemy.

295 *lumina*: literally '(rays of) light', as if here raised in challenge to the Sun.

298 *pingui* . . . *acerra*: the echo of Virg. *Aen.* 5.745 underscores the solemnity of the ritual.

300 *uri*: the flaming Sun is ironically aflame with envy.

301–2 *mille* ... *mille*: the bucolic boast is a Virgilian flourish (*Ecl.* 2.21) emulated by Calpurnius Siculus at *Ecl.* 2.68.

302–4 *Taurus* ... *Aries* ... *Canis*: witty but acerbic dual reference to the constellations and/as animals.

303 *(si vera feruntur)*: a patronizing aside with feigned ignorance, as if Syphilus speaks as one of the *vulgus rude* of 297.

304 *tanti*: sarcastic (in effect 'so small').

308 *facilesque auras*: but breezes laden with syphilis will ultimately result (see on 293).

Passage 4

326 *illuvies*: only twice in *Syph.*, the term here fulfils the prediction of its outbreak at 1.214–15 (the prediction is in Pontano's reported voice: see note on 3.8 in passage 2).

327 *Primus* (sonorously repeated for reaffirming effect in 330 and 331) ushers in a bleakly negative discovery, in contrast to the celebratory treatment of the pioneering voyages in 3.13–29.

329 *achores*: true to the appearance of *informes* ... *achores* at 1.349 in passage 1.

332 *Syphilidem*: the Latin term's first appearance.

334 *regi*: if an allegorical reference to Henry VIII is detected (see on 3.290 in passage 3) or to the Holy Roman Emperor, Charles V, Fracastoro directly alludes to the known or alleged syphilis of each.

6

A Protestant on the Attack in Latin

Martin Luther (1483–1546), *De Abroganda Missa Privata*

Lucy R. Nicholas

Introduction

The German theologian Martin Luther is one of history's giants. He is generally credited with unleashing a cataclysmic religious schism that we know today as the 'Reformation'. His act of nailing ninety-five theses to a church door in Wittenberg in 1517 has iconic status, and the impact of his revolutionary conceptions about Christianity is difficult to overstate. His written output was immense, and the spread of his ideas was greatly accelerated by the newly established Gutenberg printing press: between 1500 and 1530, Luther's works represented one fifth of all materials printed in Germany. His immense reputation rests in part on his promotion of the vernacular, and of all translations of the Bible his rendering into German is one of the best known. During his career as a reformer, Luther produced many other texts in German. However, he also utilized the medium of Latin. This section will present the influential ideas conveyed in one early Neo-Latin treatise as well as the work's relationship to the vernacular.

Luther was a monk, ordained priest and chair of theology at Wittenberg University, and a figure utterly devoted to the Church. This gave him a firm platform from which to vocalize his strong reaction to certain religious practices then currently endorsed and promoted by the Pope. His rejection of papal indulgences won rapid appeal at the start of the sixteenth century, and, thereafter, he would move to refute several aspects of doctrine and practices of the Roman Church which he perceived to be completely at odds with 'authentic' Christianity. In addition to his *Ninety-Five Theses*, he quickly became famous for several seminal works that were published in 1520 and soon circulated throughout Europe; these included *On the Babylonian Captivity of the Church*, originally written in Latin.[1] These broadsides resulted in his immediate excommunication by the Pope and condemnation as an outlaw by the Holy Roman Emperor. Yet Luther, determined to press on with reform, is famously said to have declared at the Diet of Worms in 1521: 'I cannot and will not recant anything since it is neither safe nor right to go against conscience. Here I stand, I can do no other, so help me God.'

In that same year of 1521, and amid an atmosphere of religious upheaval in Wittenberg, Luther pilloried the private mass in a tract that forms the focus of this contribution, namely the *De abroganda missa privata* ('*On the necessary removal of the private mass*'; from now on *Abroganda*). It built directly upon the arguments he had mounted in *On the Babylonian Captivity of the Church*. The tract takes the form of a letter addressed to religious members of his own community, 'the brethren of the Augustinian Convent of Wittenberg'.[2] Opening with a *protestatio*, the work was then divided into three parts, all of which attacked private masses in different ways.

The private mass had evolved during the medieval period: it was the celebration of a mass without a congregation, often in order to benefit the dead, a practice encoded in the traditional Canon of the Mass.[3] Luther's opposition to private masses centred on the twin issues of (i) the unevangelical exclusivity of the priesthood and its identification with the private sacrifice of the mass, and (ii) the absence of the true sacrament of the Eucharist that this view of the priesthood and the mass entailed. The initial part of the tract, from which the first passage is taken, comprises a forthright demolition of this medieval concept of priesthood. Luther argues that there was only one true priesthood, that of Christ, and one true sacrifice, Christ's offering of himself. Further scriptural references to 'priesthood' relate to the office of preaching; they also entail personal self-sacrifice to God, namely a contrite heart and praises, something any human could do with no need for a mediator. In sum, Luther considered all baptized Christians to be a holy priesthood.

In the second part of *Abroganda* Luther foregrounds a different but fundamental aspect of his theology, namely his firm belief that the Bible's teaching is the only source of divinely revealed knowledge. This he sets in direct opposition to the received doctrine he claimed had grown up around the practice of private masses. Placing heavy reliance on the New Testament, Luther employs a close reading of Scripture to challenge the authority and office of the Pope. He had by this time started to develop a Eucharistic doctrine that he believed would make the sacrament correspond more faithfully to Christ's inauguration of it. Luther here uses the Words of Institution collectively and individually to disprove any interpretation of the private mass as a sacrifice. The Words of Institution, from the Gospels of Mark, Matthew and Luke and the Pauline account of the Eucharist in 1 Corinthians 11, echo those of Jesus himself at his Last Supper, when he consecrated bread and wine. In passage 2 below Luther focuses on Christ's exhortations to his disciples to 'Take' and also to 'Eat' and 'Drink'.

A further means Luther used to discredit private masses was to test them against the individual commandments of the Decalogue (the Ten Commandments). The third part of the *Abroganda* contrasted the papal priesthood with Christ's. As part of this, Luther set forth a lengthy synopsis of the Decalogue, after which he catalogued a range of papal aberrations. In the third extract below we see Luther assail the Pope under the Fifth Commandment, 'Thou shall not kill'.[4] The entire third part of *Abroganda* is thus highly polemical: a potent example of how splenetic and offensive Luther's output could be. But Luther's focus on the Ten Commandments had further significance. They would become a key plank in the reform movements of the sixteenth century, and Luther was one of the first reformers to accord them a privileged place. From the 1520s the Decalogue, viewed as a moral system, quickly replaced the unscriptural Catholic code of the seven deadly sins.[5] The Commandments were also invested with a theological weight that could buttress certain doctrinal positions, and it was proposed that in some Protestant liturgies the communion service would open with the Ten Commandments.[6]

Luther's *Abroganda* was a highly theological tract, and it is not surprising that he initially opted to cast it in Latin. Latin remained the main language of the reformers for adumbrating theological ideas. Indeed, the *Ninety-Five Theses* were in Latin and intended for academic discussion and debate, not for public distribution. Yet in the same year as his Latin *Abroganda*, Luther produced a German equivalent: *Vom Mißbrauch der Messe*.[7] This was a means to broaden the appeal of his tract. Luther, it seems, had resolved that sophisticated doctrinal arguments could be shared and understood by German Christians of any rank. Indeed, a comparison of his *Abroganda* and *Vom Mißbrauch der Messe* shows little difference in content.[8] He used both languages to powerful effect, and both tracts are charged with pungent polemical energy and rhetorical verve.

While Luther's German version of this tract may have exacerbated the religious revolution in his own territory, his Latin *Abroganda* travelled. This work was read widely and sent shock waves throughout theological hubs across Europe. For example, it gripped many in England. Sir John Fisher, who established St John's College, Cambridge in 1511, reacted strongly to it upon first publication, and, as a direct response to Luther's sacerdotal attacks contained in the work, he composed his *Sacri sacerdotii defensio* ('*In defence of the sacred priesthood*').[9] In the preface to this work he referred to many 'pestilential' books of Luther, but that 'yet of all that I have seen, none is more pestilential, senseless or shameless than the one he entitled The Abrogation of the Mass'.[10] Although the issue was debated in Parliament, and there was evidently some agitation for their abolition, private masses were upheld under Henry VIII right up until the end of his reign. Yet stirrings for the abolition of the private mass resumed when Henry's young son Edward VI acceded to the throne. Serious challenges against private masses were mounted in 1547 at King's College and St John's College, Cambridge, where their legitimacy became the subject of a series of disputations.[11] The Edwardian regime subsequently decided to ban them, and they were officially revoked in the 1549 Book of Common Prayer.[12]

In many Protestant lands, the mass itself, as well as private masses, would soon be banished, with reformers restoring (as they saw it) the authentic sacrament of the Lord's Supper.[13] Doctrinal schism over the issue of the Eucharist had become irreversible, and Luther's *Abroganda* surely played a role in this. Be that as it may, Luther's target was in fact never the mass per se, and his German Mass, the text of which he published in 1526, preserved much of the structure of the medieval mass. In the year after the publication of his *Abroganda*, Luther preached against the excessive rapidity and radicalness of the changes that others had introduced in Wittenberg. Yet Luther could not control the genie he had let out of the bottle. He was, moreover, always adamant that he stood by the doctrinal case he had made in *Abroganda*

Notes

1 *De captivitate Babylonica ecclesiae* (*WA* 6, 497–573).
2 Luther joined this monastery in 1511.
3 M. Szablewski reviews the development of private masses from the sixth to the sixteenth centuries in 'Mass without a Congregation: A Sign of Unity or Division' (Wydawnictwo, PhD thesis, 2004).
4 See n. 18 below (on passage 3).
5 Bossy, J. (1998), 'Moral Arithmetic: Seven Sins into Ten Commandments' in E. Leites (ed.), *Conscience and Casuistry in Early Modern Europe*, 214–34, Cambridge.
6 Brown, W. P. (2004), *The Ten Commandments: The reciprocity of faithfulness*, London; MacCulloch, D. (1996), *Thomas Cranmer, A Life*, New Haven / London, 505.
7 *WA* 8, 477–563, translated as 'The Misuse of the Mass' in: *Luther's Works*, vol. 36, ed. Abdel Ross Wentz, 133–230.
8 It is thought that Luther did not have the Latin version when he rendered it into German, only his notes and recollection of it (*Luther's Works*, vol. 36, 131).
9 *Sacri sacerdotii defensio contra Lutherum* (Cologne 1525). In parallel, Fisher also wrote the *Defensio regiae assertionis*, in which he defended the sacrifice of the mass against Luther.
10 *The Defence of the Priesthood*, trans. P. E. Hallett (London 1953), 1.

11 For King's College see G. Haddon, *Epistles* (London 1567), 169–75; for St John's see R. Ascham, *Apologia pro Caena Dominica* (London 1577).
12 Cummings, B. (2011), *The Book of Common Prayer: The Texts of 1549, 1559 and 1662*, Oxford (p. xxviii).
13 Ascham's *Apologia*, for example, conflated private masses and the mass as a whole.

Bibliography

Croken, S. (1990), *Luther's First Front: The Eucharist as Sacrifice*, Ottawa.

Lau, F. and E. Bizer (1969), *A History of the Reformation in Germany to 1555*, trans. B. A. Hardy, London.

Luther, M. (1888/9), *Weimarer Ausgabe* (*WA*), vols 6 and 8 [Weimar edition, a critical complete edition of all writings of Martin Luther].

MacCulloch, D. (2003), *Reformation: Europe's house divided, 1490–1700*, London.

Marshall, P. (1994), *The Catholic Priesthood and the English Reformation*, Oxford.

Messenger, E. C. (1936), *The Reformation, the Mass and the Priesthood*, 2 vols, London.

Nicholas, L. R. (2015), 'Roger Ascham's *Defence of the Lord's Supper*', *Reformation*, 20: 26–61.

Rex, R. (1991), *The Theology of John Fisher*, Cambridge.

Rex, R. (2019), *The Making of Martin Luther*, Princeton / Oxford.

Wendebourg, D., ed. (2010), *Sister Reformations: The Reformation in Germany and in England*, Tübingen.

Willis, J. (2017), *The Reformation of the Decalogue: Religious Identity and the Ten Commandments in England, c. 1485–1625*, Cambridge.

Source of the Latin text

Luther, Martin: *De Abroganda Missa privata Martini Lutheri sententia* (Basel 1522), with minor amendments made in respect of punctuation.

This text has been partially translated in: *The Apostolical Succession: a Satanic invention*, by Martin Luther, London 1842; and *Misuse of the Mass* in *Luther's Works*, ed. Helmut T. Lehmann, vol. 36 (Philadelphia 1959).

Passages 2 and 3 are here translated for the first time.

All biblical references are to the Latin Vulgate.

Latin text

Passage 1 [sig. B[v]]

This passage comes from the first part of the tract. Here Luther rejects the institutional priesthood, which he argues has grown up in contravention of Scripture.

Agite, vos egregii sacerdotes, producite nobis unum iota aut apicem[1] ex universis Evangeliis et Epistolis Apostolorum, vos esse aut dici debere sacerdotes prae ceteris, aut ordinem vestrum esse sacerdotium diversum a communi Christianorum sacerdotio.[2] Quin producitis? Auditisne, surdae imagines?[3] Ite ad Parrhisienses[4] quaeso, qui pro scripturae testimoniis ponent suum magistrale sentimentum: 'Haec propositio est haeretica et ordini sacerdotali contumeliosa';[5] tum hoc sentimentum esto vobis principium fidei. Unde ergo habemus vos idolorum sacerdotes? Cur nomen commune aufertis nobis et vobis arrogatis?[6] Nonne sacrilegi estis et blasphemi in universam dei Ecclesiam, qui nomine sancto et communi violenter aliis ablato abutimini[7] non nisi ad tyrannidem et pompam avaritiae et libidinis vestrae? Iterum dico, Idola mundi, unde vos habemus sacerdotes? Proferte testimonium pro vobis, vos onera intolerabilia orbis terrarum. Sacerdotes non estis, et sacerdotes vos ipsos appellatis. Videtis quod mereamini[8] insignes vos raptores et hypocritae?

English translation

Passage 1 [sig. B^{v}]

Come, you illustrious priests. Show us one jot or tittle[1] from the entire Gospels and letters of the Apostles [to the effect] that you are or ought to be called priests above others, or that your order is a priesthood different from the common priesthood of Christians.[2] Why don't you bring forth [the evidence]? Deaf images, do you hear?[3] Go, I bid, to the Parisians,[4] who, in place of the testimony of Scripture, will assert their expert opinion: 'This determination is heretical and insulting to the priestly order';[5] then let this opinion be an article of faith for you. Why, then, do we consider you priests of idols? Why do you steal a common name from us and arrogate it to yourselves?[6] Surely you are sacrilegious and blasphemous towards the whole Church of God, you who have violently stolen away a sacred and common name from others and abuse[7] it only to [prop up] the despotism and pomp of your greed and lust? I say again, Idols of the world, why do we consider you priests? Produce a testimony in your favour, you intolerable burdens of the world. You are not priests, and you call yourself priests. Do you see what you deserve,[8] you notorious plunderers and hypocrites?

Passage 2 [sigs. Eiv^{v} – Eiv^{r}]

This excerpt is taken from the second part of Abroganda, where Luther exhaustively pits the Words of Institution against the Catholic view of the mass as a sacrifice.

Et dixit 'Accipite',[9] scilicet non solum exemplo et facto ostendit non sacrificium deo exhibitum, sed donum hominibus datum, eucharistiam[10] esse, sed et verbo confirmat, iubens ut accipiant. Cur non sic ait 'Offerte' vel 'Sacrificate'? An papistas[11] iterum ignorantia grammaticae[12] impedit, ne sciant, quid significet 'Accipere'? Neque enim 'accipere' hic sonat, ut tollant manibus, ceu alienum bonum alteri exhibituri seu oblaturi,[13] sed ut sibi ipsis vendicent[14] et in suum commodum vertant, tamquam donum ac iam rem propriam. Possessores enim facit doni, cum dicit, 'Accipite', nempe illud quod dedit et fregit. Nihil ergo offerri deo permittit hoc verbum accipiendi, sed probat a deo venire hominibus accipientibus donum. Quid potest contra tam clara verba opponi? . . . 'Comedite et bibite'.[15] Hoc est universum opus, quod in eucharistia facere iubemur. Ideo enim frangit, dat, iubet accipere ut comedamus et bibamus, et post haec memoriam eius praedicemus. Sic et Apostolus[16] nullum aliud opus in eucharistia novit nisi comedere et bibere, dum verba Christi repetit dicens, 'Quotienscumque ergo manducabitis panem hunc et calicem bibetis, mortem domini annunciabitis, donec veniat'.[17]

Passage 2 [sigs. Eiv^v – Eiv^r]

And he [Christ] said 'Take'.[9] That is to say, he not only shows by his example and action that the Eucharist[10] was not a sacrifice delivered to God, but a gift given to men, but he also affirms it in word when he commands them 'to take'. Why did he not thus say 'Offer [it]' or 'Sacrifice [it]'? Or rather does grammatical ignorance[12] once again hamper the papists[11] from knowing what 'to take' means? For 'to take' does not here signify that they should lift [it] up with their hands, as if to show or offer[13] someone else's property to another person, but that they should claim[14] it for themselves and put it to their own use, as a gift and already something that belongs to them. For he makes [you] owners of the gift when he says 'Take', namely that which he has given and broken. And so this word 'taking' does not admit anything to be offered to God, but proves that for those people who take [it], it comes [as] a gift from God. What can be said against such clear words? . . . 'Eat and drink'.[15] This is the entirety of the business we are commanded to perform in the Eucharist. For it is for that reason that he breaks, he gives, he commands [us] to take so that we eat and drink and, after this, proclaim remembrance of him. Thus, too, the Apostle[16] knows of no other business in the Eucharist than to eat and drink, while he repeats the words of Christ, saying 'Therefore as often as you shall eat this bread and drink the cup, you shall announce the Lord's death until he comes'.[17]

Passage 3 [sig. Iii^r]

An extract from the section where Luther purports to set the injunctions of the Decalogue alongside Papal decrees, in order to expose the teaching of the Roman Church as not only unscriptural but also wicked.

Quinto Moses dicit 'Non occides'.[18] Hoc vero mandatum, cum in eo caritas[19] eximie prae ceteris emineat, Papa[20] cum suis Gomorris,[21] praecipuo ludibrio habet, ut de evacuando taceam. Primum, cum omnis ira hic prohibeatur, Papa docet bellare et sanguinem fundere etiam suos Episcopos et sacerdotes. Deinde gladium et brachium seculare[22] in manu sua esse iactat, et quos bellare iusserit, coelo sublimiore donat.[23] Breviter, homicidarum Episcopus est Papa, audacter docens et iubens occidere, quoties voluerit. ... Vim vi pellere iura permittunt, inquit sua decretalis[24] sacerdotio isto dignissima. Sic iram, invidiam, et omnia mala hoc praecepto prohibita[25] alit in hominibus, et crucem Christi[26] extra mundi fines eliminat. Atque hic omitto recensere pontificum bella, Neapolitana, Veneta, Gallica, Germanica?[27] Denique ubi non bellarunt[28] furiosae istae bestiae?

Passage 3 [sig. Iii^r]

Fifthly, Moses says 'Thou shall not kill'.[18] But, since in this [commandment] love [of neighbour][19] is exceedingly important, more so than in all the other [commandments], the Pope[20] and his Gomorrahs[21] make particular fun of this commandment, not to speak of his rendering [it] null and void. First, although all anger is here forbidden, the Pope instructs the waging of war and the shedding of blood, even by his own bishops and priests. He then boasts that the sword and the secular arm[22] are in his power; and he bestows on those whom he has commanded to wage war a higher heaven.[23] In short, the Pope is a bishop of bloodbaths, recklessly instructing and commanding the act of killing, as often as he likes . . . 'The laws allow the use of force to rout force', says his own decretal,[24] very well suited to that priesthood. In this way, he promotes among mankind anger, envy and all the evils forbidden by this commandment,[25] and he banishes the cross of Christ[26] beyond the boundaries of the world. And do I here omit to recount the wars of the pontiffs in Naples, Venice, France [and] Germany?[27] To sum up, where have those furious beasts not waged war?[28]

Commentary

Passage 1

1 *iota aut apicem*: *iota* here is an indeclinable form, referring to the Greek letter of the same name. *apex* has a very specific meaning in this context, namely the point of a Hebrew letter. The combination of *iota* and *apex* appears in the Latin text of Matthew (5:18), and *apicem* is used in this sense, too, in Luke (16:17).

2 *communi Christianorum sacerdotio*: this evokes Luther's now famous notion of the 'universal priesthood of all believers', which gave lay people and clergy equal rights and responsibilities. There is a conspicuous emphasis on the ordinary Christian in this tract, Luther often deploying the Latin *laicus* ('layman').

3 *Auditisne, surdae imagines?*: Luther's rhetoric draws out the alleged fallacy of Catholic reliance on anything but the Word of God, by alluding to the inability of images, which are 'deaf', to 'listen'. It is not clear whether Luther is calling the priests 'deaf images' on the grounds that he assumes in advance they will not listen to him, or whether he is invoking the images of Christian art, which many Protestants thought the Roman Church placed too much emphasis on. In the latter case Luther probably has in mind biblical attacks on idolatry, such as Psalm 115. Luther did not in fact reject pictorial religious images, such as icons, paintings and statues, to the degree other Protestant reformers would. He did not isolate the prohibition against graven images as a separate commandment in the Decalogue, unlike Reformed Protestants (on the numbering of the commandments see n. 18).

4 *Parrhisienses*: by this Luther means the university theology faculty in Paris, which was the most authoritative of all such faculties (for more on the importance of theology faculties see Text 8).

5 *'Haec propositio est haeretica et ordini sacerdotali contumeliosa'*: Luther here is parodying his opponents. In particular, the theological faculty in Paris had in 1521 declared Luther's propositions as heretical and censured them without (according to Luther and his allies) any reasoned explanation.

6 *aufertis nobis et vobis arrogatis*: the neat chiastic arrangement underscores the gulf Luther wishes to accentuate between the institutional priesthood ('you') and the priesthood of all Christians ('us'). *nobis*: dative of disadvantage.

7 *aliis ablato abutimini*: the assonance of 'a' underscores the predatory abuses of the institutional priests. *aliis*: dative of disadvantage.

8 *mereamini*: present subjunctive in a generic relative clause.

Passage 2

9 *'Accipite'*: the injunction is found in Matthew 26:26, Luke 22:17 and 1 Corinthians 11:24; the imperative appears in Mark 14:22 as *sumite* (although the Greek in all of these verses is λάβετε). Christ here urges his disciples at the Last Supper to take the bread as his body. The precise relationship between the bread and the body was an immensely contested question throughout the Reformation.

10 *eucharistiam*: literally a thanksgiving, a traditional name for the Lord's Supper. Luther here uses the term to distinguish it from the *missa*, the private mass, and the fallacious rituals and notions he claims had grown up around the latter.

11 *papistas*: *papista, -ae* is not a classical or medieval term, but is first attested in 1413 and denotes a papal partisan.

12 *ignorantia grammaticae*: Luther scathingly and explicitly alludes to priestly ignorance, a common topos in Reformation polemics (as, for example, in Texts 3 and 8).

13 *ut tollant manibus, ceu alienum bonum alteri exhibituri seu oblaturi*: Luther uses verbs he has used above, such as *exhibeo* and *offero*, to denote the alleged priestly sacrifice. By *alienum bonum* Luther presumably has in mind Jewish and pagan sacrifices in which it is the role of the priest to take the goods of others, namely the faithful, and offer them to God.

14 *vendicent*: from *vendico*, more commonly *vindico*. Here Luther evidently has in mind all people, as opposed to just priests.

15 *'Comedite et bibite'*: the two imperatives are found in Matthew 26:26–7.

16 *Apostolus*: namely Paul.

17 *'Quotienscumque . . . donec veniat'*: 1 Corinthians 11:26.

Passage 3

18 *'Non occides'*: Exodus 20:13 / Deuteronomy 5:17. The Lutheran numbering of the Ten Commandments followed the Roman Catholic order, but deviated from Reformed Protestants who counted 'Thou shall not kill' as the sixth commandment.

19 *caritas*: often translated as 'charity', but 'love (towards God and neighbour)' conveys the notion more effectively. It is a central idea in Christianity (see Matthew 22:38–40; 1 Corinthians 13 and 1 John 4:16). Luther surely also had in mind St Augustine's idea that the Ten Commandments could be divided into those on Love of God and those on Love of Neighbour (e.g. Augustine, *Sermo* 9).

20 *Papa*: when Luther penned this tract, the Pope was Leo X.

21 *Gomorris*: Luther refers to the city of Gomorrah in the plural. In the Old Testament Sodom and Gomorrah became synonymous with sin and the divine judgement passed on it, resulting in the cities' destruction (Genesis 18–19).

22 *brachium seculare*: more commonly *bracchium* and *saeculare*. This term was developed in the medieval period for a court with a temporal jurisdiction overseen by a lay ruler. It exercised power which the Church could not, for example, in the punishing of heretics. Luther here suggests that the Pope is laying claim to ultimate authority over such courts (the relationship between the Pope's authority and that of lay rulers had been intensely disputed since the eleventh century).

23 *coelo sublimiore donat*: the use of the comparative conveys well Luther's sardonic criticism of the Pope's cavalier manipulation of ordinary Christians' faith and of orthodoxy.

24 *Vim vi pellere iura permittunt . . . sua decretalis*: *Decretalium Gregorii IX*, lib. V, tit. XII '*De homicidio voluntario vel casuali*' (see *Corpus Iuris Canonici* [1959], vol. 2, 793–804).

decretalis is strictly speaking an adjective with *epistola* ('letter') understood. A decretal is a papal decree concerning a point of canon law.

25 *iram, invidiam, et omnia mala hoc praecepto prohibita*: Luther deploys a rising tricolon.

26 *crucem Christi*: probably a reference to 1 Corinthians 1:17. Luther would develop what he termed a 'theology of the cross', namely a belief that the cross was the only source of knowledge concerning who God is and how God saves.

27 *bella, Neapolitana, Veneta, Gallica, Germanica*: in 1485–6 Pope Innocent VIII went to war against the king of Naples; a chapter in the Italian Wars of 1494–1559 saw Pope Julius II bring together the League of Cambrai in order to curb Venetian influence, but by 1510 this alliance had collapsed, causing the Pope to ally himself with Venice against France. The war with Germany possibly refers to Luther's own breach with the Pope.

28 *bellarunt* = *bellaverunt*. In this extract alone Luther uses this verb three times along with the noun *bellum* in order to underscore his argument about a bellicose papacy that utterly fails to adhere to the commandment against killing.

7

Greeting Charles V at Bordeaux, 1539

George Buchanan (1506–82), *Silvae* 1[1]

Stephen J. Harrison

Introduction

This poem of seventy hexameters was written by the Scot George Buchanan (1506–82), who spent most of the period 1520–60 on the continent of Europe. Its title indicates its origin as a contribution on behalf of Bordeaux's most significant school (the Collège de Guyenne, where Buchanan taught Latin) to a public ceremony of welcome to the city for the Holy Roman Emperor Charles V in 1539, though the poem may have been revised before its publication nearly thirty years later. Buchanan, educated largely in Paris, where he had spent much of the previous two decades, had recently arrived in Bordeaux; in his two periods there (*c.* 1539–43, *c.* 1545–7) he wrote, in addition to this and other occasional poems, his Latin translations of Euripides' *Medea* and *Alcestis* and his biblical dramas *Jephthes* and *Baptistes* for his pupils (who included Michel de Montaigne).

Buchanan was to have a remarkable public career on his later return to Scotland in the 1560s, as tutor to both Mary Queen of Scots and her son James VI/I, as principal of St Leonard's College in St Andrews (1566–70), Moderator of the Church of Scotland (1567) and Keeper of the Privy Seal (chief royal minister, 1570–8). In this last period of his life he also wrote major Latin prose works – a Cicero-style dialogue on constitutional monarchy (*De Iure Regni*, 1579) and a twenty-book Livy-style history of Scotland (1582) from its mythical beginnings until 1572. But in his earlier years he was best known as an educator and Latin poet, author of a celebrated complete version of the Psalms in the lyric metres of Horace, satirical poems against monks (*Somnium, Franciscanus, Fratres Fraterrimi*), erotic *Elegiae*, invective *Iambi*, *Epigrammata* and *Hendecasyllabi* as well as his five-book astronomical *De Sphaera*, in the style of Manilius' didactic hexameters. He was rightly regarded as one of the greatest Latin poets of his time.

Buchanan's *Silvae* ('*Forests*') is a collection of occasional poetry, which also includes other royal poems, e.g. an epithalamium for Mary Queen of Scots and François II of France (1558), a lament for the death of François II (1560) and a celebration of the birth of the future James VI/I (1566). A poem to Charles V sits well among such great figures and advertises its author's high connections. Buchanan's posthumous *Miscellaneorum liber* also contains royal encomia, in the form of Horace-style lyric odes from the 1540s and 1550s (for Henri II of France and Henry VIII of England).

Silvae 1 comes from the winter of 1539–40, when Charles V was moving across France from Spain, in order to suppress in person a rising in his native city of Ghent in Flanders. His formal reception at Bordeaux was on 1 December (McFarlane 1981: 111); later the same month he met with François I at Loches and moved with him to Paris, ultimately reaching Ghent and suppressing the rebellion in February 1540. Bordeaux was thus receiving a major neighbouring foreign head of state, indeed one who had been at war with France for much of the past twenty years, but was being allowed free passage through the country after the agreement of a ten-year truce in 1538 (in fact broken in 1542).

Consequently, the poem's high praise of Charles's martial qualities may have been more than a little ambivalent for a French audience whose armies had so often been their victim, especially in Italy (note the implicit reference to his troops' 1527 sack of Rome in lines 12–13). But the presentation of Charles as champion of Christendom against the Turks at Vienna (1529; cf. 17 *Ister*) and the Moors at Tunis (1535; cf. 18 *Bagrada*) points to a more positive view of his power; *victorem Libycae terrae* (36) casts him as a second Scipio Africanus, a common way of praising his sack of Tunis near the site of ancient Carthage. Further, the implication that the Habsburg Holy Roman Empire is the successor to both Rome and Byzantium (7–8) may reflect the passing of the claim to the Eastern Roman Imperial crown to Ferdinand II of Aragon and Isabella I of Castile (Charles's maternal grandparents) in the will of the exiled Eastern Roman claimant Andreas Palaiologos (died 1502), nephew of the last Byzantine emperor, as well as Charles's regular use of the title 'Caesar' and the view (frequently expressed since Charlemagne) that the Holy Roman Empire was the continuation of its ancient predecessor (*translatio imperii*).

Buchanan's poem (his only interaction with Charles) was first published in 1567, a generation after its composition, nearly a decade after Charles's death in 1558, and some years after its author's departure from Bordeaux. Its main impact on publication will thus have been its classicizing texture rather than its political topicality and occasion. It opens the *Silvae*, which contain seven hexameter poems that clearly look to the *Silvae* of the Flavian Roman poet Statius as their model in metre, length and topic. Its seventy hexameters match the sixty-five of Statius' *Silvae* 1.5 or the sixty-seven of Statius' *Silvae* 4.2, while a book-initial praise-poem addressed to an emperor recalls Statius' *Silvae* 1.1 and 4.1, both addressed to the emperor Domitian. The other poems in Buchanan's collection also pick up typical types from Statius' work, such as laments and birthday poems.

The poem carries some literary colour from late antique Roman Gaul, appropriate for a poem delivered in Bordeaux, which had been a major cultural centre in that period. There are clear affinities with the *Panegyrici Latini*, the collection of Latin prose orations largely from the fourth century CE. These are mainly loyal addresses to the emperor from Gaul; the theme of the emperor's *adventus* or ceremonial arrival at a city often appears there (cf. esp. 5.7–8: Constantine enters Autun; 8.6: Constantius arrives at Trier), and at least two of the late antique panegyrists seem to have been (like Buchanan) teachers of rhetoric, one probably from Bordeaux (Nixon/Rodgers 1994: 7).

A particular figure from that period who is clearly in the background of Buchanan's poem is the Bordeaux poet and teacher Ausonius (310–95 CE); his *Ordo urbium nobilium* (after 388 CE) contains forty hexameters in praise of his native Bordeaux as its final climax (24.128–68 Green), a passage used in this poem (41). Ausonius was the key figure in a cultural and educational circle in and around Bordeaux in late antiquity (cf. Matthews 1975: 69–84); Buchanan is evoking this intellectual tradition in the same place more than a millennium later.

Metre: dactylic hexameter

Note

1 A more detailed treatment of this poem was delivered at the 21st NeoLatina conference at Freiburg, June 2019, and will be published in its proceedings in due course. My thanks to all those present there, and especially Stefan Tilg and Florian Schaffenrath, for their useful comments and help.

Bibliography

Étienne, R. (1962), *Histoire de Bordeaux. 1, Bordeaux antique*, Bordeaux.
Ford, P. and R. P. H Green, eds (2009), *George Buchanan: Poet and Dramatist*, Swansea.
Matthews, J. (1975), *Western Aristocracies and Imperial Court, AD 365–425*, Oxford.

McFarlane, I. D. (1981), *Buchanan*, London.
McGinnis, P. J. and A. H. Williamson, eds (1995), *George Buchanan: The Political Poetry*, Edinburgh.
Nixon, C. E. V. and B. S. Rogers (1994), *In Praise of Later Roman Emperors: The Panegyrici Latini*, Berkeley.
Parker, G. (2019), *Emperor: A New Life of Charles V*, New Haven.

Source of the Latin text

Text, translation and brief notes are available in McGinnis and Williamson 1995, which has been used as a basis.

Latin text

AD CAROLUM V IMPERATOREM, BURDEGALE HOSPITIO PUBLICO SUSCEPTUM NOMINE SCHOLAE BURDEGALENSIS, ANNO M.D. XXXIX

Vasconidis regnator aquae, generose Garumna,
cui totiens Latios fasces totiensque curule
fas ebur, et veteres, ingentia nomina, patres
caeruleo excepisse sinu, non contigit umquam
hospitii tibi maior honos, licet usque vetusti
temporis aeterno series repetatur ab aevo;
Roma atavos quamvis, magnae licet aemula Romae
proferat antiquos tellus Byzantia patres.
Ausoniae regalis honos, decus orbis Hiberi,
Carolus, Arctoi suboles Mavortia Rheni
Vasconicam subit hospes humum, quem publica poscunt
vota orbis, famulas cui porrigit obvius ulnas
Albula, nativi quem tentat turbidus auri
deliciis revocare Tagus, quem iure paterno
caerulei repetunt prima incunabula Rheni,
cernere quem cupiunt gemino sub sole superbi
barbaricis ambo exuviis, hinc Ister, et illinc
Bagrada Marmaricae lentus sulcator harenae.
Burdigalam tamen ille tuam, tua tecta, Garumna,
ingens hospes init : tibi maiestate remissa
imperii decrescit apex, tectoque minori
Caesareus succedit honos, privata subire
culmina dignantur Latii diademata regni.
sic Hecale Aegiden, sic te Tirynthia proles
ceperunt rigidi mapalia nuda Molorchi;
sic posita quondam sceptri gravitate perustos
Iuppiter Aethiopas, canamque revisere Tethyn
gaudet, et alternis interserit otia curis.
Ergo hospes positisque minis ventisque, Garumna,
compositis, Borea non obluctante vel Austro,
tranquillus mitisque adsis, vultuque sereno
crispentur tremulae Zephyris felicibus undae.
Depositum tibi grande orbis, tibi publica vota
spemque suam credit, rectorem gentis Hiberae,
Ausoniae dominum, Boreae pugnacis alumnum,

English translation

TO THE EMPEROR CHARLES V, ON HIS RECEPTION AT BORDEAUX IN PUBLIC HOSPITALITY, IN THE NAME OF THE SCHOOL OF BORDEAUX, IN THE YEAR 1539

Ruler of the Gascon water, noble Garonne, for whom it was fitting to receive so many times in your blue bosom the Latin fasces, so many times the curule ivory chair, and the senators of old, mighty names, no greater honour of hospitality has ever been your lot, though the sequence of the age of old be repeated from time eternal; though Rome present its ancestors, or Byzantium's land, great Rome's rival, present its fathers of the past. The royal ornament of Italy, the distinction of the Spanish world, Charles, the martial issue of the northern Rhine, comes [as] a guest to the ground of Gascony, he whom the wishes of the world's peoples demand, he whom the Albula comes to meet, stretching forth her subject arms, he whom the Tagus tries to call back home, swirling with the attractions of its native gold, he whom the blue Rhine, his earliest cradle, recalls with a father's rights, he whom [two rivers] yearn to see under twin suns, both proud with spoils from savages, here the Ister, there the Bagrada, that slowly furrows the sand of Marmara.

Yet he, the mighty guest, enters your Bordeaux, your houses, Garonne; for you, his majesty set aside, the empire's crown descends, and Caesar's glory approaches a lesser dwelling, the diadem of the Latin empire deigns to enter under a private roof. So Hecale [received] Aegeus' son, so did austere Molorchus' bare hovel receive you, issue of Tiryns; [just] so does Jupiter, occasionally laying aside the weight of his sceptre, joy to visit the sunburned Ethiopians and white Tethys, and inserts leisure between the cycles of care. And so, [as] his host, lay aside your threats and calm your gales, Garonne, with no struggle of North or South wind, [and] attending in restful and kindly mode, and with serene aspect, let your rippling waves be curled by favourable Zephyrs. The world is trusting you with a deposit of great size, the people's wishes and its own hope, the ruler of the Iberian race, the lord of Italy, the nursling of the warrior north, the victor over the Libyan land, and the terror

victorem Libycae terrae Scythiaeque timorem
quem colit occasus, Boreas amat, ultimus horret
ortus, et infidi metuit sollertia Mauri.
Cernis ut effractis popularia flumina claustris
accurrant, properentque tuis se iungere Nymphae
fluctibus, Oceanus refluis ut plenior undis
maiores convolvat aquas, cupidaeque videndi
Nereides, Nereusque pater, Tritonque canorus,
et senior Glaucus, viridisque examina Phorci
discursent tremula per stagna liquentia cauda?
Tu quoque magnanimum quamvis stirps, Carole, avorum
magnanimis sis maior avis, te Gallia quamvis
obvia sollicitet, quamvis cunabula pandat
Rhenus, et Austriaci revocent molimina sceptri,
Burdigalae exiguos ne dedignere penates
hospitio sancire tuo: quae dispare quamvis
fortunae splendore tuae[1] parvoque paratu
te capit hospitio, studio in te forte fideli
atque animo regum ingentes aequaverit aulas.
At famae si danda fides, subiere minores
numina saepe casas, ac non ingrata voluntas
hospitis et magnum cepit mens grata Tonantem.
Obsequiis concede piis, concede favori
Burdigalae, totam tibi quae cum civibus urbem
devovet, ut seri possint meminisse nepotes
quae loca tu quondam, quae tecta impleveris ingens
hospes, et externis veniens peregrinus ab oris
discere magnanimi cupiat vestigia Carli.
Si locus hic superest, inter si nomina tanta
admittunt tenues communia gaudia Musas,
versibus incultis Aquitanis turba Camenis
dedita te studiis patronum et pacis adorat
auctorem, facilesque vias, facilesque recursus
exoptat, Pylios et cum superaveris annos,
iam tibi promissam super aurea sidera vitam.

[1] Here I depart from McGinnis and Williamson in adopting *tuae*, the excellent conjecture of Daniel Hadas for the 1567 first edition's *tuo*, probably corrupted by assimilation with the same form in the previous line.

of Scythia, whom the West worships, the North loves, the far East quails before, and the cunning of the faithless Moor fears. Do you see how the streams of your peoples run fast, breaking their boundaries, and how the Nymphs hasten to join themselves to your waves, how the Ocean turning back with fuller billows, rolls its waters higher, and how in their desire to see, the Nereids, and their father Nereus, and tuneful Triton, and old Glaucus and the herds of green-grey Phorcus rush through [the sea's] clear pools with trembling tails?

You too, Charles, though you are a scion of great-hearted ancestors [and] greater than those great-hearted ancestors, though Gaul comes to meet you and seeks your favour, though the Rhine offers you your cradle, and though the burdens of your Austrian rule call you back, do not disdain to honour the humble homes of Bordeaux with your visit; she, though she receives you in hospitality with a splendour unequal to your [high] fortune and with [only] slender preparations, will perhaps succeed in equalling in her faithful zeal and spirit towards you the mighty courts of kings. But if credence be given to tradition, divine powers have often entered humbler huts, and the goodwill of a host and a pleasing disposition has captivated [even] the mighty Thunderer. Yield to loyal acts of homage, yield to the support of Bordeaux, which devotes all its city and citizens to you, so that descendants far in the future may recall which places, which houses you once filled [as] a great guest, and [so that] a pilgrim coming from foreign shores may wish to learn about the traces of great-hearted Charles. If there is room left here, if our shared joys can admit my slender Muses amid such great names, a crowd dedicated to its studies adores you with rough verses, the Muses of Aquitaine, [as] its patron, and as bringer of peace, and wishes you easy travels and easy returns, and when you have surpassed the years of Nestor, the life already promised you above the golden stars.

Commentary

1 The river Garonne (here strongly personified, as often with rivers in classical Latin poetry; for the 'bosom' [*sinus*] of an anthropomorphic river see Virgil, *Aeneid* 8.712) flows north through Bordeaux to the Atlantic via the Gironde estuary in the south-western French region of Gascony. The two proper names / adjectives *Vasconidis* . . . *Garumna* elegantly enclose the Latin line (for *generose Garumna* at line end see Venantius Fortunatus, *Carm.* 1.21.1). For similar elaborate and poetic balancing or enclosing word order cf. 9 *Ausoniae* . . . *Hiberi*, 15 *caerulei* . . . *Rheni*, 19 *Burdigalam* . . . *Garumna*, the chiastic ABCBA order of 36, and 41 *fluctibus* . . . *undis*.

2–8 refer via the traditional honorific trappings of the Roman magistrate (rods of office, ivory chair, the latter echoing Statius, *Silvae* 1.2.178–9) to the many incoming Roman office-holders in Bordeaux in its late antique heyday as Burdigalia, capital of the province of Aquitania (see Etienne 1962: 112–28). These past guests are now overshadowed by the visit of a (modern, Holy) Roman Emperor, who is greater than the past emperors both of the West (Rome) and of the East (Byzantium), both empires to which Charles V saw himself as heir.

9–18 The geographical names all have contemporary political relevance of a laudatory kind. The use of river names in particular to mark foreign military victories is also a trope of the Roman triumph (cf. Tibullus 1.7.9–16). Charles was born in Ghent (seen here as in the traditionally northern region of the river Rhine; in fact some 100 km north of it), controlled much of Italy (represented by the river Albula, another name for the Tiber) and his grandparents' kingdom of Spain (represented by the river Tagus). The 'subject arms' of the Tiber points subtly to his troops' infamous sack of Rome in 1527. The Ister (Danube) alludes to Charles's victory against the Turks at Vienna (1529), while the river Bagrada (modern Medjerda, flowing across Algeria and Tunisia) and the region of Marmarica (in Libya) refer to his defeat of the Moors at Tunis (1535) and other North African campaigns, again presenting him as the champion of Christianity against non-Christian 'savages'.

19–28 These lines present the emperor's visit to Bordeaux encomiastically as parallel to the traditional classical narratives of a god or hero honouring a humble mortal home by entering it for rest and hospitality. The old woman Hecale's reception of the Athenian prince Theseus in Attica (24) was the subject of the *Hecale* of the Hellenistic poet Callimachus, a largely lost Greek work alluded to in Latin by Ovid and Petronius (*Remedia Amoris* 747; *Satyrica* 135), while the old man Molorchus' entertainment of the great hero

Hercules at Nemea (24–5) was treated by the same poet in his similarly fragmentary *Aetia* (Buchanan's language shows he gets the story from his model Statius' *Silvae* 4.6.52). The idea of the mighty (20 *ingens*) hero stooping to enter a humble home recalls Aeneas' visit to Evander in Virgil's *Aeneid* (8.362–9, esp. 367 *ingentem*). More subtly, the entry of the former enemy king Theseus, now a welcome guest, into Thebes towards the end of Statius' *Thebaid* (12.784–6) is lexically echoed in *hospes* (20), *tecto* (21) and *init* (20); this parallel suggests the similar reversal (at least for the moment) of Charles's traditional status as the enemy of France. Jupiter's visit to the Ethiopians harks back to Homer's *Iliad*, where Zeus / Jupiter goes with the other gods to enjoy that distant people's hospitality (1.423–4). Tethys (a sea goddess) perhaps suggests Bordeaux's easy access to the sea via the Garonne river and Gironde estuary.

29–45 The idea that a river should subdue its potential violence to ensure the safe carriage of a mighty hero recalls the miraculous calm and current-reversal of the river Tiber, which conveys Aeneas and his ships to the site of Rome (*Aeneid* 8.86–9), while the financial metaphor that a valued voyager is a deposit which a body of water needs to return safely recalls Horace's ode on Virgil's sailing to Greece (1.3.5–8). The idea that Charles is the 'victor over the Libyan land' presents him as a modern parallel to Scipio Africanus the Elder, the Roman vanquisher of Carthage in the Second Punic War (218–201 BCE), often so described (as at Silius Italicus 7.493, *Libyae . . . victor*). The description of the famously strong tide in the Gironde estuary (41 *Oceanus refluis . . . undis*) lexically echoes Ausonius' account of the same phenomenon (24.146 Green, *Oceanum refluo . . . aestu*). The list of places in lines 29–38 stresses the worldwide nature of Charles's power, from northern Europe to Africa and the Near East. The untrustworthiness of the pagan Moors (cf. 38 *sollertia*) is a traditional theme, picking up the similar Roman view of their local predecessors the Carthaginians (*infidus* here may also suggest 'infidels'). The group of marine deities at 43–5 recalls that at *Aeneid* 5.823–4, where Tritons, Glaucus and Phorcus all feature in the retinue of Neptune (who is about to still a storm, an appropriate matching context). The elaborate encomiastic conceit that the gods of the sea come to the Garonne to pay homage to Charles alludes once again to the sea-driven strong tides of the Gironde estuary.

46–63 The wish that Charles should be more *magnanimus* than his *magnanimus* ancestors looks to an epithet of his paternal grandfather, the Hapsburg Emperor Maximilian I (used for example in the title of *Magnanimus*, the 1519 Neo-Latin translation by Riccardo Sbruglio of Maximilian's autobiographical poem *Theuerdank*). The reprise of the theme of humble hospitality again recalls the scene of Virgil's Aeneas entering the lowly house of Evander (*Aeneid* 8.362–9): 50 *exiguos ne dedignere penates* echoes 8.364–5 *et te quoque dignum | finge deo, rebusque veni non asper egenis* ('imagine yourself, too, as worthy of divinity, and do not come with displeasure to circumstances of need'), while 61–2 *quae tecta impleveris ingens | hospes* recalls 8.364 *hospes* and 8.367 *ingentem Aenean*. Charles is thus compared to the similarly voyaging great founder of the Roman race. The reference to Jupiter being entertained incognito in a humble home (55–7) recalls Baucis and Philemon in Ovid's *Metamorphoses* (8.630–724), who make up for their poverty by their willingness as hosts (56 *voluntas* picks up 8.678 *voluntas* in the same metrical position); 55 *famae* thus refers to the tradition of Roman literature. These epic allusions are combined in lines 51–4 with the Horatian idea that a poor home can surpass a royal court in its capacity for virtue: Horace *Epistles* 1.10.32–3, *licet sub paupere tecto | reges et regum vita praecurrere amicos* ('it is possible under a poor roof to surpass kings and the friends of kings in living').

64–70 The poem's close refers with rhetorical modesty to the context of its own performance as only one small part of what was no doubt an elaborate welcoming ceremony, with other distinguished local participants (64 *nomina tanta*). The studious crowd is that of Buchanan's school pupils, represented by their master, whose elegant verses are presented with mock modesty as rough because they are provincial; the phrase *versibus incultis* (66) appropriately recalls Horace, *Epistles* 2.1.233, *incultis . . . versibus*, of poets not fit to sing the praises of Alexander the Great, another mighty conqueror. Charles is hailed as 'bringer of peace', pointing to the current truce. The final wishes for the emperor to gain eternal life after surpassing the proverbially long years of Nestor (the Homeric king of Pylos) fittingly picks up two encomiastic passages of Ovid on the future deification of the emperor Augustus, *Metamorphoses* 15.838–9, *nec nisi cum senior meritis aequaverit annos, | aetherias sedes cognataque sidera tanget* ('nor will he touch the habitations of heaven and his relations the stars except when, advanced in age, he has made his years equal to his achievements'), and *Tristia* 5.5.61–2, *di tamen et Caesar dis accessure, sed olim, | aequarint Pylios cum tua fata dies* ('still, you gods, and Caesar destined to go to the gods, but one day, when your destined span has equalled the days for the hero from Pylos'). The idea of a life 'above the stars' neatly fits both Christian heaven and pagan apotheosis.

8

Epistolae Obscurorum Virorum (1515–19)

Letter 1.37: The Converted Jew and His Foreskin

Daniel Hadas

Introduction

In 1236 Nicholas Donin, a French Jew who had converted to Christianity and become a Franciscan friar, appeared before Pope Gregory IX with a memorandum urging the suppression of the Talmud. This marked the beginning of 500 years of sporadic efforts, in the Latin West, to ban, confiscate and burn the Talmud, along with other non-biblical Hebrew religious books. Twenty-four wagonloads of books were burnt in Paris in 1244; the Counter-Reformation instigated autos-da-fé throughout the Papal States in the 1550s; the last recorded public burning of Talmuds took place in 1757 in Kamianets-Podilskyi (Poland, now Ukraine). From Donin onwards, the principal reasons given for suppressing the Talmud were the same. First, it allegedly contained passages critical of Jesus, the Virgin Mary and the Christian Church.[1] Secondly, by studying the Talmud rather than the Old Testament, the Jews were thought to be hindering their own conversion to Christianity, since they were not reading the Old Testament prophecies that pointed to Christ. There were of course also baser motives, general hatred and fear of Jews, and also extortion: Jews could often bribe Christians to refrain from confiscation or could buy back confiscated books.[2]

The *Epistolae Obscurorum Virorum* stem from one episode in this sad history.[3] In 1507 another converted Jew, the indefatigable pamphleteer Johannes Pfefferkorn, began agitating in the Holy Roman Empire for the confiscation and suppression of the Talmud and other Jewish books. In 1509–10, Emperor Maximilian, apparently reluctant to take decisive action, entrusted examination of the matter to Uriel von Gemmingen, archbishop-elector of Mainz. Maximilian ordered the archbishop to consult Pfefferkorn himself; the universities of Cologne, Mainz, Erfurt and Heidelberg; the Grand Inquisitor at Cologne, Jacob Hoogstraeten; the priest Victor of Carben (yet another converted Jew); and the lawyer Johannes Reuchlin (1455–1522),

Germany's most renowned humanist. Reuchlin was consulted for his legal expertise, but above all for his knowledge of Hebrew: he was the most prominent Christian Hebraist in Europe, and the first to produce substantial Hebrew grammatical and lexicographical aides for Latin readers.

Except for Reuchlin, all those consulted recommended confiscation of the books, either for further examination or for immediate burning. Reuchlin, too, allowed that Jewish books which contained anti-Christian blasphemies could legally be suppressed. However, he then argued that no Christian, including himself, currently knew what the Talmud said, and that, until the allegations against it could be proved, confiscation would be an illegal act against citizens of the Empire. Reuchlin's response was not meant for publication, but Pfefferkorn, who had been charged with delivering the experts' reports to Maximilian, made part of its contents known by attacking Reuchlin in his pamphlet *Handtspiegel* ('Lorgnette', Mainz 1511). This prompted the publication of Reuchlin's famous *Augenspiegel* ('Eyeglasses', Tübingen 1512), which contained the full text of his response, along with virulent attacks on Pfefferkorn and theological clarifications (in Latin).

The publication of Reuchlin's *Augenspiegel* started a war.[4] The main source of conflict was not, in itself, the recommendation against confiscation. The city of Frankfurt had also petitioned Maximilian to stop confiscation, and indeed the entire project of suppressing Jewish books was eventually dropped. However, in the *Augenspiegel*, Reuchlin had exposed the university theology faculties' ignorance of Hebrew, argued against book-burning and censorship in general, and, worst of all, shown an extraordinary ability to see Jewish–Christian conflict from the Jewish perspective. In writing against Christian beliefs, he argued, Jews were only acting consistently with their own understanding of the truth, and were therefore committing no crime.[5]

The result was Reuchlin's trial for heresy, ultimately referred to Rome, and a storm of publications on both sides. Pfefferkorn and the university theologians attacked Reuchlin. Reuchlin and his humanist allies counter-attacked. One production of the Reuchlinist side was the *Clarorum virorum epistolae* ('*Letters of illustrious men*', Tübingen 1514), a selection of letters from and (mostly) to Reuchlin, in Latin, Greek and Hebrew.[6] Ostensibly, this book was not a work of controversy: its preface states that it aims to provide epistolary models, and most of the letters included predate the *Augenspiegel* affair.[7] Nevertheless, its real purpose was to advertise Reuchlin's learning and prestige, and so contribute to his defence.

The *Epistolae Obscurorum Virorum* ('*Letters of Obscure Men*'; henceforth *EOV*), published in 1515, with a second volume appearing in 1519, was ostensibly a riposte to the *Clarorum virorum epistolae*. It, too, is an anthology of correspondence, in this case directed by university lecturers and scholars to Ortwin Gratius,[8] a Master of the Arts at the University of Cologne, and a minor contributor to the fight against Reuchlin.[9] However, as its title advertises, the *EOV* is a fake. Its aim was to ridicule Reuchlin's opponents. Most of the letter writers (the eponymous *Obscuri*), and all of the letters, are imaginary. The *EOV*'s real authors have never been securely identified, but they are to be found among Reuchlin's humanist allies: prime suspects include Crotus Rubeanus (1480–1545) and Ulrich von Hutten (1488–1523).[10] The letters focus on the war against Reuchlin, whom they constantly attack, while praising Pfefferkorn, and defending scholasticism against humanist learning. The letters are deeply grotesque: their authors and addressee are at all times mean-spirited, drunken, lecherous, miserable, stupid and, above all, ignorant. The letters teem with false erudition and chopped logic, and are written in a cruel parody of late medieval Latin, full of bad syntax, vernacular calques and inane rhyming verse. In short, the *EOV*, like François Rabelais, who imitated them, offer a savage satire of all that the humanists despised in the authoritarian and traditionalist culture of the universities.

Satire is not meant to be fair, and we must not be blinded either by sympathy for Reuchlin's position or by the *EOV*'s brilliance. Reuchlin's adversaries were neither ignorant nor stupid: scholastic theology was an immensely sophisticated discipline. 'Whatever the Renaissance and the Reformation might signify, it was not a revolt of reason against fanaticism – on the contrary, it might be more fairly described as a revolt against the over-cultivation of logic by the late Middle Ages.'[11] But that in no way detracts from the *EOV*'s literary genius. The *Obscuri* are unforgettable comic creations, greater, perhaps, than their authors intended. As with Falstaff and his companions, many readers will come to feel a perverse admiration for men whose failings are so naked and so absurd.

The letter selected offers a particularly disgusting and ludicrous example of the *Obscuri*'s mindset. It also illustrates one of the least attractive aspect of the Reuchlinists' polemics: the unrelenting mockery of Pfefferkorn's conversion to Christianity.

Notes

1 For the rare, but hostile, allusions to Jesus and Christianity in the Talmud see *Encyclopaedia Judaica* s.v.'Jesus', cols 14–17.

2 On the attempted suppression of the Talmud see Baron 1965: 62–94; *Encyclopaedia Judaica* s.v.'Talmud, Burning of'.

3 For what follows see Saladin 2004; Price 2010.

4 As Reuchlin himself calls it: *bellum hoc turbulentum, licet sine sanguine* ('this turbulent, albeit bloodless, war'), *Defensio*, B4v.

5 *Augenspiegel*, 15v; translated at *Defensio*, N2r–3r, where Reuchlin tries to obscure and distance himself from this position.
6 For the context of such publications see *Brill's Encyclopaedia of the Neo-Latin World*, 'Micropedia', ss.vv. 'Letter Collections'; 'Letter-Writing Manuals'.
7 A second edition of the *Clarorum virorum epistolae* was published as the *Illustrium virorum epistolae* (Haguenau 1519), with additional letters, almost all of which *are* concerned with the *Augenspiegel* affair.
8 Only one letter, 1.34, is 'from' Gratius.
9 Gratius' contribution was more substantial if he was Pfefferkorn's chief translator into Latin, but this is not proven. See Price 2010: 101–2.
10 Hutten was to be a prominent supporter of Luther, while Rubeanus remained faithful to the Catholic Church. Reuchlin's supporters included Luther himself, Melanchthon and others who would soon be leading Reformers, but also future Catholic polemicists such as Thomas Murner and St John Fisher (martyred under Henry VIII), and those, like Erasmus and Conrad Peutinger, who sought an elusive middle ground. The Reuchlin affair was a poignant moment of unity among humanists before the bitter divisions of the Reformation.
11 W. H. Auden, *Forwards and Afterwords*, New York 1990, 401.

Bibliography

Alessio, G. C. (2001), 'L'ars dictaminis nel Quattrocento italiano: eclissi o persistenza?', *Rhetorica* 19, 155–73.

Baron, S. W. (1965), *A Social and Religious History of the Jews*[2], Vol. 9, New York.

Böcking, E., ed. (1864: vol. 1; 1869: vol. 2.1; 1870: vol. 2.2), *Ulrich Hutteni equitis operum supplementum: Epistolae Obscurorum Virorum cum inlustrantibus adversariisque scriptis*, Leipzig.

Dionisotti, A. C. (1985), 'Beatus Rhenanus and Barbaric Latin', *Annuaire. Les amis de la bibliothèque humaniste de Sélestat*, 25, 183–92.

Kärkkäinen, P. (2017), 'Nominalism and the *Via Moderna* in Luther's Theological Work', *Oxford Research Encyclopedia – Religion* (https://oxfordre.com/religion).

Kintzinger, M. (2007), 'Licentia. Institutionalität "akademischer Grade" an der mittelalterlichen Universität', in R. C. Schwinges (ed.), *Examen, Titel, Promotion*, 55–88, Basel.

Löfstedt, B. (1983), 'Zur Sprache der "Epistolae obscurorum virorum"', *Mittellateinisches Jahrbuch*, 18, 271–89.

Pedersen, O. (1997), *The First Universities*, trans. R. North, Cambridge.

Price, D. (2010), *Johannes Reuchlin and the Campaign to Destroy Jewish Books*, Oxford.

Saladin, J.-C., ed. (2004), *Ulrich von Hutten. Lettres des hommes obscurs*, Paris.

Abbreviations

Defensio = *Defensio Joannis Reuchlin Phorcensis Ll. Doctoris Contra Calumniatores suos Colonienses*, Tübingen 1513.
DMLBS = *Dictionary of Medieval Latin from British Sources.*
DW = J. and W. Grimm, *Deutsches Wörterbuch.*
LHS = M. Leumann, J. B. Hofmann and A. Szantyr, *Lateinische Grammatik*, 3 vols, Munich 1965–79.
LLN = *Lexicon Latinitatis Nederlandicae Medii Aevi.*
LMILP = *Lexicon Mediae et Infimae Latinitatis Polonum.*
MW = *Mittellateinisches Wörterbuch.*
NG = *Novum Glossarium Mediae Latinitatis.*
Stotz = P. Stotz, *Handbuch zur lateinischen Sprache des Mittelalters*, 5 vols, Munich 1996–2004.
TLL = *Thesaurus Linguae Latinae.*
VD16 = *Verzeichnis der im deutschen Sprachbereich erschienenen Drucke des 16. Jahrhunderts* (www.vd16.de).

Source of the Latin text

The text is that of the *editio princeps* (Haguenau 1515 = VD16 E1720), with modernized spelling and punctuation. I have checked this edition against the two 1516 reprints (Nuremberg = VD16 E1721; Mainz = VD16 E1722):[1] all three are identical except for minor variants in spelling and punctuation.

Note

1 I have not had access to the 1517 reprint (Mainz = VD16 E1723).

Latin text

Lupoldus Federfusius[1] mox licentiandus[2] Magistro Ortvino Gratio tot salutes dicit quot aucae[3] comedunt gramina.[4]

Domine Magister Ortvine, est in Erphordia in quodlibetis[5] mota una[6] quaestio multum subtilis[7] in duabus facultatibus, theologicali et physicali.[8] Quidam dicunt: 'Quando[9] Iudaeus fit Christianus, protunc[10] renascitur sibi praeputium',[11] quae est cutis praecisa de membro virili in nativitate per legem Iudaeorum.[12] Et illi sunt de via[13] theologorum, et habent pro[14] se magistrales[15] rationes, de quibus est una quod[16] alias Iudaei facti Christiani in extremo iudicio putarentur esse Iudaei, si essent nudi in ipsorum membro virili, et sic ipsis[17] fieret iniuria. Sed Deus nemini vult facere iniuriam. Ergo etc.[18]

Alia ratio tenet[19] ex autoritate Psalmistae, qui dicit: 'Et abscondit me in die malorum, et protexit me in abscondito'.[20] Dicit 'in die malorum', id est in extremo iudicio in Valle Josephat,[21] quando oportet reddere rationem omnium malorum.

Alias rationes relinquo propter brevitatem, ex quo[22] in Erphordia sumus Moderni,[23] et Moderni semper gaudent brevitate,[24] ut scitis.[25] Etiam pro eo quod ego habeo malam memoriam, non possum multa mentetenus[26] scire allegando,[27] prout faciunt domini iuristae.[28]

Sed alii volunt quod illa opinio non potest subsistere. Et habent pro se Plautum, qui dicit in sua[29] poetria[30] quod facta infecta fieri nequeunt.[31] Ex hoc dicto probant: si aliquam partem corporis Iudaeus amisit in sua Iudaitate,[32] non recuperat illam in christiana religiositate. Et cum hoc[33] arguunt quod ipsorum argumenta non concludunt formaliter.[34] Alias ex prima ratione sequeretur quod illi Christiani qui perdiderunt propter suam luxuriam partem unam e suo membro,[35] ut saepe contingit in saecularibus et spiritualibus personis, etiam crederentur in extremo iudicio esse Iudaei. Sed hoc asserere est haereticum, et Magistri Nostri[36] Haereticae Pravitatis Inquisitores[37] nequaquam concedunt, quia ipsi aliquando etiam sunt defectuosi[38] in ista parte. Sed hoc non contingit ipsis ex meretrecibus, sed quando in balneis se non praevident.[39]

Iccirco precor dominationem vestram humiliter et devotarie[40] quod velitis vestra descisione[41] determinare rei veritatem, et interrogare uxorem domini Ioannis Pfefferkorn,[42] ex quo cum ea bene statis,[43] et illa non verecundatur

English translation

Lupold Scribbler[1], soon to be licensed,[2] to Master Orwin Gratius, gives as many greetings as geese[3] eat grasses.[4]

Sir Master Ortwin, in the quodlibetal[5] disputations in Erfurt a[6] very subtle[7] question was raised in the two faculties, of theology and medicine.[8] Some say: 'When[9] a Jew becomes a Christian, then[10] his foreskin grows back',[11] that's the skin cut off from the male member at birth on account of the Jewish Law.[12] And they use the theologians' method,[13] and they have magisterial[15] reasons on[14] their side, one of which is that[16] otherwise Jews who have become Christians would, at the Last Judgment, be thought to be Jews, if they were naked in their male member, and thus an injustice would be done them.[17] But God wishes to do injustice to nobody. Therefore etc.[18]

Another reason is based[19] on the authority of the Psalmist, who says: 'And he hid me in the day of evils, and he protected me in the hidden place'.[20] He says 'in the day of evils', that is in the Last Judgment in the Valley of Josaphat,[21] when we must give an account of all evils.

I leave aside the other reasons for brevity's sake, given that[22] in Erfurt we are Moderns,[23] and Moderns always rejoice in brevity,[24] as you know.[25] Also, because of the fact that I have a bad memory, I cannot know a lot of things in my mind[26] for citing,[27] like the master jurists do.[28]

But others prefer [the position] that that opinion cannot stand. And they have Plautus on their side, who says in his[29] poetry[30] that what's done cannot be undone.[31] From that saying they prove that if a Jew lost any part of his body in his Jewosity,[32] he does not get it back in Christian religiosity. And with this[33] they argue that their arguments are not formally conclusive.[34] Otherwise, it would follow from the first reason that those Christians who have lost, on account of their lust, a part of their member,[35] as often happens among lay and spiritual persons, would also be believed at the Last Judgment to be Jews. But to assert this is heretical, and Our Masters,[36] the Inquisitors of Heretical Perversity,[37] in no way concede it, since they are themselves also sometimes defective[38] in that part. But this doesn't happen to them because of prostitutes, but when they're not careful at the baths.[39]

Therefore I humbly and devotedly[40] beseech your lordliness, that you may wish to determine by your decision[41] the truth of the matter, and to interrogate the wife of Johannes Pfefferkorn,[42] given that you are on good terms with her,[43] and

dicere coram vobis quaecunque vultis, propter illam amicabilem conversationem quam habetis cum viro suo. Et ego etiam audio quod estis eius confessor. Propterea potestis eam compellere sub poena sanctae obedientiae. Dicatis: 'Domina mi,[44] nolite verecundari. Ego scio quod estis honesta persona,[45] sicut est una in Colonia.[46] Non peto inhonestum a vobis, sed ut manifestetis mihi rei veritatem, utrum maritus vester habet praeputium vel non.[47] Dicatis audacter sine verecundia,[48] amore Dei. Quid tacetis?'

Verum ego nolo vos docere. Vos melius scitis quomodo debetis vos habere cum mulieribus, quam ego.

Datum raptim ex Erphurdia. Ex Dracone.[49]

she is not ashamed to say whatever you want in your presence, on account of that friendly intercourse which you have with her husband. And I also hear that you are her confessor. Therefore you can compel her under the penalty of holy obedience. You should say: 'My lady,[44] don't be ashamed. I know that you are as decent a person[45] as any in Cologne.[46] I'm not asking for something indecent from you, but for you to make known to me the truth of the matter, whether or not your husband has a foreskin.[47] Speak boldly, without shame,[48] for the love of God. Why are you silent?'

But I don't want to teach you. You know better than I how you ought to be with women.

Written in haste at Erfurt. From the Dragon.[49]

Commentary

1 From German 'Federfuchser', literally 'feather-rascal', a derogatory term for someone whose life is devoted to writing and copying. Most of the *Obscuri* have this sort of burlesque Latinized German name.

2 *licentiandus*: Federfusius is due to receive his licence in theology, the penultimate qualification before the doctorate (Kintzinger 2007: 69–70). Compare modern English 'doctorand', and see the discussion at *EOV* 1.1 on whether someone due to become a *Magister Noster* (see below) is to be called *magister nostrandus* or *noster magistrandus*.

3 *auca* appears in late antiquity as a colloquial equivalent to classical *anser*, and Romance words for 'goose' derive from *auca* rather than *anser* (*TLL* s.v. *auca*; Stotz, vol. 1: 318). So *auca* was precisely the sort of word humanists sought to eliminate from Latin usage.

4 The *Obscuri* constantly use such flowery greeting formulae, which only slightly exaggerate genuine ones, of the sort attacked by Erasmus in his guide to letter writing (*De conscribendis epistolis*: *Opera omnia Desiderii Erasmi*, vol. 1.2, Amsterdam 1971: 284). See further Dionisotti 1985: 187–8.

5 *quodlibet* means literally 'whatever pleases'. In quodlibetal disputations a theology lecturer was required to dispute in public any question put to him by students. The disputations became increasingly notorious for frivolity. See Pedersen 1997: 261–2; Böcking 1870: 607–8.

6 *una* is used here for the indefinite article, calquing German 'eine', Italian 'una', etc. See also below: *partem unam*. The usage is common in late medieval Latin (Stotz, vol. 4: 292) and much favoured by the *Obscuri*.

7 *multum* + positive adjective is preferred to the superlative. In classical Latin this usage is colloquial; it spreads in the Middle Ages (Stotz, vol. 4: 301–2) in line with the lack of superlative forms in many vernaculars. The *Obscuri* also write, e.g., *multum profundus* ('very profound', 1.1); *multum vilis* ('very vile', 1.11); *multum pulchra* ('very beautiful', 1.39); *multum incommodosa* ('very inconvenient', 2.7); *multum difficilis* ('very difficult', 2.13); *multum proficualem* ('very profitable', 2.52).

8 *theologicalis* is late medieval: see *Glossarium mediae Latinitatis Sueciae*, s.v.; database searches show the word used by scholastic theologians, e.g. Jean Gerson, Denis the Carthusian. *physicalis* is attested from the eleventh century onwards, and from the late twelfth century in the sense 'medical' (*NG* s.v.).

For the *Obscuri*'s fondness for post-classical adjectives in *-alis* see Löfstedt 1983: 281. Note also *magistralis* below.

9 *quando* is the *Obscuri*'s preferred term for 'when', because of its Romance derivatives. Conversely, *cum* as a conjunction is very rare in the first *EOV* (only in 1.3, 15, 28). It is more common in 1.42–8, which appeared only at the third printing (= VD16 E1722) and in the second volume. This may indicate a new, less careful author.

10 The use of prepositions + *tunc* is late medieval: see *DLMBS* s.v. *tunc*.

11 This grotesque idea is perhaps inspired by 1 Corinthians 7.18: *Circumcisus aliquis vocatus est? Non adducat praeputium. In praeputio aliquis vocatus est? Non circumcidatur.* ('Was someone called when circumcised? Let him not put on a foreskin. Was someone called in the foreskin? Let him not be circumcised').

12 This explanation is of course pedantry, not a necessary clarification.

13 For *via* in the scholastic sense 'method of argument' see *LLN* s.v. *via*, B,2.b; *Glossaire du latin philosophique* (online), s.v. *via* (2).

14 *pro*: corrected from originals' *prae*. See below: *habent pro se Plautum*. *prae se* is not found elsewhere in the *EOV*.

15 *magistralis*: found already in late antiquity, but only common from the twelfth century onwards. Here it is associated with *Magistri Nostri* (see below).

16 The use of *quod* + conjugated verb, instead of accusative + infinitive, in indirect statements is characteristic of medieval Latin and slow to disappear in Neo-Latin (Stotz vol. 4: 392–4). It is of course ubiquitous in the *EOV* (eight instances in this letter).

17 *ipsorum . . . ipsis*: a classical Latin author would probably have written *suo . . . eis*. For medieval fusing of *se* / *suus* and the demonstratives see Stotz, vol. 4: 294–5. For *ipse* replacing demonstratives see Stotz, vol. 4: 407.

18 *Ergo etc.*: typically used in scholastic logic where the conclusion of a syllogism is too obvious to need spelling out.

19 For the wide range of meanings of *tenere* in the *EOV* see Böcking 1869: 272. This is surely influenced by the extraordinary variety of uses of German *halten* (see *DW* s.v.).

20 Psalm 26:5. The Bible has *in tabernaculo (suo)* ('in (His) tabernacle') after *in die malorum*: perhaps omitted here because implying that the foreskin was God's tabernacle was a step too far, even for the *EOV*.

21 The Valley of Josaphat is named as a place of divine judgement at Joel 3:2, 12.

22 *ex quó*: used by the *Obscuri* for *quoniam* (Böcking 1869: 194). This is another late medieval usage: see *DLMBS* s.v. *ex* 12d.

23 *Moderni* refers to the *Via Moderna* ('Modern Way'), a philosophical school particularly associated with the University of Erfurt, and which took a quasi-Nominalist position on the question of Universals. See Kärkkäinen 2017. Theologians' abstruse arguments in highly technical language on such abstract problems were a frequent humanist target.

24 *Gaudent brevitate moderni* is a legal commonplace (see J. Céard, G. Defaux, M. Simonin, eds, *François Rabelais: Les cinq livres*, Paris, 1994: 792). Here it is perhaps also a joke on Ockham's razor, the principle of avoiding the postulation of unnecessary hypothetical beings: this rule, which demanded a form of philosophical brevity, was embraced by the *Via Moderna*. See Kärkkäinen 2017.

25 The *Obscuri* routinely use the honorific second person plural: so, below, Federfusius calls Gratius *dominationem vestram*, and Gratius is to address Mrs Pfefferkorn in the plural. This usage is a medieval Latin development (Stotz, vol. 4: 359–61): classical authors always address single individuals, no matter how exalted, in the singular. The medieval usage was already rejected by Petrarch and his followers (Alessio 2001: 167–9), but persisted long enough to still need lengthy condemnation by Erasmus in *De conscribendis epistolis* (266–76; see also Dionisotti 1985: 188). In his 1512 letter to Conrad Kullin, a theologian at the University of Cologne who had written warning Reuchlin of the brewing *Augenspiegel* scandal, Reuchlin patronizingly explains why he is using the second person singular in response to Kullin's plural: *iam enim illud tuum ferme totum desiit et abolevit in Romana lingua, et nunc quotusquisque maiores nostros imitamur* ('for that [practice] of yours has already almost completely ceased and died out in the Roman language, and now each of us imitates our ancestors') (*Illustrium virorum epistolae*, q4v).

26 *mentetenus*: non-classical, but frequent in the *EOV* (Böcking 1869: 225). For late medieval / early modern precedents see *LLN* s.v. *tenus* B,f; *LMILP* s.v. *mens*, col. 242.55–3.5.

27 *allegando*: a dative gerund. For the gradual extension of this construction see *LHS* 2: 376–7.

28 *iurista* was coined in the thirteenth century (*DMLBS* s.v.) to designate the new class of professional lawyers then emerging from the universities.

29 *sua*: one of the *EOV*'s many redundant possessives, calqued on vernacular usage. See also below: *sua Iudaitate*, *suam luxuriam*, *suo membro*.

30 *poetria*: found from the ninth century onwards (*NG* s.v.) and frequent in the *EOV* (Böcking 1869: 242) to refer to all forms of humanist learning.

31 Does this refer to a real line of Plautus? Despite Böcking 1870 and Saladin 2004: ad loc., *Truculuentus* 728 is more relevant than *Amphitryon* 884. However, the closest classical formulation is in fact Aulus Gellius 6.3.42. The sentiment is of course a commonplace, so that alleging an authority is sheer pedantry (let alone alleging one to show that foreskins do not grow back).

32 *Iudaitas* is apparently coined for the sake of the rhyme with *religiositas*. For humanist criticism of the medieval fondness for prose rhyme see K. Polheim, *Die lateinische Reimprosa*, Berlin 1925: 460–1. Coinages are rare in the *EOV*: despite the coarseness of much of their humour, as linguistic parody, the *EOV* are careful and subtle.

33 *cum hoc*: for original printings' *cum*. Böcking (1864: 57) suggests *cum* is used for *et simul* ('and at the same time') or *etiam* ('also'). But his one parallel (1869: 181) is in fact to *cum hoc*, which is very frequent in the *EOV* (1869: 181) and suitably flat. For the need to distinguish between misprints and deliberate mistakes in the *EOV* see Löfstedt (1983: 273).

34 The language of scholastic logic: see *DMLBS* s.v. *formaliter* 2,b.

35 Ulrich von Hutten apparently suffered and died from syphilis, on which he published a treatise (*De morbo Gallico*, 1519; see also Text 5).

36 *Magister Noster*, omnipresent in the *EOV*, was a standard designation for university theology lecturers. See Löfstedt 1983: 280.

37 The full name of the Inquisition was *Inquisitio haereticae pravitatis*.

38 *defectuosus* is a late medieval adjective, frequent in scholastic literature (*LLN*, *LMILP*, *MW* s.v.).

39 *se* ... *praevident*: calqued on German 'sich vorsehen' (literally 'foresee themselves'): see *DW* s.v. *vorsehen* 7.

40 *devotarie*: also at *EOV* 1.36, but poorly attested elsewhere. J. Ramminger (http://www.neulatein.de) cites one seventeenth-century use. *devotarius/-a* are found from the fifteenth century designating a person in religious life (*LLN*, *LMILP* *ss.vv.*), and the *Latinitatis Medii Aevi Lexicon Bohemorum* records one fifteenth-century instance of *devotarius* meaning 'faithful friend'.

So the *Obscuri* appear to have coined an adverb from an actual late medieval substantive.

41 *descis(s)io*: a scholastic word, signifying 'cutting off, separation'. Its meaning, spelling and pronunciation made for easy confusion with classical *decisio*, as has happened here. See *DLMBS* s.v. 2 *decisio* 3; *MW* s.v. *descissio*.

42 The promiscuity of Pfefferkorn's wife is a running gag through the *EOV*. At 1.13 and 2.39 Gratius (who was in holy orders) is said to be sleeping with her, as is also implied here.

43 *bene statis*: calqued on German *gut stehen mit* (literally 'stand well with'): see *DW* s.v. stehen 14.b.

44 *mi* is properly a masculine vocative, but is found already with feminines in early Christian texts (Stotz, vol. 4: 124).

45 *honesta persona*: a stock phrase with a legal flavour: see, s.v. *persona*, *TLL*, col. 1728.73–4; *NG* IV.C.3; *LMILP*, col. 466.50–1.

46 *estis . . . Colonia*: literally 'You are an honourable person, just as is one (woman) in Cologne'. The Latin is as bad as that, but the sense must be either as translated or 'You are a more honourable person than any woman in Cologne.' Similar idioms, with the same sense, at 1.21 (*vos estis speciosissima, sicut est una in toto mundo* – literally 'you are most beautiful, just as is one [woman] in the entire world'); 1.36 (*ipse est bonus et zelosus Christianus, sicut est aliquis in Colonia* – literally 'he is a good and zealous Christian, just as is anybody in Cologne'; *ipsa vero est ita honesta matrona, sicut est una in Colonia* – literally 'but she is so honourable a matron, just as is one [woman] in Cologne'); 2.12 (*est ita pulchra civitas, sicut est in mundo* – literally 'the city is so beautiful, just as there is in the world'). These expressions possibly calque the German construction 'wie nur (irgend) ein' ('as any of them') – I thank Henrike Lähnemann for this suggestion, and Carlotta Dionisotti for pointing out a parallel to the *aliquis* usage in the fourteenth-century *Logic* of Albert of Saxony (ed. H. Berger, Hamburg 2010: 304).

47 The reader already knows from *EOV* 1.36 Mrs Pfefferkorn's view on foreskins: *Audivit frequenter a sua matre quod viri praeputiati faciunt feminis minorem* [conjectured for originals' *maiorem*] *voluptatem quam non praeputiati. Eam ob causam dicit, quando suus maritus moritur, et ipsa alium accipiet, ille debet etiam nullam cutam habere in membro* ('She has frequently heard from her mother that men with foreskins give women less pleasure than men without foreskins. For this reason she says that, when her husband dies, and she shall take another, he too should have no skin on his member').

48 *audacter sine verecundia:* such useless pleonasms abound in the *EOV*, in 'imitation of scholastic and legal prose' (Löfstedt 1983: 276).

49 For the identification of the Dragon drinking house in Erfurt see Böcking 1870: 609. Although the *Obscuri* spend much time in taverns, this is the only one of their letters actually said to have been written in one. Federfusius was surely drunk when he wrote it.

9

The Pleasures of the Hills

Conrad Gessner (1516–65), *Descriptio Montis Fracti sive Montis Pilati, iuxta Lucernam in Helvetia*, pp. 47–9

William M. Barton

Introduction

Swiss physician, natural philosopher and humanist Conrad Gessner (1516–65) was born and died in Zurich. He came from a modest family, but gained access to schooling and a rich education through the support of reformers Huldrych Zwingli and Heinrich Bullinger, among others. After travelling to Bourges and Paris for his studies, Gessner took up a teaching post in his home town, before being appointed Professor of Greek in Lausanne in 1537. Gessner's next step took him to Montpellier to study for a medical degree, which he was awarded in Basle in 1541. He then returned to his home town to settle, initially as Professor of Natural Philosophy at the city's Collegium Carolinum, one of the forerunners of Zurich's university, and later as a private doctor. After practising medicine in the city for several years, Gessner was appointed Zurich's city doctor in 1554.

Gessner wrote on an extraordinarily wide range of topics throughout his lifetime. For example, he published a Greek dictionary in 1537, wrote a linguistic tract comparing world languages, the *Mithridates*, in 1555, and produced the *editio princeps* of Marcus Aurelius' *Meditations* in 1559. Among contemporaries, but still also today, Gessner was best known, however, for his encyclopedic works. With the *Bibliotheca universalis* (1545) Gessner attempted the first complete bibliography of all known Hebrew, Greek and Latin printed books to his time. The *Historia animalium* (1561–5) offered extensive descriptions and numerous woodcuts of the world's animals, in five volumes and nearly 5,000 pages. His unfinished *Historia plantarum*, complete with detailed drawings from Gessner's own hand of numerous plants, attempted the same for the world's flora. The manuscript was only published posthumously in 1750, having been largely forgotten after his death. Alongside these larger works, Gessner also published numerous smaller studies on everything from fossils and the mountain landscape of his native Switzerland to medieval authors and central Europe's hot springs.

The following extract is taken from one of Gessner's best-known pieces of mountain-writing, the description of Mount Pilatus, also known as the *mons fractus* ('broken mountain'), Fräckmünt, a mountain range just south of Lucerne ('*A Description of the Fräckmünt or Mount Pilatus, near Lucerne in Switzerland*'). The mountain's name, and to some extent its fame, came from a local legend, which held that the marshy area under one of the range's peaks was the resting place of the Roman Prefect Pontius Pilate. The story went that Pilate had been recalled from Judea to Rome under Caligula, but chose exile over the terrible fate that awaited him in the capital. He then died abroad, either at his own hand or having drowned in a river. In the several places where his corpse was thought to have ended up – this legend was connected to a number of locations in Europe – the area was said to suffer from horrendous storms and poor weather. Gessner relates the legend towards the end of his letter (pp. 53–4). By Gessner's own time, the legend meant that the city of Lucerne required visitors to the mountain to obtain permission for their ascent from the mayor – Gessner 's group was granted this permission in 1555 from Nicolaus a Meggen. Visitors were also to be accompanied by 'an honest townsman' (*probus aliquis vir ex civibus*, p. 46), who would act as the group's guide on their journey, and would also guarantee their behaviour around Pilatus' marshy lake.[1] On account of the legend, it was forbidden to throw any object into the water, in order to protect the city against the threat of storms or flooding. Gessner sensibly expresses his doubts over this 'belief of the locals' (*incolarum persuasio*, p. 52) in his description of the mountain.

As his writing on mountains shows, Gessner knew his country's Alpine landscape well. He undertook regular walking trips to the mountains to collect new data on their plant and animal life, for the sake of his health and simply to 'get away from it all'. Aside from publishing his own eulogy to the peaks in the well-known *Epistola de montium admiratione*, '*Letter on the Wonder of the Mountains*' (Zurich 1541), Gessner also printed shorter pieces on the mountains from his friends and colleagues, often as appendices to his larger publications. In this way he contributed significantly to a growing interest and enthusiasm in mid-sixteenth-century Europe for the mountain landscape. This extract from his *Descriptio Montis Fracti* represents another vibrant expression of Gessner's enjoyment of the peaks. The letter is dedicated to one of his Swiss medical colleagues, Johannes Chrysostomus Huber, and opens with a brief sketch of the city of Lucerne (p. 45), before moving on to a general overview of the mountain terrain. Gessner first offers an image of the peak surrounded by shepherds' huts and their herds among the forests, valleys and snow-capped mountains (pp. 45–6). He then switches to a narrative of his group's ascent, which sees them spend the night in a local chalet, before embarking on the last part of the climb (p. 46). His report of the hike itself takes Gessner into a discussion of the delights available for all the senses on the mountains (pp. 47–50). After this aesthetic excursus, Gessner writes a short eulogy of mountain life in general (pp. 50–1), before bringing himself back to a more formal, topographic description of Mount Pilatus (pp. 52–3). Having finished this geographical section, he deals with the legend of Pilate and the names of other local natural features (pp. 53–4), before closing the letter in a short paragraph on the group's return to the city of Lucerne by night as it started to rain (pp. 54–5).

Note

1 Gessner employs both the words *palus* ('marsh') and *lacus* ('lake') to describe the area in his letter. He uses, however, *palus* in the subtitle to his letter (see translated title below), and in narrating his group's descent to visit the area, he comments in more detail on its character (p. 52): *per clivum descendimus aliquandiu donec tandem ad lacum, aut verius paludem Pilati pervenimus* ('we descended a slope for some time until at last we arrived at the lake, or more correctly the marsh of Pilatus').

Bibliography

Backus, I. (2016), *Life Writing in Reformation Europe: Lives of Reformers by Friends, Disciples and Foes*, Abingdon.

Barton, W. M. (2016), *Mountain Aesthetics in Early Modern Latin Literature*, London.

Boscani Leoni, S. (2004), 'La montagna pericolosa, pittoresca, arretrata', *Schweizerische Zeitschrift für Geschichte*, 54: 359–83.

Boscani Leoni, S. (2019), 'Conrad Gessner and a Newly Discovered Enthusiasm for Mountains in the Renaissance', in U. B. Leu and P. Opitz (eds), *Conrad Gessner: Die Renaissance der Wissenschaften – The Renaissance of Learning*, 119–28, Berlin / Boston MA.

Cappeller, M. A. (1767), *Pilati Montis Historia, figuris aeneis illustrata*, Basel.

Coolidge, W. A. B. (1904), *Josias Simler et les origines de l'alpinisme jusqu'en 1600*, Geneva.

Leu, U. B. (2016), *Conrad Gessner (1516–1565). Universalgelehrter und Naturforscher der Renaissance*, Zurich.

Leu, U. B. and M. Ruoss, eds (2016), *Facetten eines Universums: Conrad Gessner 1516–2016*, Zurich.

Simmler, J. (1566), *Vita clarissimi philosophi et medici excellentissimi Conradi Gesneri Tigurini a Josia Simlero*, Zurich.

Wellisch, H. (1975), 'Conrad Gessner: A Bio-Bibliography', *Journal of the Society for the Bibliography of Natural History*, 7.2: 151–247.

Source of the Latin text

Conrad Gessner, *Descriptio Montis Fracti iuxta Lucernam, et primum chorographica, praesertim quod ad paludem Pilati in eo memorabilem* ('*A Description of the 'Fräckmünt' near Lucerne, principally a chorographical [description] concerning especially the remarkable marsh of Pilatus*'), in: C. Gessner, *De raris et admirandis herbis, quae sive quod noctu luceant, sive alias ob causas, Lunariae nominantur, commentariolus* ('*A short tract on the rare and wonderful herbs, which are called 'moon-herbs' either because they shine at night, or for other reasons*'), Zurich (A. and F. Gessner) 1555, pp. 47–9 (with some adjustments to spelling and punctuation).

Latin text

Quis enim sensuum hic sua voluptate non fruitur? Nam quod ad tactum,[1] corpus universum aestu affectum, frigidioris per montes aeris occursu, qui et superficiem corporis undique aspirat, et plenis hauritur faucibus,[2] unice recreatur, iuxta illud Homeri Ζώγρει ἐπιπνείων ψυχρὸς βορέαο ἀήτης[3] Idem rursus ventos et frigora expertum,[4] sole, ambulatione vel igne in casis pastorum calefiet.

Visus mirabili montium, iugorum, rupium, sylvarum, vallium, rivorum, fontium, pratorum,[5] aspectu insolito delectatur. Quod ad colorem, virent et florent pleraque omnia, quod ad eorum quae videntur figuras, mirae et rarae sunt scopulorum, rupium, anfractum, aliarumque rerum species, tum figura, tum magnitudine altitudineque admirandae. Si oculorum aciem[6] intendere, visum dispergere, et longe lateque prospicere et circumspicere omnia libeat, speculae scopulique non desunt, in quibus capite iam inter nubes versari tibi videaris. Si contra colligere visum malis, prata sylvasque virentes aspectabis, aut ingredieris quoque: vel ut amplius colligas, valles opacas, rupes umbrosas, speluncas obscuras inspicies. Est autem cum omnium rerum vicissitudo et varietas, tum vel maxime sensibilium iucunda. Tanta vero varietas alibi nusquam, quanta in montibus, intra quidem tam breve spatium reperitur: in quibus, ut alia iam non dicam, quatuor anni partes, aestatem, autumnum, ver, hyemem, uno die videre ac ingredi licet. Adde quod ex summis montium iugis, universum caeli nostri hemisphaerium libere conspectui tuo patebit, et ortus occasusque siderum absque ullo impedimento facile observabis: et solem longe tardius occidentem, exorientem vero citius[7] animadvertes.

Auditum suaves sociorum sermones, ioci facetiaeque oblectabunt, et avicularum in sylvis suavissimi cantus, et ipsum denique solitudinis silentium. Nihil hic auribus molestum esse potest, nihil inportunum, nulli tumultus aut strepitus urbani, nullae hominum rixae.[8] Hic in profundo et religioso quodam silentio ex praealtis montium iugis, ipsam fere caelestium, si quae est, orbium harmoniam exaudire[9] tibi videberis.

English translation

Indeed, which of the senses doesn't experience its own delights here? For as far as the sense of touch is concerned,[1] the entire body suffering with the heat is especially restored by the current of cooler air through the mountains, which both blows from all sides over the body's surface and is inhaled in healthy gulps.[2] As Homer put it, 'the cold breath of the northern wind revives [us] when it blows'.[3] On the other hand, the same [body], once tested by the winds and the cold,[4] will be warmed by the sun, by walking, or at the fireside in the houses of [local] shepherds.

One's sight is delighted by the unusually astonishing view of the mountains, ridges, cliffs, forests, valleys, brooks, springs [and] meadows.[5] As for colour, almost everything is full of vigour and in blossom. As for the forms of the things one can see, the views of the crags, cliffs, ledges and other things are wondrous and distinctive. They are to be admired for their shape as well as for their size and height. Should you enjoy widening your eyes' gaze,[6] spreading out your view, and observing both far and wide in the distance, and seeing everything all around [you], there is no shortage of viewpoints and crags upon which you can seem now to touch the clouds with your head. Should you prefer, on the other hand, to concentrate your gaze, you will observe pastureland and verdant woods – you can even go into them. And as you gather your gaze further in, you will see sheltered valleys, shady cliffs [and] dark caves. There is, then, both variety and diversity in everything, as well as especially delightful [variation] for the senses. There is no such great variety to be found anywhere else than in the mountains, [and] in such small a space as well. In the mountains – not to mention the rest – you can see and even experience the four parts of the year, summer, autumn, spring [and] winter all in one day. I would add that from the summits of the mountain peaks the whole half-dome of our skies will lay itself out freely before your eyes. And you will see the rising and the setting of the stars easily, without any obstacle, and you will notice that the sun sets far later but rises earlier.[7]

The pleasant chatter of friends, their jokes and gibes will delight the ear, along with the very sweet birdsong in the woods and, in fact, the very silence of solitude. Nothing here can be a nuisance to the ears, nothing is troublesome. There is none of the hustle and bustle of the city, nor the quarrels of men.[8] Here you will believe you are listening to the harmony of the celestial spheres itself (if such a thing exists[9]), in a deep and reverent silence, from the tops of the highest mountains.

Odores etiam suaves ex herbis, floribus ac stirpibus montanis se offerunt; eaedem enim plantae in montibus, tum odoratiores, tum ad medicamenta efficaciores, quam in plano proveniunt.[10] Aer hic longe liberior et salubrior, nec adeo vaporibus crassis infectus, ut in planitie, nec ut in urbibus et aliis hominum habitationibus contagiosus aut foetidus. Hic naribus ad cerebrum derivatus, arteria ad pulmones[11] et cor, non solum non offendit, sed etiam iuvat.

Gustus oblectamentum eximium iam supra celebravi,[12] frigidae potum: qui quidem defessos ac sitientes nulla aut multo minore noxa hic delectabit, quam in planitie vel domi fieret. Primum[13] enim ipsa aqua in montibus purior et melior est, praesertim circa medium, ni fallor: ubi neque frigida nimis aut nivalis est, et tamen pura et percolata, et libero adhuc exposita aeri.

The sweet smells of herbs, flowers and mountain plants also offer themselves up. Indeed, the very same plants on the mountains are both more pungent and more effective for making medicines than when they grow in the lowlands.[10] The air here is far freer and healthier: It is neither so contaminated by thick vapours as it is in the plains, nor so diseased and foul-smelling as it is in the cities and in the other settlements of men. Here [the air], drawn through the nose to the brain and from the windpipe into the lungs[11] and the heart, not only does not vex [us], but in fact delights.

I have, above, already sung the praises of [that] extraordinary delight for the palate,[12] a draft of cold [water], which will certainly give pleasure to the tired or thirsty here, [and] with none, or much less of the harmful effect than there would be in the lowlands or at home. This is first of all[13] because the water in the mountains is purer and of better quality, especially that found around its middle [sections] (unless I am mistaken), where the water is neither too cold nor icy, but nevertheless pure and well-filtered. It is, moreover, still exposed to the free air.

Commentary

1 *quod ad tactum*: the following excerpt is arranged according to the five human senses. After Gessner's opening rhetorical question – *Quis enim sensuum hic sua voluptate non fruitur?* – each section discusses a different sense: in the original edition, each sense is named in italics in the margin. In the main text, *tactus*, *visus*, *auditus* and *gustus* are the normal Latin words for the respective senses. Gessner deviates from his use of such abstract nouns only in *odores*, 'smells', in paragraph three, where the reader might have expected *odoratus* or *olfactus*, 'the sense of smell'. Indeed *olfactus* is used in the marginal note.

2 *plenis . . . faucibus*: literally 'with a full throat'. The word *faux*, *faucis* (f.) was used in medical terminology often in the plural (*fauces*, *faucium*) to designate the pharynx or gullet.

3 *iuxta illud Homeri*: like many humanists, Gessner often included passages of Greek in his writing to put his learning on display, but also, in line with humanist ideas of literature, because the ancients were simply thought to have said it best. Gessner's Greek was excellent: he had taught Greek in Lausanne (1537–41) and relied frequently on ancient Greek authorities for his natural philosophical work. In this passage of Greek, however, Gessner muddled Homer's words. The citation, as Gessner has it, is nowhere to be found either in our texts of the *Iliad* and *Odyssey* or in the early modern editions Gessner would have known. Most likely, then, our author was attempting to quote Homer from memory or from a commonplace book (a collection of popular quotes on numerous topics), where the phrase had been poorly recorded. Gessner perhaps had in mind one or a mixture of the following Homeric passages for his version: Hom. *Il.* 5.697–8: αὖτις δ' ἐμπνύνθη, περὶ δὲ πνοιὴ Βορέαο | ζώγρει ἐπιπνείουσα κακῶς κεκαφηότα θυμόν ('Again he recovered, and the gusty breath of the North Wind | reinvigorated his wheezing soul'); *Od.* 4.567–8: ἀλλ' αἰεὶ Ζεφύροιο λιγὺ πνείοντος ἀήτας | Ὠκεανὸς ἀνίησιν ἀναψύχειν ἀνθρώπους ('But it is always the gusts of the clear-blowing Zephyr | that Oceanus sends up to refresh mankind'). Or he had mixed up the phrase with a similar one from another author, e.g. Pindar, *Ol.* 3.31–2: τὰν μεθέπων ἴδε καὶ κείναν χθόνα πνοιᾶς ὄπιθεν Βορέα | ψυχροῦ ('Pursuing her, he saw even that land beyond the gusts of the cold North Wind').

4 *expertum*: the participle *expertum* qualifies *corpus*, carried over from the previous sentence, which is constructed in parallel to this one: . . . *corpus universum aestu affectum*.

5 *montium . . . pratorum*: this is the first of several sentences in the present passage where Gessner attempts to express his wonder at the abundance of the natural world which he finds in the mountains by formulating long lists of vocabulary. There follows another example in the following sentence (*figuras . . . species*) and yet another (*valles . . . obscuras*) just before Gessner sums up his feelings about this marvellous variety in the instructive *est autem . . . iucunda.* Europe's 'arch-humanist' Erasmus of Rotterdam, basing himself on Quintilian's *Institutio oratoria*, had laid down guidelines for this 'abundant style' of writing – particularly popular among humanists in the sixteenth and seventeenth centuries – in his rhetorical handbook *De duplici copia verborum ac rerum commentarii duo* ('*Two treatises on the double supply of words and things*' 1512). We hear numerous echoes of this idealized rhetorical style in this passage, where Gessner's use of this verbal abundance effectively mirrors his astonishment at the mountain landscape's scenic abundance.

6 *oculorum aciem*: the basic meaning of *acies* is a 'point' or 'sharp edge'. It is therefore frequently used to denote a sword or other weapon, but also, in the context of the eyes or the act of seeing, to describe a 'glance', 'focus' and then by extension 'vision' or 'sight' more generally (*OLD* s.v.). In the image of a 'point' or 'sharp edge' of the eyes we hear echoed in Gessner's use of this standard Latin phrase the vocabulary of the emissive theory of sight. This held that vision occurred by means of rays or beams emitted from the eyes onto an object to be viewed. While some ancient thinkers upheld this model (e.g. Plato, *Tim.* 45b), the emission theory was contested already, for example, in Aristotle (*De anim.* 418a–19b), in favour of models moving towards that of intromission which we rely on today. Nonetheless, debates over the intro- and emissive ideas of sight continued well into the early modern period.[1] Where exactly Gessner stood on this question is not clear from this passage.

7 *longe tardius . . . vero citius*: in these two comparative adverbs it is necessary to understand the words' secondary meanings – *tarde*, 'late', and *cito*, 'early'. Their primary senses of 'slow' and 'fast' would paint a confusing picture of the sunrises and sunsets, as seen from the tops of mountains.

8 *nihil . . . hominum rixae*: in his comparison of the mountain's quiet atmosphere with the hustle and bustle of life in the town, Gessner picks up on the ancient opposition of *rus*, 'the countryside', and *urbs*, 'the city'. Among classical authors, this idea famously found expression in Horace's *Epist.* 1.10, for example, where the simple blessings of the country (2–14) are set against the luxury of the city (19–23). The contrast between *rus* and *urbs* became, indeed, so commonplace that it was even set as a topic for debate among schoolboys in ancient Rome (Quintilian, *Inst.* 2.4.24). In Gessner's time this

opposition was still very much at the forefront of readers' minds: in Battista Spagnoli Mantovano's (Mantuan's) enormously successful collection of ten Latin eclogues, the *Adolescentia* (1498; see Text 1), the two characters Cornix and Fulica debate the theme in poem six. Gessner's equation of *mons* with *rus* in the present passage is indicative of the gradual inclusion of the high Alpine landscape in later ideas of the 'pastoral'.

9 *caelestium . . . orbium harmoniam exaudire*: the concept of the 'harmony of the spheres', 'music of the spheres' or 'universal harmony' held that the relative proportions of the movements of celestial bodies represented a coherence akin to that of musical harmonies. While a number of early thinkers indeed thought that bodies in space – the sun, moon and the planets – emitted sounds corresponding to their respective orbits (cf. Plin. *HN* 2.20 on Pythagoras), the idea of an audible celestial music had met with resistance already in ancient thought (cf. Aristotle, *De caelo* 2.9). Gessner's expression of his doubts (*si quae est . . .*) shows that he, too, had thought critically about the presence of a true audible harmony. But that the orbits of celestial bodies were arranged according to a congruent, harmonious schema remained a popular concept in natural philosophical thought until much later. Johannes Kepler's *Harmonices mundi* (*'On the harmony of the world'*, Linz 1619), for example, dealt with the world's geometric and physical harmonies in everything from shapes and music to astronomical features. The work's fifth book studies the harmony of the motions of the planets.

10 *plantae in montibus . . . in plano proveniunt*: among Gessner's principal motivations for undertaking his trips to the mountains was his interest in their rich plant life. He would not only collect data (descriptions, drawings and seeds, for example) on the plentiful plants he found on the slopes for his botanical publications; he would also collect simples of numerous flora for the preparation of medicines and remedies back at home. This study of plant life and gathering of 'simples' for the purpose of pharmacopoeia were occupations shared by a widespread community of natural philosophers, physicians and apothecaries – among others – who drove the intensive early modern interest in botany. As is characteristic of the humanist effort in various other fields of study, early modern botany focused in its earliest phases on the preservation and understanding, then (later) expansion and improvement, of ancient treatises on the topic. For botany, the work of the ancient authors Aristotle, Theophrastus, Galen, Dioscorides and Pliny the Elder were of primary interest. Just as in the present passage from Gessner, the mountain's special place in this botanical fascination, as a pure and particularly fertile 'garden of nature', was often emphasized in contemporary reports of trips to the hills. The various letters and descriptions of Swiss

mountains that Gessner collected from colleagues and appended to his own publications contain, almost without exception, similar praise of the wonderful mountain plant life. This botanical admiration for the mountain, in particular its praise as 'nature's garden', constituted an important early modern innovation on the images to be found among ancient authors.[2]

11 *Hic naribus ... ad pulmones*: this part of the sentence is, as occasionally elsewhere in Gessner's Latin writing, rather compact. *naris*, 'nostril', is often used in the plural to mean simply 'nose'. The word *arteria, -ae* (f.) – also often *arterium, -i* (n.) – can be a 'false friend'. It is used generally for any type of 'pipe' or 'tubing' in the body (hence 'artery' in English today) but designates in Latin principally, as here, the windpipe. In the first part of this clause, the subject *aer* is carried over from the beginning of the sentence; so *hic* [*aer*] *naribus ad cerebrum derivatus* [*est*]. In the second part, constructed in parallel to the first in the same way as we have seen already above in n. 4, the same must again be understood; so [*aer*] *arteriā ad pulmones* [*derivatus est*].

12 *Gustus oblectamentum ... supra celebravi*: in the paragraphs just before Gessner's turn to the aesthetic pleasures of the mountain (p. 47 in the original) he had described a moment where the hike to Mount Pilatus had become steeper and more difficult, just before the group arrived at a mountain 'Sennhütte' (Swiss chalet). Here the group discover a spring where the fresh mountain water works wonders to restore the hot and tired walkers from their toils: *Paulo infra quam fons est ad dexteram in latere clivi, in exiguo terrae cavo abditus, cuius purissima gelidissimaque aqua a lassitudine, siti et aestu mirifice refecti sumus* ('A little below which [the *Sennhütte*] there is a spring to the right in the side of the slope, hidden away in a narrow hollow in the ground. We were wonderfully refreshed from our tiredness, thirst and overheating by this [spring's] very pure and icy-cold water').

13 *Primum*: this word introduces the first of a longer list of arguments for the benefits of mountain water over that to be found in the plains. In the continuation of this section, not included here, Gessner builds his case in favour of mountain water by defending its cooler temperature, the benefits of drinking it while performing physical activity as well as its effective use against fevers and gout.

Notes

1 On the history of theories of vision in general see the standard work of D. C. Lindenberg, *Theories of Vision from Al-Kindi to Kepler*, Chicago, 1976. For

discussion over the question of intro- or emission among early modern thinkers see pp. 137–9; 156–61; 180–1.

2 See M. Korenjak, '*Pulcherrimus Foecundissimusque Naturae Hortus*: Berichte über botanisch motivierte Bergbesteigungen im 16. Jahrhundert', *Neulateinisches Jahrbuch*, 15 (2013): 197–218.

10

Neo-Latin Love Elegy

Joachim Du Bellay (*c.* 1522–60), Selection from *Amores* (1558)

Paul White

Introduction

Joachim Du Bellay (*c.* 1522–60) is best known for his poetry in the French language (most notably the 1558 sonnet collections *Les Antiquitez de Rome* ['*The Antiquities of Rome*'] and *Les Regrets* ['*The Regrets*']) and for his authorship of the influential 'manifesto' of the group of poets that came to be known as the Pléiade, the *Deffence et illustration de la langue françoise* ('*Defence and Illustration of the French Language*', 1549). In the *Deffence* he had criticized those who composed Latin poetry at the expense of their native vernacular, but during his Roman 'exile' in 1553–7 (in fact a period spent as secretary to his uncle, Cardinal Jean Du Bellay, at the Papal court) it seems he had a change of heart. The four collections of Latin poems he composed during his stay in Rome were published in Paris in 1558, as were the French sonnet collections for which he is famous today. Both the Latin and the French poems explore, among other things, the French poet's often ambivalent relationship with Rome's history, literature and contemporary culture. Fruitful comparisons may be made between the differing treatments of these themes in the Latin and in the French poems.

In the Latin collections published in 1558 (*Elegiae*, *Varia Epigrammata*, *Amores* and *Tumuli* – '*Elegies*', '*Various epigrams*', '*Love poems*', '*Epitaphs*' – all in one volume) Du Bellay undertook a complex interrogation of his own choice to write Latin poetry. In the first poem of the *Elegiae*, titled *Cur intermissis Gallicis Latine scribat* ('Why, having paused with French, he writes in Latin'), he emphasized the difficulty and foreignness of Latin: the image he used was that of a dangerous sea voyage undertaken against his will. In another poem, addressed 'To the reader', at the head of his *Epigrammata*, the emphasis was quite different: here, Du Bellay defended himself against implied criticism of his choice to abandon his French 'wife' (*nupta*) for a Latin 'girlfriend' (*puella*), thus linking poetic composition in Latin with sensuality and pleasure.

The terms Du Bellay used in that poem to figure his relationship with Latin, *puella* and *domina* ('mistress'), are keywords of the genre of Roman love elegy. The poems of the *Amores*, which describe a love affair with a Roman *puella* named Faustina, develop the connection further.

My title presents Du Bellay's *Amores* as belonging to the genre of Neo-Latin love elegy. This requires some explanation. Walther Ludwig gave a useful working definition of the Latin love elegy collection as 'a group of middle-sized poems collected within one artistically arranged book and, at least to a large extent, dealing with the passionate and devoted love of the poet for a specific girl' (1976: 172). It is certainly the case that Du Bellay's *Amores*, whose title is bound to evoke the love elegies of Ovid, adopts both the central conceit and the language and conventions of the Roman love elegy book: the poet-lover persona is denied access to his beloved by a series of obstacles (her jealous husband, locked doors, her own *duritia* or hard-heartedness); he laments his suffering and complains of his enslavement to love (*servitium amoris*). However, generically, the *Amores* is not precisely a love elegy collection on the model of those of the canonical Roman elegists Propertius, Tibullus and Ovid. Although it adheres to the Roman elegiac model in terms of its settings, themes and underlying narrative structure, the individual poems are not quite like classical elegies. They are on the whole shorter, and structured more like epigrams (or like Du Bellay's own French sonnets): they often focus on one central image or conceit, rounded off with a final *pointe*. They are metrically varied and show a pronounced Catullan influence: indeed, the collection is prefaced by a hendecasyllabic dedicatory poem *Ad Gordium*, which is wholly Catullan in style. The *Amores* also contains political and satirical epigrams, and other poems not concerned with the Faustina narrative. (This last feature was not a departure from the classical models: the Roman love elegists had also included non-amatory poems in their collections.)

The generic hybridity of the *Amores* is not in itself unusual. Some of the first Neo-Latin love elegy collections, such as the *Cinthia* of Aeneas Silvius Piccolomini, had mixed elegies with epigrams and with poems modelled on the non-elegiac parts of Catullus. More generally, recent criticism on Renaissance love poetry has tended to complicate any picture of generic stability, by emphasizing the promiscuous use of elements drawn from a broad range of Latin and vernacular traditions, which were themselves complicatedly intertwined (Roman love elegy and lyric, medieval *fin' amor* and troubadour poetry, Petrarchism, Neoplatonism). This does not mean that poets like Du Bellay did not conceive of themselves as writing squarely in the

Roman elegiac tradition of Propertius, Tibullus and Ovid: indeed, self-conscious play with other modes and genres is a hallmark of the ancient genre of love elegy; its Renaissance practitioners recognized and developed this characteristic.

Five of the thirty-three short poems in Du Bellay's *Amores* were selected for inclusion here: the four opening poems, and the eighth in the sequence. The poems, taken together, give a clear sense of the elegiac framing of the collection and its underlying narrative; they also exemplify some of the characteristic themes, images and set pieces of Neo-Latin love elegy.

Metre: elegiac couplet

Bibliography

Bizer, M. (1995), *Imitation et conscience de soi dans la poésie latine de la Pléiade*, Paris.

Demerson, G., ed. (1984), *Joachim Du Bellay: Œuvres poétiques VII: Œuvres latines: Poemata*, Paris.

Ford, P. (2003), *The Judgement of Palaemon: The Contest Between Neo-Latin and Vernacular Poetry in Renaissance France*, Leiden (esp. Ch. 2, 'Joachim Du Bellay: Language and Culture').

Galand-Hallyn, P. (1995), *Le 'Génie' latin de Joachim Du Bellay*, La Rochelle.

Ginsberg, E. (1980), 'Joachim du Bellay's Latin poem *Patriae desiderium* and his vernacular poetry', in J.-C. Margolin (ed.), *Acta conventus Neo-Latini Turonensis*, 529–36, Paris.

Hinds, S. (1987), *The Metamorphosis of Persephone: Ovid and the Self-Conscious Muse*, Cambridge.

Hoggan, Y. (1982), 'Aspects du bilinguisme littéraire chez Du Bellay: le traitement poétique des thèmes de l'exil dans les *Poemata* et *Les Regrets*', *Bibliothèque d'Humanisme et Renaissance*, 44: 65–79.

Houghton, L. (2013), 'Renaissance Latin Love Elegy', in T. S. Thorsen (ed.), *The Cambridge Companion to Latin Love Elegy*, 290–305, Cambridge.

Ludwig, W. (1976), 'Petrus Lotichius Secundus and the Roman Elegists: Prolegomena to a Study of Neo-Latin Elegy', in R. R. Bolgar (ed.), *Classical Influences on European Culture A.D. 1500–1700*, 171–90, Cambridge.

Parker, H. (2012), 'Renaissance Latin Elegy', in B. K. Gold (ed.), *A Companion to Roman Love Elegy*, 476–88, Malden / Oxford / Chichester.

Smith, M. (1979), 'Joachim Du Bellay's Renown as a Latin Poet', in P. Tuynman, E. Kessler and G. C. Kuiper (eds), *Acta conventus Neo-Latini Amstelodamensis*, 928–42, Munich.

White, P. (2019), *Gallus Reborn: A Study of the Diffusion and Reception of Works Ascribed to Gaius Cornelius Gallus*, London.

Source of the Latin text

The Latin text has been taken from Demerson 1984: 135–9, 141; checked against *Ioachimi Bellaii Andini Poematum Libri Quatuor* (Paris 1558): fols 34^{r}–35^{r}, 36^{r}. Some adjustments have been made to spelling and punctuation.

Latin text

[I] *Ad Venerem*

Bella per Emathios non hic civilia campos,
fraternas acies, arma virumque cano.
Nec quoque fert animus mutatas dicere formas,
raptoris Stygii nec memorantur equi.
Aeneadum genitrix causa est mihi carminis una:
materiam vati da, Venus alma, tuo.
Tu quoque Faustinam nobis, formosa, dedisti,
qua nihil est tota pulchrius Ausonia.
Hac mihi sublata, periit mihi pristinus ardor
et quicquid mentis vel fuit ingenii.
Redde ergo ingenium solitasque in carmina vires,
Faustinam potius sed mihi redde, precor.

English translation

To Venus

I sing not here of civil wars over Emathian plains, of fraternal battles, of arms and the man. Nor does my mind bring [me] to speak of changed forms, nor are the horses of the Stygian ravisher [here] related. The mother of the line of Aeneas is the only cause of my song: kind Venus, grant a subject to your poet. You, lovely [goddess], also gave me Faustina: nothing in all of Ausonia is more beautiful than her. When she was taken from me, the fire I once felt died in me, along with whatever intelligence or talent I possessed. So please give back my talent and my former poetic force, or better still: give me back Faustina.

[II] ***Raptus Faustinae***

Qualis Tartareo quondam Proserpina curru,
 dum vaga discurrit saltibus, Enna, tuis,
nocturnis nuper rapta est Faustina quadrigis,
 dum tenet, ah demens, limina aperta domus.
Rapta est, me miserum, et caeco sub carcere clausa
 coniugis ingrato nunc gemit in thalamo.
Et nunc ille ferus tanquam de virgine rapta
 exultat, nostris heu fruiturque malis.
Interea infelix mater lymphata per urbem
 currit, et ignotas excubat ante fores,
te solam, Faustina, vocans, tua limina quaerens,
 quaesisse ut natam dicitur alma Ceres.
Ast ego, quem assiduo torret malus igne Cupido,
 deferor, ut noto concita Baccha Deo.
Nec dubitem aeratos liceat si rumpere postes
 duraque nocturna solvere claustra manu,
irruere armatus, vel, si hoc mala nostra ferat sors,
 perferre audacis vincula Pirithoi.

The rape of Faustina

Just as, long ago, Proserpina was abducted by a chariot of Tartarus as she ran roaming through your pastures, Enna, so, recently, was Faustina abducted by a four-horse car in the night, while her house – foolish [girl]! – had its doors open. She was abducted (to my sorrow) and now, incarcerated in a dark prison, she groans in the unwanted bed of a husband. And now that savage revels as if in the rape of a virgin and delights alas! in my misery. Meanwhile her poor, frantic mother runs about the city, and keeps vigil by strangers' doors, calling out only for you, Faustina, searching for your abode, just as kind Ceres, they say, searched for her own daughter. As for me, wicked Cupid burns me with unceasing fire, [and] I am carried away like a Bacchante roused [to a frenzy] by the familiar god. Nor would I hesitate, if it were granted to me to break down doors of bronze and unlock hard bolts with my hand by night, to take up arms and force my way in, and even, if unlucky fate should require it of me, to suffer the chains of bold Pirithous.

[III] *Faustinam primam fuisse quam Romae adamaverit*

Ipse tuas nuper temnebam, Roma, puellas,
nullaque erat tanto de grege bella mihi.
Et iam quarta Ceres capiti nova serta parabat,
nec dederam saevo colla superba iugo.
Risit caecus Amor. 'Tu vero hanc', inquit, 'amato':
Faustinam nobis indicat ille simul.
Indicat, et volucrem nervo stridente sagittam
infixit nobis corda sub ima puer.
Nec satis hoc: tradit formosam in vincla puellam,
et sacrae cogit claustra subire domus.
Haud prius illa tamen nobis erepta fuit quam
venit in amplexus terque quaterque meos.
Scilicet hoc Cypris nos acrius urit, et ipse
altius in nostro pectore regnat Amor.

That Faustina was his first love in Rome

I once used to scorn your women, Rome, and not one of that great crowd was beautiful to me. And already for the fourth time Ceres was preparing fresh garlands for her head, and I had not yielded my proud neck to the cruel yoke. Blind Cupid laughed. He said: 'Love *her*, then', just as he pointed out Faustina to me. He pointed [her] out, his bowstring twanged, and the boy buried his flying arrow in the very depths of my heart. Nor was that enough [for him]: he consigned my beautiful girl to chains, and forced her to enter the bounds of a holy house. But she was not snatched away from me before coming three or four times to my embrace. To be sure, by this it is that Cypris burns us more intensely, and Cupid himself reigns all the more supreme in our hearts.

[IV] *Ad ianuam Faustinae*

Haec domus, haec illa est, nostros quae claudit amores:
ah nimis atque nimis ianua dura mihi.
Tu veneres, ingrata, meas lususque, iocosque,
tu cohibes vinclis gaudia nostra tuis.
At nunc ille senex forsan rosea illa labella
sugit, et amplexu mollia membra premit.
Interea vagus atque excors, sine mente animoque,
limina nocturnis nota tero pedibus.
Et circunspicio Lyncaeo lumine, si qua
rimula sit nostris forte patens oculis.
Nulla patet, vel si qua patet, sunt omnia muta,
vocibus ac nostris pervia nulla via est.
Hei mihi quod Dominae nulla ratione potis sum
me dulce in gremium mittere per tegulas.

At Faustina's door

This is the house, the one that confines my love: o door, you are hard, all too hard on me. Unyielding, you keep bound up in your chains my desires, and my frolics and laughter, and [all] our joy. And maybe now that old man is sucking those rosy lips and pressing her soft limbs in his embrace. Meanwhile, erratic and senseless, my wits and reason lost, I pace all night the familiar doorway. And I inspect it with the gaze of Lynceus, in case a little crack might open up before my eyes. No [crack] appears, or if one does, all is silent, and there is no way for my voice to penetrate. What torment, that I cannot by any means thrust myself through the roof tiles [and] into the soft lap of my mistress.

[V] *Cum Faustina inclusam esse Venerem et Amorem*

Claustra tenent nostram (sic dii voluere) puellam:
  Felix quem clausum ferrea claustra tenent.
Illic sunt Charites lususque iocique leporesque,
  Et quicquid sedes incolit Idalias.
Casta Venus sancto corpus iam velet amictu,
  Sacraque iam discat relligiosus Amor.

That Venus and Cupid were imprisoned together with Faustina

Bolts confine my girl (so the gods willed it): happy the one whom [those] iron bolts imprison. There the Graces are, and frolics, and laughter, and delights, and whatever dwells in the Idalian abode. Venus should now be chaste and veil her body with a holy habit, and Cupid should now be a monk studying theology.

Commentary

[I] *Ad Venerem*

1–5 Du Bellay opens his collection with a conventional elegiac *recusatio*: the 'refusal' of grand themes and the high style in favour of love poetry (cf. Propertius 2.1, 10, 13, 34.61–94; 3.1, 3, 9; 4.1.71–150; Ovid, *Amores* 1.1; 2.1.11–22, 18; 3.1). Strikingly, he expresses this refusal in the form of a *cento* (a 'patchwork' poetic composition), stitching together phrases from the first lines of all of the major Roman epics: in order, Lucan, *Pharsalia* 1.1; Statius, *Thebaid* 1.1; Virgil, *Aeneid* 1.1; Ovid, *Metamorphoses* 1.1; Claudian, *De raptu Proserpinae* 1.1; Lucretius, *De rerum natura* 1.1. Lines 1–4 use the first four quotations to evoke the epic language and subjects that are being rejected; in line 5 the quotation from Lucretius expresses the preference for the subject matter of love elegy. The irony of taking line 5 from an epic and not from an elegiac source highlights the instability of the generic scheme on which the *recusatio* relies: Latin elegy tends to blur genre boundaries even while asserting their importance.

7 *Faustina*: the name means 'fortunate', 'auspicious'. Goethe later chose the same name for his Roman beloved in his *Römische Elegien* (1788–90).

8 The comparative construction and the indefinite construction in line 10 are features of the Neo-Catullan style (cf. poem 5.8).

Ausonia: the term strictly designates the southern part of the Italian peninsula, but was sometimes used in ancient poetry, and very often in Neo-Latin poetry, to mean Italy in general (see Text 7, ll. 9, 35).

9 *sublata*: acts here as past participle of *tollo*, not *suffero*.

9–12 In identifying the beloved Faustina with the poetry itself (6–7), and with his own poetic talent and power, Du Bellay establishes in this opening poem a metapoetic framework that will inform the collection as a whole. The identification of the *puella* with the elegist's Muse, inspiration or poetic talent, or with poetry itself, was a feature of ancient Roman elegy.

[II] *Raptus Faustinae*

The title of the poem, 'The Rape of Faustina', and much of the language Du Bellay uses allude to Claudian's *De raptu Proserpinae* (already evoked in the previous poem, line 4). 'Rape' is meant in the sense of 'abduction'. Ovid's two treatments of the rape of Proserpina (*Met.* 5.341–661; *Fasti* 4.417–620) are also relevant.

1 *Qualis* . . .: the epic diction of the opening, contrasting with the elegiac language of the rest of the poem, sharpens the comparison between mythological and domestic situations. Cf. Hinds 1987 on the generic complexity of Ovid's treatments.

2 *Enna*: a city in Sicily, the setting for Proserpina's abduction by Dis that prompted the goddess Ceres' anxious search for her missing daughter.

5–10 The run-on from hexameter to pentameter in these three couplets is suggestive of the persona's overflowing emotion.

5–6 The repetition of *rapta est* (from line 3) and the striking alliteration in *c* convey the distress and anger of the poetic persona at the harshness of the beloved's situation.

9–12 That Faustina's mother takes on the role of Ceres is a logical continuation of the mythological comparison on which the poem is based. However, that the mother lies down in doorways while calling out Faustina's name means that she also seems, oddly, to be assuming the normal role of the elegiac lover engaged in the *paraklausithyron* (the lament before the locked door: see poem 4). The elegiac lover himself, in this poem, wants a more heroic role: that of Theseus or Pirithous.

12 *dicitur*: in the context, this word functions as a marker of an 'Alexandrian footnote' (a term coined by David Ross), signposting an instance of intertextuality. The technique was much favoured by Ovid.

14 Gender confusion persists, as the persona compares himself to a Bacchante or Maenad, a female follower of the god Bacchus/Dionysus.

15–18 The persona now attempts to reassert a masculine identity, giving voice to a desire for violent irruption. The poet-lover's fantasy of storming the house in which his beloved is confined may bring to mind Du Bellay's famous exhortation, in the conclusion to the *Deffence et illustration de la langue françoise*, that the modern poet should storm the citadels of Rome and ransack its literary heritage.

18 *vincula Pirithoi*: cf. Horace *Carm.* 4.7.27–8. The reference is to the punishment of Pirithous, friend of Theseus, for his attempt to abduct Proserpina from the underworld.

[III] *Faustinam primam fuisse quam Romae adamaverit*

This poem develops the elegiac *recusatio* theme of the opening poem, by staging another typical elegiac scene, the appearance ('theophany') of the god Cupid, who compels the poet to write of love.

1–2 perhaps recall Maximianus' scorning of the women of Rome in his youth (*Eleg.* 1.63–100). Maximianus was a late antique elegiac poet, but his works were in the sixteenth century attributed to the first Roman elegist, Gallus, and Du Bellay knew them well. He had himself translated 'Gallus' *Eleg.* 1.89–100 into French for Louis Le Roy (White 2019: 27). More generally, the idea that the poet-lover had no interest in love or women before his enslavement to the *puella* is a commonplace of elegy (e.g. Prop. 1.1.1–2) as well as of Petrarchan love lyric.

3 The reappearance of Ceres, here as part of poetic periphrasis for the passing of a year, provides a link with the previous poem.

5 *Risit caecus Amor*: cf. Ovid, *Am.* 1.1.3–4.

5–7 The repetition of *indicat* emphasizes that Cupid merely 'points out' Faustina: this is not a dramatic revelation or *coup de foudre*. The apparent casualness of the selection of the beloved ('Love *her*, then') shows that we are quite far from the spiritual seriousness of the Petrarchan *innamoramento*: love elegy often advertises the fact that the beloved *puella* is little more than a pretext for the writing of love poetry (cf. Ovid, *Am.* 1.1 and Johannes Secundus, *Eleg.* 1.1).

10 *sacrae . . . domus*: the statement that Faustina was sent to a convent seems to conflict with the initial narrative of her abduction and forced marriage in the previous poem. Both versions remain in play in the poems that follow. The separation of the elegiac *puella* from the poet-lover (whether because of protective husbands, locked doors or her own *duritia*) was a fundamental feature of Roman love elegy, Du Bellay multiplies the obstacles that stand between him and the beloved and so amplifies Faustina's elegiac unattainability.

11–12 *Haud prius . . . quam*: when *priusquam* goes into tmesis, the position of *quam* marks the temporal clause: therefore the lovers' meetings must have occurred before Faustina's confinement. However, the sentence is constructed in such a way as to introduce a degree of confusion about the sequence of events.

13 *hoc*: ablative of means.

[IV] *Ad ianuam Faustinae*

The figure of the *exclusus amator* ('shut-out lover') is fundamental to love elegy. This poem stages the elegiac set piece known as the *paraklausithyron*, the lament before the locked door (e.g. Tibullus 1.2; Propertius 1.16; Ovid, *Am.* 1.6; cf. Catullus 67). See also note on poem 2.9–12.

9 *Lyncaeo lumine*: Lynceus ('lynx-like'), one of the Argonauts, was famed for his sharp vision.

9–12 Propertius, too, wishes that his voice might penetrate some crack in the door (1.16.27–8). Ovid (*Am.* 1.6.3–6) wants the door to open just a chink to admit his slender body: the joke is that he is emaciated from pining away for love.

13–14 The image of the sorrowful lover crashing in through the roof tiles is a humorous one. Du Bellay perhaps had in mind here the comic description of Jupiter's seduction of Danae in Terence, *Eunuchus* 584–9: the character Chaerea imagines the god creeping over the tiles of another man's house and coming in through the skylight.

[V] *Cum Faustina inclusam esse Venerem et Amorem*

inclusam: As is usual in Latin, the adjective agrees in gender, number and case with the nearer of the two nouns it qualifies.

1 *Claustra*: locks, bolts and cloisters are prominent in this collection. Du Bellay runs through several variations on the elegiac theme of the confinement and enclosure of the beloved. The metapoetic reading of Faustina as a symbol for Latin poetry, or the Latin poetic tradition, is again in play here.

3 *Charites*: the three Graces, goddesses of charm and beauty.

lususque iocique leporesque: the vocabulary of the Neo-Catullan style (the indefinite construction in line 4 is also characteristically Catullan; cf. note on poem 1.8). Note the elision at the end of the hexameter. The qualities enclosed in the convent with Faustina evoke eroticism and sensual pleasure, but they also have a pronounced literary and aesthetic dimension.

4 *sedes . . . Idalias*: Idalium in Cyprus was sacred to Venus.

5–6 *sancto . . . amictu . . . relligiosus*: here, as throughout the collection, Du Bellay uses properly classical vocabulary, rather than Ecclesiastical Latin coinages, to designate Christian concepts and things.

The subjunctives *velet* and *discat* have a jussive or optative meaning. The sense of the epigrammatic *pointe* is that Faustina's enclosure in the convent, instead of isolating her from love and sex, has had the effect of transforming the cloistered space into a realm of erotic delights. Venus' and Cupid's imagined adoption of the garb of a nun or a theologian is not therefore an expression of the triumphant Christianization of pagan figures, along the lines of St Jerome's famous image of the reclothing of captive women (*Epistle* 70). Rather, pagan eroticism infiltrates the sacred space in the guise of religiosity. The association of the convent with eroticism is a theme taken up in other poems in the collection.

11

A Jesuit Encounter with an Indian Yogi

Francesco Benci (1542–94), *Quinque Martyres* 5.96–132

Paul Gwynne

Introduction

A scholar of international reputation, Francesco Benci SJ (1542–94) was appointed first professor of rhetoric at the new Jesuit University in Rome, the Collegium Romanum. He was thus at the very heart of European intellectual, political and religious life during the stormy period of the late sixteenth century, when the nascent Jesuit order was struggling to establish itself across the globe. Close association with a series of popes (particularly Gregory XIII Boncompagni [r. 1572–85] and Sixtus V Peretti [r. 1585–90]) reveals that Benci was at the epicentre of papal politics in the 1580s and 1590s, and was directly able to translate papal policy into Jesuit pedagogy across the curriculum. This would have profound effects not only upon the Jesuit education system, but also upon global politics, as the Jesuits engaged in their worldwide missions.

What little is known about Benci's life can be summarized as follows. He was born Plauto Benci on 21 October 1542 at Acquapendente (*c*. 150 km north of Rome along the Via Cassia). He entered the Jesuit order on 18 May 1570, was ordained on 17 March 1576 and took the four vows on 7 May 1587. For obvious reasons, he changed his name from the pagan Plauto to Francesco when he entered the Order. He studied with the French philologist Marc-Antoine Muret (1526–85), then specialized further in philosophy and canon law. He taught *lettere* (the classical canon) at Siena and then Perugia, before going on to teach rhetoric at the Collegium Romanum (1583–4; 1585–90). From 1586 to 1591 he composed the *Annuae Litterae Societatis Iesu* (the annual bulletin of Jesuit news disseminated across the globe). He died at Rome on 6 May 1594 and was buried in the church of the Gesù. A prolific poet, playwright, essayist and correspondent, Benci composed the first Jesuit epic of martyrdom, the *Quinque martyres e Societate Iesu in India* ('The Five Martyrs from the Society of Jesus in India') in response to the news from Goa of the massacre of a missionary expedition to Salcete and the call for the missionaries' beatification. As editor of the *Annuae Litterae* Benci had access to Jesuit correspondence from all corners of the globe. His information about events in India is derived from these sources.

In summer 1583 five Jesuit brothers led by Rodolfo Acquaviva (1550–83) set out for the province of Salcete with the intention of founding a new church and mission in India. Unfortunately, their dream was almost immediately, and brutally, terminated by local opposition; almost all members of the expedition (including the local Christians and native collaborators who had accompanied the Jesuits) were killed on Monday, 15 July, as they attempted to construct a new mission upon the site of a Hindu temple complex which some members of the expedition had previously helped to destroy with the aid and military support of the Portuguese authorities. When the news reached Rome, the massacre was immediately celebrated as martyrdom. Francesco Benci, who was, in all likelihood, personally acquainted with at least three of the unfortunate missionaries, set about composing a six-book epic on their time in India: *Quinque martyres e Societate Iesu in India*, first published at Venice in 1591, with a second, corrected version issuing from the Vatican Press a year later. This poem is compelling not only for its competence, polish and classical resonances, but also for its subject matter and the decision to document such a gory incident in over 5,500 Latin hexameters.

Benci's epic follows the journey of Rodolfo Acquaviva to India and documents his time at the court of the Mughal Emperor Julāl-ud-Dīn Muhammad Akbar (1542–1605). Both interested in comparative theology and apprehensive about the threat posed by Portuguese maritime power, Akbar was keen to learn about the religion professed by the Europeans on the coast, and so invited the Portuguese to send representatives from Goa to debate their Christian beliefs with Muslim doctors at the weekly discussions held in the 'Ibādat-khāna ('Hall of Worship') at his court in Fatehpur Sikri. On realizing the impossibility of converting the Mughal hierarchy to Christianity, the Jesuits switched their attention to the lower classes. In Benci's poem the cordial reception afforded at the emperor's court contrasts with violent local opposition, as a group of five Jesuit brothers attempt to found a new church and mission among the Hindu population at Cuncolim in the south of the territory of Salcete, on the borders of the state of Bijapur. The Jesuit missionaries' journey through Salcete to Cuncolim, their violent martyrdom and reception in Paradise form the climax of Benci's narrative.

The *Quinque martyres* was immediately popular. The poem was reprinted throughout the seventeenth century in Benci's collected poems and afterwards in his collected works. It was also included in the massive anthology of Jesuit epic poetry, the *Parnassus Societatis Iesu* printed at Frankfurt in 1654.

Written as part of the campaign for the beatification (and eventual canonization) of the five main protagonists, the *Quinque martyres* is the first of a long line of Jesuit epics of martyrdom. These long poems are distinct from, yet dependent upon, the classical tradition. Here, Aeneas' divinely ordained mission to found Rome is remodelled in terms of the hazards and glory of the Jesuit vocation. Classical epic thus is recast as Christian panegyric, and the didactic nature of the genre is deliberately emphasized to teach lessons of moral choice, endurance and salvation for the Jesuit seminarians. For they would perhaps face similarly dangerous missions, especially when fulfilling their 'Fourth Vow', which bound members of the Society to do ministry anywhere in the world (see also Text 12).

Yet Benci's epic was not only intended for repeated perusal among the Jesuit seminarians to remind them of their vocation. It was also designed as a model for the composition of hexameter verse and to teach Virgil's sublime style at the Collegium Romanum (and at other Jesuit Colleges in Europe and further afield), thus reducing the dangerous influence of Virgil's pagan gods and unwholesome subject matter.

The text chosen here forms part of a long narrative intended to alleviate the tedium of the missionaries' journey by describing previous attempts by the Jesuits at conversion in the area. It records the often ambivalent and contradictory attitude of the first Jesuits towards the native Indian population, and in particular the ascetics known as Yogis, although it should be noted that the Yogis played no part in the Jesuit massacre. The prejudice on display in Benci's account (often through subtle intertextual reference) is echoed later in the letters of the Italian aristocratic traveller Pietro della Valle (1586–1652) reporting the Yogis he had seen on 3 March 1623 at a Vaishnava temple outside Cambay, in the village of Causary. Della Valle labelled their unworldliness studied arrogance, and their chastity hypocritical 'since it is known that in secret many of them do vile acts when they have an opportunity', and above all their books and exercises, whether spiritual or erudite, 'consist in nothing but the arts of divination, the secrets of herbs and other things of nature, and magic and spells' (from Joan-Paul Rubiés, *Travel and Ethnology in the Renaissance: South India through European Eyes, 1250–1625*, Cambridge 2000: 374).

In the extract chosen, Benci would clearly expect his pupils to recognize the intertextual references and draw their own conclusions about the Indian Yogis. The passage continues with the miraculous conversion of this Yogi in the new church and his own proselytizing mission as a recent convert to Christianity (otherwise undocumented).

Source of the Latin text

No autograph manuscript of the *Quinque martyres* has yet been identified. The Latin text here reproduces (with minor revisions to the punctuation) the second, corrected edition (Rome: Typographia Vaticana, 1592) as it appears in Paul Gwynne, *Francesco Benci's 'Quinque martyres'. Introduction, Translation and Commentary* (Leiden / Boston 2017). The translation and the commentary have been completely revised.

Latin text

Est genus hic hominum miserabile, quos tamen Indi
mirantur miseri et titulis ingentibus ornant.
Nam quia semiferos artus setosaque membra
veste tegunt lacera, solisque in montibus errant
duriter e vulsis ducentes stirpibus aevum,
caelicolum in terris dicuntur degere vitam,
quin etiam instinctu superum eventura profari.
Hos illi dixere Iogues, vatesque salutant,
horum consiliis uti meditantur et arte.
Ipsi autem raro conspecti et pauca locuti,
incautam ficto deludunt numine plebem.
Atque horum e numero egregio studioque virorum,
haud dudum huc quemdam memini concedere, cultu
se talem, talem se animis, talem ore ferentem,
posset ut ignaras tacitus pervertere mentes.
Ibat inops, vestitu humilis, sed mente superbus,
torva supercilio gravitas fastusque dolosam
pauperiem ostentans. Barba capitisque revulsis
crinibus extabat supremo in vertice rara
canicies, circlum extollens. Traiecerat unco
multiplici auriculas, digitos manuumque pedumque
brachiaque et crura armillis ex aere rigenti
vinxerat. Ex humero confertis rebus onusta
mantica, sed levior pendebat fistula collo.
Idem etiam, ut nulla inciderent oblivia mortis,
extinctam gestabat avem, cui corpore plumae
nondum detractae. Curvatum dextra ferebat
praeterea cornu, quod sparsa per oppida rauco
adventum celebrans cantu vulgusque moneret
officii et cupidum portis exciret apertis.
Hac pompa, his armis, hac sese mente ferebat
inflatus plausuque hominum numeroque sequentum,
et templum ingressus magna stipante caterva,
stultus avi similis, quam circum turba volucrum
ludendi studio late strepitantibus alis
pervolitat, demens fert partem lumina in omnem,
et nova quae facies aedis miratur et usus.

English translation

In this place there is a pitiable race of men. Yet the wretched Indians admire them and honour them with great titles. For since they wrap their brute bodies and bristling limbs with ragged clothes and wander among the deserted mountains, eking out a hard existence on torn-up roots, they are said to live the life of gods on earth. Indeed, they are even said to predict future events by the inspiration of the gods. They have named these men Yogis, and greet them as prophets, [and] constantly take their advice and employ their skills. Those men, however, are rarely seen and say little, deceiving the credulous mob with their false divinity. And I still recall that a certain member of this infamous band and sect had recently come hither bearing himself in such a way in discipline, life [and] appearance that he could pervert their ignorant minds without saying a word. He went about penniless, in humble dress, but arrogant in his demeanour; grim authority showing in his stern looks and contempt in his dubious poverty. With his beard and the hair of his head wrenched out, he wore the few grey hairs atop his head looped into a topknot. He had pierced his earlobes with many hooks and fettered his fingers and toes, and his arms and legs with bangles of rigid bronze. A heavy knapsack, stuffed full, was hanging upon his shoulder and a light flute from his neck. This same man also, so that no forgetfulness of death should occur, was carrying a dead bird with its feathers not yet plucked from its body. In addition, in his right hand he held a curved horn, whose raucous note announced his advent throughout the scattered villages, and would remind the common people of their duty, and summon them eagerly from their open doors. Bearing himself with this ceremony, with these accoutrements, with this attitude, puffed up by the crowd's applause and by the number of his followers, and having entered the church with a great mob thronging around him, foolish, like a bird around which a flock of birds flit about on flapping wings keen to play, the madman turns his gaze upon everything and marvels at the shrine's new appearance and its use.

Commentary

96 *miserabile*: the Yogis deserve pity, for as non-believers and unbaptized they are outside God's grace. Benci perhaps recalls Ovid's use of the phrase *genus miserabile leti* ('a wretched type of death') with reference to drowning (*Tristia* 1.2.51). The Yogis are a miserable race of men who are dead to the Christian message; yet there is always hope for their conversion and salvation, as this story reveals. Note, too, that the indigenous population who admire the Yogis are also referred to as *miseri* ('wretched').

97 *mirantur miseri*: perhaps recalling Laocoön's words to the citizens of Troy (Virgil, *Aeneid* 2.42) as they admire the Wooden Horse (*molem mirantur equi*, *Aen.* 2.32). Both the Trojans and the Indians are doomed to destruction for their vain beliefs.

98 *Nam quia*: a regular hexameter incipit as at Virg. *Aen.* 4.696.

semiferos artus: the compound adjective *semiferus* (used throughout classical literature to refer to mythical hybrid beasts such as the centaurs and satyrs) betrays Benci's opinion of the Yogis. This is reinforced by the frequent intertextual references that associate the Indian ascetics with the inhospitable and uncivilized Cyclops.

setosaque membra: note the suppressed diphthong (classical spelling *saetosa*); the phrase is used by Horace to describe Odysseus' sailors transformed into swine by Circe (*Epodes* 17.15).

99 *solisque in montibus errant*: cf. *et altis montibus errant*, a half-line at Virg. *Aen.* 3.644 to describe the Cyclops.

100 *duriter*: adverb, not found in Virgil and only once in Lucretius; the alliteration of *d*s, against the repetition of *t*s, helps paint the harshness of the Yogis' existence.

e vulsis . . . stirpibus: cf. *et vulsis pascunt radicibus herbae*, Virg. *Aen.* 3.650 (the Greek Achmaenides describing his life when he had been marooned on the island of the Cyclops).

ducentes . . . aevum: *ducere aevum*, literally 'to lead a life', hence 'to live'.

101 *caelicolum*: contracted genitive plural for *caelicolarum*; literally 'an inhabitant of heaven'. This is the term commonly used by Benci to describe the Christian saints. It is used ironically here to emphasize the preposterousness of the idea of the Yogis' divinity.

degere vitam: literally 'to pass life', hence 'to live'; the phrase is found at Virg. *Aen*. 4.550–1, where the distraught Dido is describing her own situation to her sister Anna, and continues *more ferae* ('like a wild creature'). Benci would expect his students to be able to make such associations.

102 *instinctu superum eventura profari*: the phrase recalls *instinctu videbantur futura praedicere*, from Quintus Curtius Rufus, *History of Alexander* (8.6.16), where Alexander is saved from a palace conspiracy by 'a woman of unsound mind' who 'seemed by inspiration to predict the future'. If Benci had this passage in mind, then the suggestion is that all those who claim clairvoyance are similarly 'of unsound mind'.

instinctu superum: the phrase is found at Statius, *Thebaid* 5.104.

superum: contracted genitive plural for *superorum*.

103 *Iogues*: the Latin form for Yogis; corrected from *Ioques* in the first edition (1591). The change in spelling does not affect the scansion.

106 A variation upon the classic golden line (abVBA). Although Benci would not have been aware of the term 'golden line', the patterned combination of two adjectives, two substantives and a verb only in a single line of hexameter is an extreme form of the rhetorical figure hyperbaton.

107 *studioque virorum*: literally 'school of men' (a slightly changed meaning of *studium*, found in late Latin).

108 *memini*: 'I recall'; the speaker is the Italian Jesuit Pietro Berno (*c*. 1550 – 15 July 1583) from Ascona, at the foot of the Alps. After being ordained a priest at Rome, he entered the Society of Jesus in 1577, arrived in Goa in October 1579 and was soon appointed to Salcete. He accompanied the first missionary expeditions to Cuncolim, and assisted in destroying the Hindu temples and sacred anthill, and killed a cow which was an object of Hindu worship. It was these actions that caused such hatred among the Indian population. Berno was killed with his companions at Cuncolim as they attempted to establish a Christian mission upon the remains of the Hindu sacred site that had previously been destroyed.

109 *se talem, talem se*: an example of the rhetorical figure called chiasmus.

110 *ignaras . . . mentes*: the phrase is found at Virg. *Aen*. 4.65 to describe the empty prophecies of seers.

111–26 Early Jesuit correspondence is replete with warnings against immoderate missionary zeal. The temptation towards extreme asceticism and excessive renunciation is to be avoided. The Yogis are therefore presented as arrogant 'false prophets'. It is also, perhaps, no accident that the description recalls depictions of St Francis (see n. on 116). The Franciscans were the Jesuits' main rivals in their proselytizing missions in the East, and there were frequent disputes between the two orders.

115 *canicies*: for *canities*; the word recalls the description of the squalid ferryman Charon (Virg. *Aen.* 6.300–1): *canities inculta iacet, stant lumina flamma, | sordidus ex umeris nodo dependet amictus* ('his grey hair lies unkempt, his eyes are fixed with flame, a dirty cloak hangs from his shoulder in a knot').

circlum: contracted form of *circulum*.

116 *digitos manuumque pedumque*: literally 'digits of his hands and feet'. The description of the Yogi recalls one of Francis of Assisi (Henry of Avranches, *Legenda Sancti Francisci Versificata* 11.60–4): *Raris barba pilis nigra, laxis guttura fibris | marcida, subvectis humeri cervicibus alti, | brachia parva, manus tenues, subtilia crura, | exiguique pedes, digiti manuumque pedumque | proceri, carnemque domans asperrima vestis* ('His beard was black with few hairs, his throat withered in loose folds, tall shoulders on a curved neck, small arms, thin hands, slender hips, and small feet, his fingers and toes long, and the roughest clothes taming his flesh').

117 *ex aere rigenti*: echoing Virg. *Aen.* 8.621 (the description of Aeneas' breastplate).

119 *pendebat fistula collo*: a half-line (now considered spurious) completing the unfinished verse at Virg. *Aen.* 3.661 describing the shepherd Cyclops Polyphemus. This half-line, or a variation upon it, is not found in the primary witnesses but included in some medieval manuscripts and the first printed editions of the *Aeneid*; it was obviously considered genuine by Benci who copied it here.

120 *ut nulla*: breaking the usual rule of classical Latinity for a final clause; *ne qua* would be more correct.

121 *corpore plumae*: a line end at Virg. *Aen.* 4.181 describing the feathered goddess *Fama* (Rumour).

123 *cornu*: perhaps here quite literally 'the bill of a bird', used to trumpet the Yogi's arrival, rather than a military bugle. The bathos continues in the following line.

123–4 *rauco … cantu*: found at Virg. *Aen.* 8.2, as Turnus calls his men to arms.

124 *adventum celebrans*: the elevated language of a royal or imperial entrance is here used ironically.

125 *portis exciret apertis*: recalling *iamque adeo exierat portis equitatus apertis*, Virg. *Aen.* 8.585 ('and now the cavalry had marched from the open gates').

126 *Hac* ... *his* ... *hac*: an example of polyptoton, a favourite rhetorical device of Benci. Compare also *sic oculos, sic ille manus, sic ora ferebat*, Virg. *Aen.* 3.490 ('he had the same eyes, the same gestures, the same expression'). Benci subverts the language of the Roman triumph as the Yogi progresses towards the shrine now converted into a Christian church.

128 *templum*: the Church of the Holy Spirit at Margão was built on the site of the ancient Hindu temple to the deity Damodar (a form of Lord Shiva). Following a pattern of enforced conversion and destruction across the area, which was sanctioned by the Portuguese authorities and supported by their troops, the original temple was demolished, and the temple tank was infilled and replaced by the Church of the Holy Spirit in 1564.

magna stipante caterva: a half-line at Virg. *Aen.* 4.136, describing Dido surrounded by her attendants; cf. *Aen.* 1.497 (also of Dido); also *magna comitante caterva*, *Aen.* 2.40 (the priest Laocoön).

129 *avi similis*: in this metrical position at Virg. *Aen.* 4.254, to describe the flight of the god Mercury.

turba volucrum: cf. Statius, *Silvae* 1.2.61, where the phrase describes Cupid.

130–1 *late* ... *pervolitat*: the combination is found at Virg. *Aen.* 8.24, to describe the flickering light of the moon's rays.

strepitantibus alis: found at Tibullus 2.2.17, to describe the noise of Cupid's wings.

132 *miratur et usus*: a clever echo of *miratur et usum* | *nescit* ('he marvels and knows not its use'), Ovid, *Fasti* 6.703–4, where the satyr marvels at the discovery of the pan pipes.

12

Mary, Liturgy and Missions

Francisco Enzinas' Correspondence with Robert Bellarmine (1605–07)[1]

Jan Machielsen

Introduction

When the Jesuit Francisco Enzinas (or Encinas; 18 July 1570–10 January 1633) arrived in the Philippines in August 1596, he was about as far from home as a Spaniard was likely to get: two oceans away from his native Ávila (Uriarte and Lecina 1925: 2.485–6). The Philippines, named after Philip II of Spain, had been claimed for the king in 1565 by forces that had sailed from Mexico, and they continued to be governed from and via the New World. Enzinas, however, had arrived for a different conquest: that of the souls of the natives rather than their possessions. The Society of Jesus, one of the new religious orders of the Counter-Reformation, was as renowned for its global missionary activity as it was for its vast network of colleges and the quality of the (free!) classical education that its members provided (O'Malley 1993; Clossey 2008; see also Text 11).

The first three Jesuits only arrived in the Philippines in 1581. Theirs was a small mission, originally answering to Mexico. Only in 1605, the same year that Enzinas picked up his pen to write to Cardinal Robert Bellarmine (1542–1621) in Rome, did they become their own province (Schumacher 2001). Even in 1606, a year for which we have a full inventory of personnel, there were just ninety-three Jesuits across the vast archipelago, with Enzinas one of five in Carigara, on the island of Leyte, nearly 350 miles south of the Spanish capital of Manila, from which the galleons left annually for Acapulco, on Mexico's west coast.[2]

It was from Carigara that, in 1605, Enzinas wrote to one of the most famous living members of the Society of Jesus. Robert Bellarmine was only the second Jesuit to be elected cardinal (it was an honour they were meant to eschew), and he was one of the towering intellects of early modern Catholic reform. Best known for the *Disputationes de controversiis Christianae fidei* (1586–93), a powerful refutation of the Protestant heresies, he was among those charged by Pope Clement VIII to oversee reforms to the liturgy. Despite the obvious difference in resources between Carigara and the Eternal City, Enzinas wrote to Bellarmine with a liturgical contribution of his own. This chapter includes his letter and the cardinal's encouraging but firmly negative reply.

The communication lines that connected the two men were long and fragile. Enzinas' letter to Bellarmine was carefully crafted not only because it sought to influence a member of the sacred college of cardinals, but because space on the page was limited, and one could wait a long time, even an eternity, for a response. One needed to write with both maximum impact and economy in mind. Thus, it took Bellarmine twenty-one months to answer Enzinas' first letter, and Enzinas twenty-eight months to offer his reply (excited that a cardinal of the Church deigned to take any notice of him). It took another twenty-two months for him to resend that letter when he learned that the ship carrying it had sunk.[3] Enzinas' own experiences after he was elected in April 1627 to represent the interests of his province in person in Rome also shed light on the tedium, danger and length of the journey. Leaving Manila on 9 August, he arrived in Acapulco on 31 December. The Pacific crossing was notorious for its endless monotony, and in a letter to Mutio Vitelleschi, the Superior General of the Society, Enzinas reflected on the many months when 'it appeared that there was almost nothing other than sky and sea everywhere'.[4] Making his way over land to Vera Cruz, on 7 August 1628, nearly a year to the day after his initial departure from Manila, he boarded the Spanish treasure fleet which was heading first for Havana, and then on to Spain. At least that had been the intent. 'If only it had sailed later, or not at all!' Enzinas reflected afterwards.[5] On 9 September, the Dutch, then Spain's mortal enemy, captured this unhappy fleet, loaded with silver, off the coast of Cuba. Enzinas wrote his travel account on 29 January 1629 from a Rotterdam prison, partly to raise funds for his release. Remarkably, these adventures did not stop his return – he died in Manila on 10 January 1633.

The original impetus of Enzinas' letter had been the reform of the Roman Breviary, one of the principal liturgical outputs of the Counter-Reformation. Breviaries contain all the readings, hymns and prayers, both biblical and otherwise, required to be recited by religious and secular clergy during the canonical hours (such as matins, lauds and vespers) for every day of the year. The Council of Trent (1545–63) had mandated the Breviary's revision, along with that of the other office books, such as the Missal, and handed the task over to the papacy. With some exceptions, the Roman Breviary promulgated by Pius V in 1568 became the Church's standard prayer book. It nevertheless was subject to alteration, which often reflected the Church's uneasy relationship with the pious legends of the past. For instance, the Virgin's apocryphal parents, Joachim and Anne, were missing in the Pian version, but were restored under Pope Gregory XIII (1572–85). Another commission, headed by two of the most influential Counter-Reformation scholars, Cardinals Robert Bellarmine and Cesare Baronio, published the Clementine Breviary in 1602. It notoriously brought into question whether the Apostle James (Santiago), the patron saint of Spain, had ever visited the Iberian peninsula during his lifetime (Ditchfield 1995; 2007).

Word of this revision of the Breviary prompted Enzinas to write (though he soon discovered he was too late), because he had long felt aggrieved that the liturgy did not sufficiently praise the Virgin Mary. Of course, her many feasts, from her own Nativity to her Assumption into Heaven, already dotted the Church's liturgical calendar. Yet this was not enough for Enzinas, whose devotion to the Virgin was legendary among his fellow Jesuits. A posthumous manuscript *Vita* ('Life'), composed by one of his peers, reported that he fasted on water and bread in her honour every Saturday and on all her feast days, and that he would sleep for only one or two hours, to spend the rest of the night in prayer.[6] Among the few objects that he was able to keep out of greedy Dutch hands in 1628 were his Breviary and 'an amazing image of the Most Holy Virgin, my best companion during thirty-two years of traversing Indian villages'.[7] Upon his death, Enzinas left behind a 'pretty corpulent' manuscript, in both Latin and Spanish, on the Virgin, 'in which this devout and learned father showed no less his devotion than his reading'.[8]

While Enzinas' piety was remarkable for its intensity, even among Jesuits well versed in Marian devotions, it was not unusual. Protestants, hostile even to the hint of worship of someone other than God, frequently charged Catholics with Mariolatry. The basilica of Santa Maria della Vittoria in Rome was consecrated in the Virgin's honour after she ensured Catholic victory over the Protestants at the battle of White Mountain in 1620. The cult of the Virgin of Guadalupe in Mexico (a site of an alleged miraculous appearance) shows her tremendous appeal in the New World. The popularity of pilgrimages to the Holy House of Loreto on Italy's east coast, where the Virgin was believed to have relocated her family home with some angelic assistance, further testifies to her role as a lodestone of Catholic identity (Heal 2007; Rubin 2010; Vélez 2018).

Enzinas' letter, then, points to the importance of both Marian devotion and liturgical reform within the Catholic Church's global mission. Just as significantly, it shows the role played by an individual in the larger project of Catholic reform. Historians, especially in Italy, have traditionally cast the Counter-Reformation as a repressive institutional project, emphasizing the role of the Inquisition and the Index of Prohibited Books. Yet these institutions did not provide the Church's lifeblood. In Enzinas' letter and Bellarmine's reply we can see the interplay between the individual and the institutional. Enzinas is unusual only for the vast distance separating him from Rome – the pet projects of European Catholics feature regularly in the correspondence of Roman scholars. Bellarmine, who fielded many such letters, especially from fellow Jesuits, replies here with a polite rejection. Yet he made no attempt to restrict Enzinas' private devotions, and he offered reasons for his inability to help. Some of these – the desire for decorum, the need to keep changes to a minimum – vividly illustrate the ambiguities at the heart of the early modern Catholic Church, as an institution that was at once the custodian of age-old traditions and undergoing rapid change, and one that was dependent on the initiative and the devotions of the faithful but worried where those might lead (Machielsen 2017).

Notes

1 My thanks to Simon Ditchfield, Francis Young and P. G. Maxwell-Stuart for comments and advice, to Father Martín M. Morales SJ and Lorenzo Mancini of the Archives of the Pontifical Gregorian University (APUG) for their support of the British Academy-funded project out of which this contribution emerged and for permission to reproduce the two letters in question.

2 Rome, Archivum Romanum Societatis Iesu [ARSI], Philipp. 5, fols 240, 249–51.

3 This last letter, not included here, was dated 31 May 1609 and resent on 8 April 1611: Rome, ARSI, Philipp. 11, fol. 1r–v, at 1r.

4 Rome, ARSI, Philipp. 11, fols 142–3, at 142r: *tot enim menses nihil fere videtur aliud nisi caelum undique et undique pontus* (cf. Virgil *Aen.* 3.192).

5 Rome, ARSI, Philipp. 11, fol. 142r: *Atque utinam serius exisset, vel nullo modo exisset.*

6 Rome, ARSI, Philipp. 20, fol. 419.

7 Rome, ARSI, Philipp. 11, fol. 143r: *praeclaram Sanctissimae Virginis imaginem meorum discursuum in Indorum oppidis per duos et triginta annos optimam comitem.*

8 Backer et al. 1890: 3.391. This manuscript appears to have been lost after the dissolution of the Society in the late eighteenth century.

Bibliography

Backer, A. de et al. (1890), *Bibliothèque de la Compagnie de Jésus*, 12 vols, Brussels.

Clossey, L. (2008), *Salvation and Globalization in the Early Jesuit Missions*, Cambridge.
Danieluk, R. (2018), 'Il ritorno delle carte gesuitiche dall'Archivio Segreto Vaticano all'Archivio Romano della Compagnia di Gesù', in A. Gottsmann et al. (eds), *Incorrupta monumenta ecclesiam defendunt*, 253–63, Vatican City.
Ditchfield, S. (1995), *Liturgy, Sanctity and History in Tridentine Italy*, Cambridge.
Ditchfield, S. (2007), 'Tridentine Worship and the Cult of Saints', in R. P. Hsia (ed.), *Cambridge History of Christianity*, Vol. 6, 201–24, Cambridge.
Heal, B. (2007), *The Cult of the Virgin Mary in Early Modern Germany*, Cambridge.
Le Bachelet, X.-M., ed. (1911), *Bellarmin avant son cardinalat, 1542–1598*, Paris.
Le Bachelet, X.-M., ed. (1913), *Auctarium Bellarminianum*, Paris.
Machielsen, J. (2017), 'Counter-Reformation', in P. Ford et al. (eds), *Brill's Encyclopaedia of the Neo-Latin World*, Leiden.
Noyes, R. S. (2017), *Peter Paul Rubens and the Counter-Reformation Crisis of the Beati Moderni*, Basingstoke.
O'Malley, J. W. (1993), *The First Jesuits*, Cambridge MA.
Restall, M. and K. Lane (2018), *Latin America in Colonial Times*, Cambridge.
Rubin, M. (2010), *Mother of God: A History of the Virgin Mary*, London.
Santi, A. de (1910), 'Litany of Loreto', in *The Catholic Encyclopedia*, Vol. 9, New York (http://www.newadvent.org/cathen/09287a.htm).
Schumacher, J. N. (2011), 'Filipinas', in C. E. O'Neill and J. M. Domínguez (eds), *Diccionario histórico de la Compañía de Jesús*, Vol. 2: Costa Rossetti–Industrias, 1422–9, Rome.
Uriarte, J. E. de and M. Lecina (1925), *Biblioteca de Escritores de la Compañía de Jesus pertenecientes a la antigua Asistencia de España desde sus orígenes hasta el año de 1773*, 2 vols, Madrid.
Vélez, K. (2018), *The Miraculous Flying House of Loreto*, Princeton.

Source of the Latin text

In the late nineteenth century the French Jesuit Xavier-Marie Le Bachelet (1855–1925) prepared a full edition of Robert Bellarmine's correspondence and unpublished works, although only a small part appeared in print (Le Bachelet 1911; 1913). The project was revived after Bellarmine's canonization in 1930 by the Dutch Jesuit Sebastiaan Peter Cornelis Tromp (1889–1975), who had Le Bachelet's handwritten transcripts typed up. Even these volumes remained accessible only in the reading room of the Gregorian Archives. Only now is the correspondence being made more widely available through the digitization efforts of Gregorian Archives Texts Editing (GATE): https://gate.unigre.it/mediawiki/index.php/Monumenta_Bellarmini.

The manuscript that should have contained our two letters is now Opera NN 242 in the Jesuit Archives in Rome (ARSI), which contains original letters received by the Jesuit cardinal, who usually drafted his response in fine print on the verso side. Le Bachelet, who consulted the manuscript in the Vatican Archives, described Enzinas' letter as a 'loose folio' ('feuille détachée') folded inside the manuscript; this presumably accounts for its disappearance (Rome, APUG, MS 1611, item no. 670). The typewritten version available online can thus be collated only against Le Bachelet's transcription, not the original. Collation shows that Tromp or an assistant misread Enzinas' last name as 'Lucinas' (as also proven by the survival of Enzinas' second letter, not included here). The name has been corrected in the text below, but only one minor correction to Tromp's typescript appeared necessary. Abbreviations have been resolved, some punctuation has been changed and paragraphs added to improve legibility.

The manuscript of Marian devotions that accompanied Enzinas' letter has not survived, and its contents are difficult to establish. (Bellarmine clearly did not read it.) The letter suggests that if it is not incorporated into the Breviary, it could still stand on its own. If that is the case, then Enzinas' letter can also be read as a prefatory epistle that could be appended to the text, if Bellarmine had chosen to publish it.

Latin text

Letter 1

Cum audissem novo breviario excudendo operam dari, curamque eam tibi (quae tua est sapientia) Cardinalis amplissime, demandatam fuisse, ausus sum has ad te lucubrationes[1] mittere, ad quas, dum animarum ministerio vaco, aliquid temporis suffuratus sum, Sanctissimae studio stimulatus. Dolebam enim, ornatissime praesul, et vehementer angebar, quod Sanctissimae Virginis officia omnino plena non essent, nativitatis[2] eiusdem officium aliis eiusdem Deiparae diebus festis accommodari;[3] multa matutinarum horarum responsoria[4] vacua videri, utpote in quibus eaedem sententiae repeterentur, omnes etiam antiphonas ad matutinas horas in omnibus Virginis beatissimae officiis easdem esse; quasi vero materia desit, ut nova diversis eiusdem Deiparae festis diebus adhibeantur. Quapropter in eam operam incubui, ut ex his quae in sacra Scriptura habentur, et Sanctissimae Virgini ab ecclesia accommodari solent, antiphonas et responsoria conficerem, quibus explere optabam quod in plerisque Virginis beatissimae officiis requirebam, gaudeoque quod paene omnia quae collegi sint Spiritus Sancti,[5] non mea, licet paucula quaedam ex sanctissimis viris subiecerim, in quibus tamen concinnandis totum, quod potuit, meum desudavit ingenium, quod quidem quam sit exiguum sentio; simulque video hoc meum opusculum impar omnino esse tantae virgini Dei Optimi Maximi[6] parenti dignissimae ac totius ecclesiae amplissimae matri. Quare tuum erit Cardinalis amplissime, quod minus apposite et concinne dictum sit, componere, exornare, excolere et perpolire, ut qui sapientia et eloquentia polleas plurimum.

Atque hanc quidem epistolam anno superiori scripseram, quae tamen a Patribus Manilae degentibus missa non est, quod scirent additiones ad breviarium excusas iam esse,[7] oportereque ut eas ipse, qui tamen procul Manila aberam, prius viderem, quas tamen non vidi. Sed neque despondi animo, quin potius ausus sum nihilominus hoc ad te opusculum mittere, si forte maxima tua ista auctoritas transigeret cum summo Ecclesiae praesule, ut hoc opus in laudem Sanctissimae Virginis vel seorsim excuderetur, ut eo ecclesia in diebus Virgini sacris uteretur. Ridebis fortasse homunculi audaciam, temeritatem, arrogantiam importunamque imprudentiam, sed amanti mihi meae Deiparae nihil non licere vel audere visum fuit. Nam

English translation

Letter 1

When I heard that work had started on the printing of a new Breviary and that its oversight had been entrusted to you, such is your wisdom, most honoured Cardinal, I was bold enough to send you these lucubrations,[1] for which I had stolen some time, urged on by my zeal for the Most Holy [Virgin], while I was occupied with ministering to souls. For it hurt and greatly distressed me, Most honoured Prelate, that the Offices of the Most Holy Virgin were not altogether complete; that the Office of her Nativity[2] does not fit with the other feast days of the God-Bearer;[3] that many of the responsories[4] during matins appear empty, in as much as the same lines are repeated during them; also that the antiphons for matins are all the same in all the Offices of the Most Blessed Virgin. It is truly as if material were missing, for new things to be added to the God-bearer's various feast days. For this reason, I settled upon the task of composing antiphons and responsories from those [passages] which are found in Holy Scripture and which are usually applied by the Church to the Most Holy Virgin. I wanted to fill in with these what I missed in most of the Offices of the Most Blessed Virgin, and I am delighted that almost everything I have put together comes from the Holy Spirit,[5] and not from me, although I have added one or two things [I culled] from very saintly men, in the arrangement of which my whole mind strained itself as much as it could, [although] I am well aware of how feeble [my mind] is. And at the same time, I realize that my little work is altogether undeserving of the most worthy and outstanding Virgin Parent of the best [and] greatest God[6] and the most honoured Mother of the whole Church. Consequently, it will be your task, most honoured Cardinal, to arrange, embellish, develop and polish what I have said less appropriately and less beautifully, since you are extremely rich in wisdom and eloquence.

Moreover I had actually written this letter last year, but it was not sent by the Fathers resident in Manila, on the grounds that they knew that the additions to the Breviary had already been printed,[7] and that I should see these first myself, even though I was a long way from Manila – however, I have not seen them. Still I have not lost heart, but rather have nevertheless ventured to send you this little work in the hope that perhaps that great authority of yours might prevail upon the Supreme Prelate of the Church to get this work in praise of the Most Holy Virgin printed, even separately, so that the Church could use it on days sacred to the Virgin. You will perhaps smile at a poor little fellow's audacity, temerity, arrogance and impertinent thoughtlessness, but it seemed to me, in my love, that there was nothing I was

immorior quidem desiderio, cupiditati, studio, omnia ut officia Sanctissimae Virginis sint quam elegantissima et aptissima. Itaque, quamvis additiones ad breviarium editae sint, et aliquid circa officia Sanctissimae Virginis additum, ut accepi ab his qui viderunt, sed his adhuc locus esse potest, qui locus ut sit tu faxis, quod totum non ego, qui nihil sum, sed Sanctissima ipsa Virgo commendat tibi.

Res est profecto dignissima in qua tuae sapientiae industriaeque et diligentiae vires exeras. Potes, o praesul ornatissime, obsequium hoc praestare Deiparae, potes quidem; praesta igitur, siquidem potes, et gaude quod possis. Quid enim felicius, quam aliquid in honorem Sanctissimae matris edere? Hoc vero, quod ad eius officia attinet, magnum profecto est. Tu vero, qui eximia in lucem ad haereticorum tenebras dispellendas in lucem edidisti,[8] si hoc opusculum propter Sanctissimam virginem apostolica auctoritate edi curaveris, magnus quasi cumulus, sin minus tuis accedet laudibus, tuis certe in gloriosissimam matrem meritis accedit quidem.

Sed satis iam sit, precor audaciae meae parcas. Homo enim e Societate Iesu licet omnino indignus ausus sum scribere amplissimo viro, qui ex eadem Societate Iesu ad ecclesiasticos honores assumptus[9] est. Te Deus Optimus Maximus servet incolumem augeatque ad maius totius ecclesiae bonum. Ex Philippinis insulis insula Leyte, idibus Aprilis anno a partu Virginis[10] 1605.

Tuus humillimus et indignus servus
Franciscus de Enzinas e Societate Iesu

not allowed [to do] or was not bold enough [to do] for my God-bearer. For I really am dying with desire, longing [and] eagerness for all the Offices of the Most Holy Virgin to be as elegant and suitable as possible. Therefore, even though the additions to the Breviary have been published, and something has been added with respect to the Offices of the Most Holy Virgin, as I have learned from those who have seen [it], there can still be a place for these. Please arrange for such a place to be [made]. It is not I who am recommending all this to you – I am nothing – but the Most Holy Virgin herself.

The matter is undoubtedly a most worthy one in which you can make use of the [full] force of your wisdom and your assiduity and diligence. Most distinguished Prelate, you can do the God-bearer this service, you really can. So do it, since you can, and be glad that you can, because what can be more propitious than to publish something in honour of the Most Holy Mother, and surely this, which relates to her Offices, is something great? But if you, who have published remarkable things to scatter into the light the darkness of the heretics,[8] would arrange for this little work for the Most Holy Virgin to be published with Apostolic authority, even if this crowning glory, as it were, adds little to your renown, it certainly adds to your merits in the eyes of the Most Glorious Mother.

But let this now suffice. I beg you to forgive my audacity because, even though I am an entirely unworthy individual from the Society of Jesus, I have been bold enough to write to a most honoured man, who from the same Society of Jesus has been raised[9] to high honours in the Church. May the best [and] greatest God protect you from harm and exalt [you] for the greater good of the entire Church.

From the Island of Leyte in the Philippine islands, 13 April in the 1605th year after the Virgin gave birth,[10]
Your most humble and unworthy servant,
Francisco de Enzinas of the Society of Jesus.

Letter 2

Admodum Reverende Pater

Accepi litteras Reverentiae Vestrae et quae de officio, et litaniis Beatissimae Virginis Mariae ad nos transmisit. Non possum non vehementer commendare studium Reverentiae Vestrae in celebranda memoria sanctissimae patronae nostrae, quam omni laude dignissimam esse nemo pius negare potest. Ceterum de adiungendis officiis propriis festorum eiusdem Beatissimae Virginis ad breviarium, multis de causis hoc tempore agi non potuit.

Primum, quod iam breviarium sit editum, recognitum, et reformatum auctoritate Clementis Octavi summi Pontificis, magno labore, et annotationibus virorum doctorum, ex omnibus fere christianis provinciis, mature discussis et consideratis, neque deceat tam cito aliam reformationem tentare.

2° Quod in reformatione Breviarii non defuerint, qui similia officia propria inseri voluissent, et iustis de causis auditi non fuerint.[11]

3° Quod reformatoribus breviarii a Summo Pontifico mandatum sit, ut nihil nisi necessario immutarent, id est ea sola demerent vel mutarent quae manifesti erroris convinci poterant; ea sola adderent quae necessaria omnino viderentur.[12]

4° Quod ecclesiae gravitatem et constantiam deceat, non facile mutare quae a maioribus instituta sunt.

5° Quod antiphonae et responsoria propria addi non possint sine gravissimo sumptu ecclesiarum et monasteriorum, in quibus habentur libri magni precii cum notis cantus Gregoriani ad veteres antiphonas et cetera responsoria.

Itaque poterit Reverentia Vestra pro sua devotione privatim legere officia illa propria, sed quod ea in communem et publicum usum recipiantur, nulla spes apparet. Quod ad litanias attinet, cum sanctum generalis Inquisitionis officium maturo iudicio vetuerit in publico usu recitari litanias alias praeter eas, quae habentur in breviariis, et missalibus et eas quae in aede sacra Lauretana[13] assidue concinuntur, non videtur tentandum ut aliquid ad eas addatur. Oro autem Reverentiam Vestram ut non moleste ferat quod non audeam ea proponere summo Pontifici vel sacrae Congregationi[14] quae certe scio non esse admittenda.

Valeat Reverentia Vestra, in ista Domini vinea[15] fructum facere pergat, meque Deo precibus suis commendet.

Datum Romae, die 30 ianuarii 1607.

Letter 2

Very Reverend Father,

I have received the letter from Your Reverence and what you have sent us on the Office and Litanies of the Most Blessed Virgin Mary. I cannot but greatly commend Your Reverence's enthusiasm in celebrating the memory of our Most Holy Patroness, whom no devout person can deny is most worthy of every praise. At this time, however, it is not possible, for many reasons, to discuss adding Proper Offices of the feasts of the Most Blessed Virgin to the Breviary.

First, because the Breviary has already been published, [after being] examined and reformed, by the authority of the Supreme Pontiff Clement VIII, after a great deal of effort and with the comments of learned men from almost all the Christian provinces fully discussed and considered. So it cannot be right to attempt another reform so quickly.

2° Because during the reform of the Breviary, there was no shortage of people who wanted to insert similar Proper Offices and they, for good reasons, were not listened to.[11]

3° Because the reformers of the Breviary were ordered by the Supreme Pontiff to change nothing unless it was necessary [to do so]: that is, they were to take out or change only what they could clearly demonstrate was a manifest error, [and] they were to add only what they thought was absolutely necessary.[12]

4° Because it befits the gravity and constancy of the Church not to be too quick to change what was established by our ancestors.

5° Because it would not be possible to add the proper antiphons and responsories without very great cost to churches and monasteries which [already] hold very expensive books containing the notation of the Gregorian chant for the ancient antiphons and the other responsories.

Therefore Your Reverence will be able to read these Proper Offices privately for your own devotion, but there appears to be no hope that they can be taken into general and public use. As far as the Litanies are concerned, since upon mature judgement the Holy Office of the General Inquisition banned the public recitation of Litanies other than those contained in Breviaries and Missals, and those which are continually sung in the Holy House of Loreto,[13] it seems one should not attempt to add anything to them. I pray, then, that Your Reverence will not take it ill that I do not venture to propose to the Supreme Pontiff or to the Sacred Congregation[14] what I know for certain will not be permitted.

I wish Your Reverence good health [and] to carry on producing fruit in that vineyard of the Lord,[15] and [I beg you] to commend me to God in your prayers. Dated Rome, 30th day of January 1607.

Commentary

Letter 1

1 *lucubrationes*: given the noctural nature of Enzinas' devotions, we could take this word (which means 'work done by lamplight') literally.

2 The Virgin's Nativity falls on 8 September. Other prominent feast days include the Annunciation (25 March), the Visitation (31 May), the Assumption (15 August) and the (since 1854, Immaculate) Conception (8 December).

3 Enzinas felt that the different Offices of the Virgin deserved less repetition and greater embellishment. Different (pre-/post-)Tridentine versions of the Divine Office (with English translation) can be consulted at https://divinumofficium.com.

4 *responsoria*: a responsory is a type of chant in Western Christianity, usually a reading led by a cantor or small group, which elicits a repetition or response from the whole congregation.

5 *Spiritus Sancti*: Enzinas means Scripture. The bride in the Song of Songs, in particular, was read allegorically to refer to Mary.

6 *Dei Optimi Maximi*: a title the Romans reserved for Jupiter, but frequently applied to the Christian God in Neo-Latin sources.

7 As noted in the introduction, the Clementine Breviary appeared in 1602, well before Enzinas picked up his pen.

8 'published' is for *in lucem edidisti*, literally 'you have brought out into the light', a standard early modern phrase for 'publishing'. The doubtless conscious repetition of *in lucem* links two metaphors: dispelling (heretical) darkness with light and bringing a book into the light.

9 *assumptus*: probably a conscious choice of words, establishing a parallel between Bellarmine's 'assumption' and that of the Virgin.

10 *anno a partu Virginis*: a Mary-centric version of *anno Domini*.

Letter 2

11 Bellarmine may also be alluding to the 'crisis of the *Beati moderni*', which engulfed the later years of Clement VIII's reign, when pressure was mounting for the swift canonization of leading Counter-Reformation figures, such as Teresa of Avila, Philip Neri and Ignatius of Loyola (Noyes 2017).

12 Bellarmine's statement captures the paradoxical rhetoric of early modern Catholic reform. The Catholic Church was rapidly changing, as demonstrated by Bellarmine's and Enzinas' efforts, while claiming not to, as exemplified by the motto of Bellarmine's colleague, Cesare Baronio: *semper eadem* ('ever the same').

13 *litanias … in aede sacra Lauretana*: the so-called Litany of Loreto, in praise of Mary, was approved by Pope Sixtus V in 1587 and was associated with that particular shrine since at least the 1550s (Santi 1910).

14 *sacrae Congregationi*: Bellarmine was a member of the Congregation of Rites, which oversaw both the liturgy and processes of canonization.

15 *Domini vinea*: a biblical metaphor (see Isaiah 5:7; Matthew 20:1–16).

13

Seneca's Death Dramatized

Matthew Gwinne (1558–1627), *Nero: Tragaedia Nova* (1603), Act 5, Scene 6

Emma Buckley

Introduction

Matthew Gwinne (1558–1627) was an eminent physician and one of Oxford University's major academic playwrights. Of Welsh descent, but born in London, he attended Merchant Taylors' School and St John's College, Oxford, both famous cradles of academic drama, and he rose through the ranks at Oxford before taking up the post of Professor of Physic at the new Gresham College in 1597. In 1605, he was appointed Physician to the Tower and elected as fellow of the College of Physicians. In the latter years of his career he served as one of James I's tobacco regulators, as well as contributing to the publication of the College's *Pharmacopoeia Londoniensis* (1618), which became the standard textbook on pharmacology for centuries. Gwinne was also involved in foreign service in the 1580s and 1590s, first travelling with Fulke Greville on a mission directed by Sir Francis Walsingham in 1587–8 and later accompanying Sir Henry Unton in his ambassadorship to France in 1596.

In addition to his flourishing medical practice, Gwinne was at the heart of Oxford's literary and theatrical scene. He was friends with John Florio and Giordano Bruno and formed part of the 'Sidney circle', a loose group of artists and writers who shared religious, literary and political sympathies with Philip Sidney (the eminent courtier, poet and soldier who became a national hero when he died after sustaining a wound at the battle of Zutphen in 1586) and his sister, Mary, Countess of Pembroke. In addition to providing verses for the Oxford anthology *Exequiae illustrissimi equitis, D. Philippi Sidnaei* ('*Commemorations for the most distinguished knight, Sir Philip Sidney*', ed. William Gager, 1587), he collaborated with Fulke Greville in editing Sidney's *The Countesse of Pembrokes Arcadia* (1590). He also helped with John Florio's

1603 translation of the *Essays* of Michel de Montaigne, with Florio praising him for his learning in Greek, Latin, Italian and French. On several occasions Gwinne took part in model academic disputations before distinguished visitors and royalty, including Elizabeth I, and for James VI/I's state visit to Oxford in 1605 Gwinne also wrote the comedy *Vertumnus, sive Annus recurrens* ('*Vertumnus, or the Recurring Year*'), which was staged at Christ Church.

Much of Gwinne's work was never printed, and is now lost, but his monumental *Nero: Tragaedia Nova* ('*Nero: A New Tragedy*') was first published in 1603, with reprints in 1638 and 1639. A gargantuan chronicle-history of Nero's rise and fall in more than five thousand lines of Latin verse, it features an equally monumental cast of eighty-four named characters. In this compendious work Gwinne claims that he has simply transformed history into verse ('they [Tacitus, Suetonius, Cassius Dio, Seneca] also say nearly everything: I've simply made it metrical', *nam et loquuntur ipsi fere omnia: ego tantummodo modos feci*, ¶2^{v}), and his play text is buttressed by a system of marginal annotation that references a wide range of ancient and contemporary authorities. No less deeply embedded is *Nero*'s allusive relationship with Augustan and early imperial literature, above all Senecan tragedy. In particular, in his creation of a tyrannical emperor Nero who behaves like and speaks as the Atreus of *Thyestes*, Gwinne emulates the pseudo-Senecan historical play *Octavia*, a fundamental source of inspiration for early modern historical drama. Indeed, in his commendatory poem to the play, John Sandsbury addresses the great Renaissance scholar Justus Lipsius, claiming that he now has a play far superior to the 'puerile' *Octavia*, and asserting 'Seneca was as Gwinne is' (*talis Seneca, qui Gwinnus, fuit*, sig. A1^{r}).

To Gwinne's evident chagrin (¶4^{r}), the play was never staged, though both the attention to stage management and the preface's defence of theatre speak to its performative potential, while the precedent set by Thomas Legge's highly successful *Richardus Tertius* ('*Richard the Third*'), staged in 1579 and probably involving more than a hundred performers, might have led him to hope for a similarly dazzling dramatic spectacle. In its style and subject matter the piece is, moreover, very much a revenge drama of its time. Nemesis promises at the outset *caedem, ultionem, lacrimas, cladem, nefas* ('slaughter, revenge, tears, calamity, unspeakable crime', sig. A3^{v}); a whole host of revenging ghosts and Furies frame the action; and ghastly onstage scenes of torture, suicide and murder abound. The play's exuberance is also expressed in its adherence to the euphuistic style (a term derived from John Lyly's 1578 prose romance *Euphues*): it is playful and ingenious in its use of antithesis and balance, elaborately attentive to sound effects, and heavy on assonance and alliteration. In declaring that the play is a *new* tragedy – a self-conscious marker of departure from Aristotelian norms, experimentation with mixing of genres, and constant flirtation with a slide into parody – Gwinne signals his own ambition to innovate within the moralizing, educational frame of academic drama.

The extract below, part of Act 5, Scene 6, concentrates on a famous site of early modern interest: the death of Seneca. Gwinne's version is very closely modelled on Tacitus' famous death scene (*Ann.* 15.61–4), but there are some pointed departures from Tacitus' account. In particular Gwinne chooses not to present the philosopher as the disinterested sage with a close eye on posterity (*Ann.* 15.63.1). Instead, he portrays an emotional Seneca in need of the support of his brave wife Paulina, who is responsible – through judicious deployment of Stoic philosophical maxims as well as the Christianizing assurance that heaven awaits them – for inspiring his self-controlled demise. And while Gwinne follows Tacitus in offering a Seneca who self-consciously models his death on Socrates, he innovates in creating a similarly self-aware Paulina, who does not just look to and quote examples of wifely virtue in death, but even cuts her wrists first, 'leading the way' for Seneca. This is no doubt partly inspired by Montaigne's essay 'Of three good women', which praised Paulina's heroic participation in this shared bid for suicide, but it also reflects Gwinne's larger interest in the heroic female – surely no mistake in a play that explicitly celebrates Elizabeth as 'salvation of empire' and 'glory of monarchs' (*imperii salus … regum decus*, sig. T3^r). The result is a fascinating conglomeration of Tacitus, Senecan tragedy and philosophy, with a hyper-tragic early modern sensibility, amounting to a unique reception of Seneca's death.

Metre: iambic trimeter

Bibliography

Allen, S. (2015), '*Ulysses Redux* (1591) and *Nero* (1601): *Tragedia Nova*', in E. M. Dutton and J. McBain (eds), *Drama and Pedagogy in Medieval and Early Modern England*, 131–58, Tübingen (SPELL 31).

Binns, J. W. (1974), 'Seneca and Neo-Latin Tragedy', in C. D. N. Costa (ed.), *Seneca*, 205–33, London.

Binns, J. W. (1990), *Intellectual Culture in Elizabethan and Jacobean England: The Latin Writings of the Age*, Leeds.

Boas, F. S. (1914), *University Drama in the Tudor Age*, Oxford.

Buckley, E. (2013), 'Matthew Gwinne's *Nero* (1603): Seneca, Academic Drama, and the Politics of Polity', *Canadian Review of Comparative Literature*, 40: 16–33.

Buckley, E. (2016), 'Drama in the margins – academic text and political context in Matthew Gwinne's *Nero: Nova Tragœdia* (1603) and Ben Jonson's *Sejanus* (1603/5)', *Renaissance Studies*, 30: 602–22.

Fisher, C. D., ed. (1906), *Cornelii Taciti Annalium ab excessu divi Augusti libri*, Oxford.

Florio, J. (1603), *The essayes or morall, politike and millitarie discourses of Lo: Michaell de Montaigne . . .*, London.

Ker, J. (2009), *The Deaths of Seneca*, New York / Oxford.

Norland, H. B. (2009), *Neoclassical Tragedy in Elizabethan England*, Newark DE.

Sutton, Dana F., ed. and trans. (1997 / 2017), *Matthew Gwinne, Nero (1603). A hypertext critical edition*, Birmingham Philological Museum (http://www.philological.bham.ac.uk).

Wright, I. (2008), 'Gwinne, Matthew (1558–1627), physician and playwright', *Oxford Dictionary of National Biography* (https://doi.org/10.1093/ref:odnb/11813).

Source of the Latin text

I have used the hypertext critical edition by Sutton (1997/2017), itself a transcription of *Nero tragaedia noua. Matthaeo Gwinne Med. Doct. Collegii Diui Ioannis Praecursoris apud Oxonienses socio collecta è Tacito, Suetonio, Dione, Seneca* ('*Nero: a new tragedy. By Matthew Gwinne, Doctor of Medicine, Fellow of St John the Forerunner's College, Oxford, gathered out of Tacitus, Suetonius, Dio, Seneca*'). Impress: Londini: [By R. Read] impensis Ed. Blounte, 1603. STC (2nd ed.) / 12551. Sigs. Q1^{r}–Q2^{r}. I have made some changes to punctuation.

Latin text

Seneca. Maerere duret degener, fortis mori.
Moeror mulierem si deceat, at non decet
moerere Senecae coniugem: in sexu tuo *Lucan. l.5.f.*
materia laudis unica est coniux miser.
Foelicem amasti, nunc ama, quod sum miser.
Nec miser: at aditus non recessurae patet
foelicitati. Spirat animus aeternum: dies
vitae prioris ultimus, primus novae.
Natalis hic est vitae inextinctae dies.
Sic vita mortem sequitur, ut vitam mori:
et vita melior, quam nec eripiat Nero.
Non flentem iniquum est flere: nil Senecae novum,
cui vita stadium mortis, an studium fuit.
Abstergit ille lacrimas qui non fleat:
indignus ille lacrimis qui se fleat.
Tu chara coniux, memor, ut in vita mihi
virtus praeierit, charior vita mihi,
desideratum coniugem, ut par est, feras,
viduos honesta mente solando lares.
Hoc solo amara mors dolet, siqua dolet,
quod rapit amatae coniugis amatum virum.
Paulina. An ergo sine te, mi Seneca, vivam tua?
An ergo sine me, Seneca, morieris meus?
An foedus id pepigimus? An nullum mihi
cor, quia mulieri? Monita sic memini tua?
Hoc vita solo placuit, ex quo uxor tua,
quod tibi placebam: nulla sim, ni sim tua.
Tecum volebam vivere, et tecum mori.
Sic destinatum est, una mors perimet duos.
Mecum potes perire, sine me non potes.
Percussor, in me prima figatur manus.
Uterque meriti pariter: ego tantas opes,
quibus inhiatur, iure retinebo meo,
si sim superstes longius. Age ergo, feri.
Portia peribit igne, si ferrum negas. *Martial. l.1. epigr. 43.*
Seneca. O mira virtus foeminae: an laudi tuae
Seneca resistat? An sibi adamatam unice
iniuriis relinquat expositam feris?

English translation

Seneca. Let the base be resolved to grieve, the brave to die. Even if grief is seemly for a woman, yet it is not seemly that Seneca's wife grieves: for your sex, a wretched husband is the sole stuff of glory. You have loved me happy: now love me because I'm wretched. Nor [am I] wretched: on the contrary, an entrance to never-receding happiness lies open. My spirit lives forever; the last day of my old life is the first of my new one. This is the birthday of inextinguishable life. Thus life follows death, as dying follows life: and a better life, which not even Nero can snatch away. It is unjust to weep for one not weeping: nothing is new for Seneca, for whom life was a stage for death, or rather a study. As one who does not weep, he wipes away your tears. The one who weeps for himself would be unworthy of your tears. You, dear wife, mindful of how in my life virtue (dearer to me than life) led the way, endure your longing for your husband, as is proper, by caring for an empty home with honest mind. Bitter death hurts in this alone - if it hurts at all - in that it snatches away a beloved wife's beloved husband.

Paulina. Therefore, my Seneca, shall I live, yours without you? Therefore Seneca, will you die, mine without me? Is this the bargain we struck? Do I have no heart, because I am a woman? Is this how I remember your teachings? Life pleased in this alone, from the time I was your wife, that I was pleasing to you. Let me be nothing, if I'm not yours. With you I wanted to live, and with you to die. Thus it has been resolved: one death shall kill two. You can perish with me, without me you cannot. Executioner, direct your hand against me first. Both of us are equally deserving. I will retain in my own right the great wealth, which is coveted [by Nero], if I am to live longer. Therefore come, strike. Portia will perish by fire, if you deny the sword.

Seneca. O wondrous woman's virtue: can Seneca stand in the way of your glory? Can he leave behind the one loved by him with singular devotion, [to be] exposed to savage injury? I advised what makes for a good life; you prefer

Monui ego, vitam quae iuvent: mortis decus
mavis, ut inde bona feras, vites mala.
Non invidebo tam bono exemplo: praei.
Sit penes utrosque par animus isto exitu,
sed claritudo maior in letho tuo.
Paulina. Ergo ictus idem solvat utrique illico *Paulinae brachia*
venas easdem. Ah! Quid tibi? ah! Seneca? *Seneca.* An dolet, *ferro exolvuntur.*
Paulina? *Paulina.* Seneca, non dolet vulnus meum,
sed vulnus illud, quod premet Senecam, dolet.
Mihi magis exit, quam meus, sanguis tuus:
et versat animas sanguis idem una duas. *Senecae venae secantur.*
Seneca. Natura, quam me frangis, invitum quoque! Ah.
Quam vel philosophum! Ah. Mors, ut absentem fui
te despicatus, appropinquantem horreo?
Tumidus sereno nauta, timidus cum tonat?
Philosophus homine maior, aegre hominem exuit.
Maiora hominibus dicimus; at homines sumus.
Senile corpus, tenue deductis cibis,
effugia lenta sanguini praebet meo.
Euge cruciatus, te malum ut fatear, facis.
Paulina. Ah ne fatere. *Seneca.* Sentio. *Paulina.* At sensus malus
rerum aestimator, mollis, et blandus sibi.
Gladiator ullus fortius, quam tu, cadet?
Consta, nec arma proiice, nec alto gradu
deiicere: morere, qua decet Senecam mori.
Effugium hoc habeas a malis. *Seneca.* Sed per mala.
Paulina. Per amara, dicas; quibus et accipitur salus.
Iam mihi videmur victimae ante aras sacrae.
Ut taurus et iuvenca se ferro induant,
Caedamur, et cadamus, ut par est, piae,
Placidae, innocentes, supplices, gratae Deo.
Piaculum sit, si reluctetur mori
devota morti victima, ut scelera expiet.
Si trahat eculeus, strangulet laqueus, cremet
flamma, grave ferrum membra membratim secet,
quid Seneca faciat, si nimis mollis gemat
sanguine fluente molliter, ut optat, mori?
Virtute clarus si vir haud praestet virum,
mirumne, mulier mollior siquid labem?

the honour of death, so that you may take from this world the good, avoid the bad. I will not begrudge [you the display of] so good an example: take the lead. May each of us have equal courage in that death, but let there be more glory in your dying.

Paulina. Then let the same blow open the same veins for both of us right away. [*Paulina's arms are opened with the knife*] Ah! What's wrong with you – ah! – Seneca?

Seneca. Does it hurt, Paulina?

Paulina. Seneca, my wound does not hurt, but that wound which will oppress Seneca, [that] hurts. Your blood gushes more for me than my own; and the same blood flow spurts out two souls at once. (*The veins of Seneca are cut.*)

Seneca. Nature, how you break me, even against my will! Ah. How you break even a philosopher! Ah. Death, just as I scorned you in your absence, shall I shudder at your approach? Is the sailor cocky in calm [waters], terrified when it thunders? A philosopher is super-human, [yet] he finds it hard to cast aside his humanity. We say super-human things; but we are human. My old body, thin from meagre portions, grants [only] a slow escape to my blood. Bravo, torture! You are making me confess that you are an evil.

Paulina. Ah, don't confess that.

Seneca. [It's what] I feel.

Paulina. But feeling is a bad judge of things, delicate and soft on itself. Will any gladiator fall more bravely than you? Be strong: neither throw down your weapons, nor be toppled from your exalted station. Die in the way it befits Seneca to die. You can have this escape from your evils.

Seneca. But *through* evils.

Paulina. You should say through bitter times, through which salvation is also gained. Now we seem to me to be sacral victims before the altars. Like the bull and heifer who throw themselves onto the blade, let us be killed, and let us fall, as is right, pious, calm, innocent, suppliant, dear to God. Call it a sin, [even] if the victim struggles against dying who is condemned to death, in order to expiate his crimes. If the rack should drag, the noose strangle, the flame burn, the heavy blade cut limbs limb-by-limb, what would Seneca do, if he, excessively soft, groans as his blood flows, though he is dying softly, as he wishes? If the man famous for his virtue doesn't prove himself a man, is it any wonder if I, a weaker woman, should falter in any way?

Commentary

1 *Maerere ... mori*: gnomic *sententia*, modelled after pseudo-Seneca, *Hercules Oetaeus* 1836, *fortes vetant maerere, degeneres iubent* ('brave men forbid grieving; base men command it').

2–3 *Moeror ... coniugem*: another formulation Seneca is fond of in both tragedy and philosophy, an impersonal *decet* clause (cf. v. 63). The self-referential mode via a third-person address, together with prominent acts of self-naming, is a feature of Senecan tragedy (cf. e.g. Sen. *Oed.* 1003) but also of the self-defining heroes of the Elizabethan vernacular stage (cf. vv. 12, 36).

2 *Moeror* = *Maeror* (cf. *moerere*, v. 3).

3–4 *in sexu tuo ... coniux miser*: despite Gwinne's side note, a reprise of Lucan, *BC* 8.70–85, in which Pompey scolds his wife Cornelia for showing immoderate grief and claims: 'You have an entrance to fame that will last through the ages; for your sex there is no glory from the rights given by law nor from arms: your only stuff [of glory] is a wretched husband' (*habes aditum mansurae in saecula famae. | laudis in hoc sexu non legum iura nec arma, | unica materia est coniunx miser*, 8.74–6).

4 *coniux* = *coniunx*.

5 *Foelicem* = *felicem* (cf. v. 7).

6–8 *at aditus ... novae*: a reworking of Lucan, *BC* 8.74 (see note on vv. 3–4): but the language of eternal bliss, an everlasting soul and a new life after death conjures, instead of pagan glory (*fama*), a Christian-looking vision of 'new life' or afterlife. These lines gesture to the deep implication of ancient ideas of the afterlife (including Plato's *Phaedo*, whom Gwinne cites later in this scene) in Christian writing about the soul. And, thanks to the apocryphal correspondence between Seneca and St Paul (a late-fourth-century work), Gwinne's Renaissance audience would be primed to see a 'Christian' Seneca onstage.

Spirat animus aeternum: Seneca uses *animus* of the 'active' mind or controlling centre of the soul; this phrase may also recall the Stoic notion of *pneuma*, the breath pervading the whole universe. However, Gwinne's lines seem more reminiscent of Christian *spiritus*, esp. John 3:8: *Spiritus ubi vult spirat* ('The wind bloweth where it listeth').

9 *Natalis ... dies*: cf. Sen. *Ep.* 102.26. There may be more Christianizing emphasis here: in martyrologies saints were commemorated on the day of their death, which was celebrated as their 'birthday' (*dies natalis*) into heaven.

13 *stadium ... studium*: it is hard to render this pun in English, which plays on *stadium* (a unit of length or racecourse).

14–15 *Abstergit ... fleat*: more sententious moralizing. *qui* with subjunctive indicates a characteristic.

16 *Chara* = *cara* (cf. v. 17).

19 *viduos ... lares*: Lares were the tutelary deities of the home. The phrase *honesta mente* comes from Seneca, *Phoen.* 97. Gwinne may also have been thinking of Deianira's lament at *Hercules Oetaeus* 755, *O lares, miseri lares! Nunc vidua, nunc expulsa, nunc ferar obruta* ('O home, wretched home! Now I will be borne away widowed, cast out, overwhelmed').

26 *ex quo* = *ex quo tempore*.

28 *Tecum ... mori*: cf. Horace *Carm.* 3.9.24.

29 *Sic ... duos*: cf. Tacitus, *Ann.* 15.63.5–6; the line ending recalls Seneca, *Agam.* 200, *et perimat duos*.

30 *Mecum ... potes*: cf. Seneca, *Phoen.* 66.

31 *Percussor, ... manus*: cf. Tacitus, *Ann.* 15.63.6–7.

32–4 *ego tantas opes ... longius*: this point seems to have been inspired by the fate of Annaeus Mela (Tac. *Ann.* 16.17.4–5), ordered to kill himself since Nero coveted his wealth (*opibus eius inhians*).

35 *Portia ... negas*: Paulina quotes the example of Porcia, Cato's daughter and wife of Brutus, who decided not to live after her husband's defeat at Philippi. Cf. Martial 1.42, which concludes: *dixit et ardentis avido bibit ore favillas. | i nunc et ferrum, turba molesta, nega!* ('She spoke and drank burning ashes with greedy mouth. Go now and deny [her] the sword, you troublesome crowd!'). In some early modern editions this poem was numbered 1.43. Gwinne's use of Porcia may compete with Montaigne (*Essayes* 2.35 [1603: 416–20]; see Ker 2009: 317–21).

36 *O mira virtus foeminae*: on *mira virtus* cf. Lucretius, *De rerum natura* 5.966; Statius, *Silvae* 4.5.37; the collocation is also a favourite of Valerius Maximus (2.7.15; 3.2.9; 5.2.8).

foeminae = *feminae*.

37–43 *An ... tuo*: cf. and contrast Tac. *Ann.* 15.63.8–12.

39 *Monui ... iuvent*: supply a demonstrative like *haec* after *monui* to serve as antecedent for the relative clause that follows; the subjunctive implies

characteristic or purpose, with the sense 'I advised these things in order that they may help life' or, more narrowly, 'I advised these things (as opposed to others)' . . .

43 *letho* = *leto*.

44–5 *Ergo . . . easdem*: contrast Tac. *Ann*. 15.63.12.

45–6 *An dolet . . . dolet*: Gwinne dramatizes Martial 1.13, the words of Arria, wife of Caecina Paetus, who rebelled unsuccessfully against the emperor Claudius (Pliny, *Ep*. 3.16; cf. Montaigne, *Essayes* 2.35): *Casta suo gladium cum traderet Arria Paeto, | quem de visceribus strinxerat ipsa suis, | 'si qua fides, vulnus quod feci non dolet,' inquit, | 'sed tu quod facies, hoc mihi, Paete, dolet.'* ('When chaste Arria was handing the sword to her Paetus, which she had withdrawn from her own flesh, she said: "Trust me, the wound I have made does not hurt, but the one which you will make – that hurts me, Paetus"').

49 *et versat . . . sanguis*: this expression is not found in classical Latin. *verso* can mean 'spin', and perhaps Gwinne puns on the sense of 'gushing' or 'spurting' for 'spin' in early modern English (*OED* s.v. 6b, 'to send forth in a stream').

50 *Natura . . . quoque!*: cf. Sen. *Phaedr*. 1117, *natura, quam te colimus inviti quoque* ('Nature, how we worship (you), even against our will').

54 *aegre hominem exuit*: cf. Seneca, *De Ben*. 4.17.4. Several early Christian writers also use the phrase, in respect of man's potential to cast off human form on entry to heaven, but also of man's capacity to act as less than human.

56–8 *Senile corpus . . . facis*: cf. Tac. *Ann*. 15.63.13–15.

Euge cruciatus . . .: Seneca's 'confession' that death *is* an evil contradicts (his own) Stoic teaching, both about death itself and the process of dying. Cf. *Ep*. 82.11: *Tamquam indifferentia esse dico (id est nec bona nec mala) morbum, dolorem, paupertatem, exilium, mortem . . . laudatur non dolor, sed ille quem nihil coegit dolor; nemo mortem laudat, sed eum cuius mors ante abstulit animum quam conturbavit.* ('I say that illness, pain, poverty, exile, death are "indifferents" (that is to say, neither good nor bad) . . . Pain is not praised, but he whom pain can in no way coerce; no one praises death, but him whose death took away his soul before it troubled it').

61–3 *Gladiator . . . mori*: Paulina reminds Seneca of his own remarks on the bravery and virtue of gladiators, especially in facing their own deaths (cf. e.g. *De Ira* 1.2.4–5). Gwinne may be thinking in particular of *Ep*. 37.1, where Seneca contrasts the gladiator, able to lower his weapon and try the goodwill of the people, with Lucilius, who must face death upright and unbeaten.

nec alto gradu | deiicere: this, too, is a gladiatorial image ('to be knocked off one's feet'), but is also often used in a transferred sense (cf. Cic. *Off.* 1.80).

64 *Effugium . . . malis*: cf. Sen. *Agam.* 590–1.

65 *Per amara . . . salus*: the notion that salvation is achieved through suffering is a staple of Scripture (cf. e.g. Romans 5:3; 8:17–18; Philippians 1:29). While Seneca sees hardship as an opportunity to practise virtue, Stoic thought does not see suffering as a virtue in itself (see note on vv. 56–8).

66–9 *Iam mihi . . . gratae Deo*: Gwinne fuses Roman ritual (the importance of the victim's 'willingness' to be sacrificed) and the language of Senecan tragedy (cf. esp. Sen. *Oed.* 336–7, 341–4) with Christian inflections.

piae . . . gratae: these five adjectives are in agreement with *victimae* (66).

70–1 *Piaculum sit . . . expiet*: Cf. Sen. *Oed.* 247. On *devota morti*, cf. Hor. *Carm.* 4.14.18.

72–5 *Si trahat . . . mori?*: Senecan tragedy offers limb-slicing (Sen. *Med.* 476; *Thy.* 760); Seneca also reflects on the fear induced by torture in his philosophy (e.g. *Ep.* 14.3–6).

eculeus: a 'foal', but also the rack, an instrument of torture (in the shape of a horse) (*L&S* s.v. II.B). It is tempting to see Gwinne here evoking ghastly contemporary methods of torture and execution, in contrast with Seneca's less painful end, as the play does elsewhere (as in, e.g., Act 2, Scenes 1–3).

14

Virgilian Commentary

Juan Luis de la Cerda (1558/60–1643), on Aeneas' First Appearance in the *Aeneid*

Fiachra Mac Góráin

Introduction

Juan Luis de la Cerda (1558/60–1643), a Spanish Jesuit priest and humanist, was a founding figure in the modern tradition of Virgilian commentary. He was born in 1558 or 1560 in Toledo (seat of the Royal Court before Philip II moved it from there to Valladolid in 1561) and entered the Society of Jesus aged 16. He held professorships of grammar, poetry, rhetoric and Greek at Murcia, Oropesa and Madrid. He revised successive editions of Elio Antonio de Nebrija's much-used Latin Grammar; produced an edition with commentary of Tertullian (a Christian convert and author of the phrase *anima naturaliter Christiana*, 'a naturally Christian soul' [*Apol* 17.6], that was later applied to Virgil); edited the apocryphal Psalter of Solomon in Greek with a Latin translation; and composed devotional works, including a treatise on the ministry of guardian angels. Manuscript works survive on Aldhelm of Malmesbury's *In Praise of Virginity* and on the Gospels.

The monumental Virgil edition with commentary was published in three folio volumes, with a combined total of 2,210 pages, including 150 pages of indices across the three volumes. The first (Madrid 1608) begins with prolegomena (see Roberts 2013) and presents the *Eclogues* and *Georgics*; volumes 2 and 3 cover *Aeneid* 1–6 (Lyons 1612) and 7–12 (Lyons 1617) respectively. As is characteristic of the age, the *mise-en-page* harks back to preprint manuscripts: the commentary sections are tightly packed, with two columns of text on each printed page, each of these flanked with marginal indications as to the content of the notes. La Cerda's practice is to preface each *Eclogue* or poetry book with a synopsis, and to divide the text into chunks of between ten and thirty lines, punctuated with letters (a, b, c etc.). Each chunk is followed by a brief *argumentum* ('summary'), a longer *explicatio* ('critical analysis'), divided according to the lettered subsections of the passage, and *notae* ('notes') on the text, which substantiate and build on the *explicatio*.

The work is a marvel of erudition and insight (see Mazzocchi 1990 and Casali 2008 for examples). La Cerda presents abundant parallels from Greek and Roman literature, drawn from a list of 301 ancient authors (varied and unpredictable, among them scholiasts and ancient critics of Virgil), whose names stand at the head of his prolegomena. Among the most-cited authors are Homer, the Greek tragedians, Greek and Roman historiography, especially Livy, Quintus of Smyrna (whom La Cerda erroneously thought had preceded Virgil), later Latin poets and Plutarch. Pre-Virgilian texts are treated either as models for imitation or comparative sources of information; citations of post-Virgilian authors, including Christian authors, illustrate how the Virgilian tradition developed or show Virgil's relevance to contexts beyond his own time.

La Cerda's work is a mirror of its time. He occasionally refers to recent events, including the Spanish conquest of the New World, or to Spanish customs (see Laird 2002). He follows Renaissance taste in frequently arguing for Virgil's poetic superiority to Homer (on the relative status of Homer and Virgil in debates on literary aesthetics see Vogt-Spira 2002). He regularly cites prior commentators, from Servius to the humanist critics, often to disagree with and sometimes to ridicule them. Indeed, La Cerda is also valued for his lively and occasionally mischievous critical voice.

La Cerda's illustrations of Virgil are strongly didactic. By revealing Virgil's excellence, he aims to teach poetics (and to a lesser extent, rhetoric), but he also elucidates the moral dimensions of Virgil's heroic characters. The present extract shows La Cerda's interest in Aeneas' character and virtues, and reflects his preoccupation with the *Aeneid*'s status in the Augustan age. It also showcases his exegetical method, which involves confronting Virgil's poetry with texts from diverse contexts.

This excerpt gives one of La Cerda's chunks of Virgil followed by the *explicatio* as well as notes on the first three lines. The amplitude of the commentary gives a sense of La Cerda's expansive style (*copia verborum*); he is at his most exuberant when commenting on significant passages such as this one, which describes Aeneas' first appearance in the epic. Alongside La Cerda's exuberance, however, the Latin style suggests haste of composition: as is typical of note form, he often omits words, his connecting adverbs sometimes betray logical ellipsis, and his sentences tend to agglutination (note his frequent use of *tum . . . tum* in this extract).

Bibliography

Casali, S. (2008), '*Agudezas* virgiliane nel commento all'*Eneide* di Juan Luis de la Cerda', in C. Santini and F. Stok (eds), *Esegesi dimenticate di autori classici*, 233–62, Pisa.

Casali, S. and F. Stok (2019), 'Postclassical Commentary', in F. Mac Góráin and C. Martindale (eds), *The Cambridge Companion to Virgil. Second Edition*, 95–108, Cambridge.

Laird, A. (2002), 'Juan Luis de La Cerda and the Predicament of Commentary', in R. Gibson and C. S. Kraus (eds), *The Classical Commentary: History, Practices, Theory*, 171–203, Leiden.

Martínez de la Escalera, J., SJ (2011), 'Cerda. Juan Luis de la', in *Diccionario biográfico español*. Vol. 13, 176–7, Madrid (http://dbe.rah.es).

Mazzocchi, G. (1993), 'Los comentarios virgilianos del Padre Juan Luis de la Cerda', in M. García Martín (ed.), *Estado actual de los estudios sobre el Siglo de Oro (Actas II Congreso AISO)*, 663–75, Salamanca.

Roberts, J. (2013), 'The Prolegomena of La Cerda's Commentary on Virgil. A Commented Edition from the Cologne 1642 Imprint, with English Translation and Explanatory Notes', Warwick PhD dissertation (http://wrap.warwick.ac.uk/59456/).

Sirchich von Kis-Sira, A. (2020), *Der Aeneis-Kommentar von Juan Luis de la Cerda (1612): Kritische Edition, Übersetzung und Erschließung des ersten Buchs*, Hildesheim (Noctes neolatinae 36) [*non vidi*].

Stevens, J., SJ (1931–2), *Le Père Juan de la Cerda S. J. (1558–1643), commentateur de Virgile*, Louvain.

Stevens, J., SJ (1945), 'Un humaniste espagnol: le Père Juan-Luis de la Cerda', *Les Études Classiques*, 13: 210–21.

Vogt-Spira, G. (2002), 'Warum Vergil statt Homer? Der frühneuzeitliche Vorzugsstreit zwischen Homer und Vergil im Spannungsfeld von Autorität und Historisierung', *Poetica*, 34: 323–44.

Source of the Latin text

The text has been manually transcribed from the first edition, J. L. de la Cerda, *P. Virgilii Maronis priores sex libri Aeneidos argumentis, explicationibus notis illustrati* ('*The first six books of the Aeneid of P. Virgilius Maro, illustrated with summaries, critical analyses [and] notes*'), Lyons 1612, and standardized.

Later editions are online at http://sceti.library.upenn.edu (*Bucolics* and *Georgics*, Cologne 1647; *Aeneid* 1–6, Cologne 1642; *Aeneid* 7–12, Cologne 1642).

Latin text

[**a**] Extemplo Aeneae solvuntur frigore membra.
Ingemit, et duplices tendens ad sidera palmas,
Talia voce refert: [**b**] O TERQUE QUATERQUE BEATI,
Queis[1] ante ora patrum Troiae sub moenibus altis
Contigit oppetere. [**c**] o Danaum fortissime gentis [2]
Tydide, mene Iliacis occumbere campis
Non potuisse? tuaque animam[3] hanc effundere dextra?
Saevus ubi Aeacidae telo iacet Hector, ubi ingens
Sarpedon, ubi tot Simois correpta sub undis
Scuta virum, galeasque, et fortia corpora volvit?

ARGUMENTUM.

Aeneas ad subitum malum expavescit, ingemit, sublatisque ad caelum manibus, illos beatos putat, qui cum gloria ceciderunt ad Troiam sub diro hoste.

EXPLICATIO.

[**a**] Expavescit Aeneas ad subitum malum. Pavoris huius duplex est nota, videlicet solutio membrorum, et gemitus. In persona Aeneae servatur decorum, nam hic timet, tum post alios, praecessit enim *Praesentemque viris intentant omnia mortem*, tum post emissos ventos, mare erutum, tenebras densissimas, tonitrua, fulgura.[4] Alii[5] suos duces timentes inducunt in ipso aditu tempestatis, praeter decorum. Tendit vero manus ad caelum, nihil precaturus, sed quia sequitur, *o terque quaterque beati*, quasi ipsa manus sublatione ad sidera, indicet illos esse beatos, qui occubuerunt, cum in sideribus iam sint.[6]
[**b**] Sequitur oratio affectibus magnis plena.[7] Incipit ab exclamatione, felices indicans illos, qui ceciderunt in bello Trioano, tum quod ceciderint ante ora suorum parentum, tum quod in conspectu Troiae: nam quid felicius morienti, quam habere testem suae virtutis, quo carent, qui misere in mari pereunt?
[**c**] Apostrophe ad Diomedem, qui filius Tydei. Optat vero cecidisse sub illo hoste, cum quo ad Troiam pugnaverat.[8] Est vero in istis tacita Aeneae laus, tum quia cum fortissimo Graecorum pugnaverit, neque victus fuerit: tum quia ita pugnaverit ut voluerit occumbere, sed non potuerit.[9] Nam quantum in se fuit,

English translation

[La Cerda translates or paraphrases most Greek quotations; duplications are avoided here.]

[**a**] Suddenly Aeneas' limbs slacken with the cold. He groans, and stretching out both his palms to the stars, speaks out loud as follows: [**b**] 'O thrice and four times blessed, whose[1] lot it was to fall before the faces of their fathers beneath the high walls of Troy. [**c**] O bravest of the Greek people, son of Tydeus [Diomedes], could I not have lain down on the plains of Ilium? Poured out this soul[3] by your right hand? Where savage Hector lies because of the spear of Aeacus' grandson [Achilles], where massive Sarpedon [lies], where the [river] Simois has whipped away and rolls beneath its waves so many shields of men, and helmets, and strong bodies?

SUMMARY.

Aeneas is stricken with fear at the sudden calamity, he groans, and having raised his hands to heaven, thinks that those who fell in glory at Troy at the hands of a fearsome enemy were blessed.

ANALYSIS.

[**a**] Aeneas is stricken with fear at the sudden calamity. There are two markers of this terror, viz. loosening of the limbs and groaning. In the character of Aeneas decorum is maintained, for he feels fear at this point, both after the others, as made clear by the preceding line, 'all things threaten the men with immediate death' [1.91/95], and after the winds had been released, the sea churned up, thickest darkness, thunderclaps, bolts of lightning.[4] Others [i.e. poets][5] make their leaders enter fearful at the very beginning of the storm, exceeding the boundaries of decorum. Moreover, he raises his hands to heaven, not because he intends to pray, but because there follows 'O thrice and four times blessed', as if by the very act of raising a hand to the stars, he shows that those who have fallen are blessed, since they are now among the stars.[6]

[**b**] There follows a speech full of strong feelings.[7] He begins with an exclamation, calling blessed those who fell in the Trojan War, both on the grounds that they fell before the faces of their fathers, and because [they fell] within sight of Troy: for what is happier for a person dying than to have a witness of their valour, as lacked by those who die wretchedly in the sea?

[**c**] Address to Diomedes, who [was] son of Tydeus. He wishes he had fallen at the hands of that enemy with whom he had fought at Troy.[8] In fact these words conceal praise of Aeneas, both in that he had fought with the bravest of the Greeks and not been beaten, and because he had fought in such a way that he wished to die but could not.[9] For as far as he was concerned, he wished to die.

ipse voluit mori. Versum illum *tuaque animam hanc effundere dextra*, nota, totum fere exprimi cum hiatu oris: ut declaret Poëta ipsum actum animae volentis exire. Fugit enim vates consulto illas litteras, quae compressis labiis efferuntur.[10] Exaggerat ad finem calamitatem suam ab Hectore, Sarpedone, Troianis reliquis: quibus contigit tanta felicitas, ut ad Troiam caderent sub hoste nobili, Hector ab Achille interfectus, Sarpedon a Patroclo. Assumitur Simoëntis mentio cum emphasi.[11] Quasi dicat: Si moriendum aquis erat, quanto melius oportuerat cadere Troianum hominem apud Troiam, et in Troiae flumine, ubi alii fortissimi ceciderunt. Multa subierant expendenda, quae omisi tamen, ne quis me nimium scrutatorem putet.[12] Non omittam dignissimum esse laude Virgilium, qui toties in hoc sermone laudet Aenean ore ipsius Aeneae, et tamen ita ingeniose, et tecte, ut decebat laudantem se.

Notae.

[marg: Frigus constringens cur dicatur solvere.]

1. SOLVUNTUR FRIGORE MEMBRA] Oppianus 5. Hal.

Δείματι καὶ καμάτῳ θυμαλγέϊ γυῖα λέλυνται.

Timore, et dolorifico labore soluta sunt membra.

Homerus. Ὀδυσσῆος λύτο γούνατα. *Ulyssis solvebantur genua*. Roges, frigus quod astringit, qui potest membra solvere? Adi Corradum,[13] qui late hunc nodum.[14] Summa est, calore, quo alimur, deficiente, membra solvi: inde est, ut fortissimi quoque abeunte calore a membris, et succedente frigore, contremiscant. Ideo Homerus Odyss. 12.

—λίπε δ᾽ ὀστέα θυμὸς ἀγήνωρ.

deseruit ossa animus generosus.

Calabro[15] in sua tempestate placuit ad animum confugere non ad corpus, Κατέκλαστο (inquit) Ἀχαιῶν θυμὸς ἐνὶ στέρνοισιν:[16] *frangebatur Graecorum animus in pectoribus.*

[marg: Gemitus virorum fortium.]

2. INGEMIT] Viris fortibus datur ex decoro gemitus, nunquam lacrymae, nisi ex misericordia. Ingemit autem (ait Servius) non propter mortem, nam statim ait, beatos esse, qui obierunt, et ipse obiisse cupit, sed propter genus mortis; nam anima, quae igneae est naturae, contrario perit elemento. Servianum hoc plausibile est doctis, praesertim Nannio, Germano, Delrio, aliis. [marg: Mors in aquis exitiabilis.] Itaque credebant veteres mortem in aquis exitiabilem esse animae, illique adducere interitum sempiternum. Nituntur hi testimonio Homeri Odyss. 4 qui de interitu Aiacis Oilei,

Note that almost that entire verse, 'Poured out this soul by your right hand', is pronounced with the mouth wide open, so that the Poet is expressing the very action of a soul that wishes to leave the body. You see, the bard deliberately shuns those letters which are pronounced with the lips pressed together.[10] At the end he heightens [the sense of] his own misfortune with reference to Hector, Sarpedon [and] the other Trojans whose happy lot it was to fall at Troy at the hands of an illustrious enemy: Hector killed by Achilles, Sarpedon by Patroclus. Emphatic mention is made of the [river] Simois.[11] As if he were saying, 'if it was necessary to die in water, how much better should it have been for a Trojan person to fall at Troy, and in the river of Troy, where other most brave men fell. Many other points to be assessed had suggested themselves, but I have left them out, so that no one should think I am being overanalytic.[12] I shall not omit that Virgil is most deserving of praise, since so often in this speech he praises Aeneas out of Aeneas' own mouth, and yet in such a clever and concealed fashion, as was appropriate for one praising himself.

Notes.

[marginal note: Why cold that tightens is said to dissolve.]

1. LIMBS SLACKEN WITH THE COLD] Oppian, *Halieutica* 5[.664].

With fear and painful toil limbs were loosened.

Homer [*Od.* 5.406]. *Ulysses' knees were loosened.* You might ask how cold that tightens can loosen limbs? Consult Corradus,[13] who expands on this knot.[14] The basic point is that when heat, by which we are nourished, fails, the limbs are loosened. So it happens that even the bravest, when heat fails from their limbs, and cold takes its place, shudder violently. Hence Homer in *Odyssey* 12[.404]:

his noble spirit left his bones.

The Calabrian[15] was content in his tempest to appeal to the spirit, not to the body, 'The Greeks' spirit,' he said,[16] 'was broken in their breasts.' [*Posthomerica* 14.491–2]

[marginal note: The groans of brave men.]

2. HE GROANS] Decorum allows groans to brave heroes, [but] never tears, unless from pity. He, however, groans (Servius says) not because of death, for he says immediately that those who died are blessed, and he wishes that he had died himself, but because of the nature of the death: for the soul, which is of a fiery nature, perishes in its opposite element. This dictum of Servius is considered plausible by the learned, especially Nannius, Germanus, Delrius, others. [marginal note: Death in water is pernicious.] So the ancients believed that death in water was pernicious to the soul and that it made it perish permanently. They rely on the testimony of Homer in *Odyssey* 4[.511], who [says] of the death of the Oilean Ajax:

Ὣς ὁ μὲν ἔνθ' ἀπόλωλεν ἐπεὶ πίνεν ἁλμυρὸν ὕδωρ.
Sic ille quidem periit, postquam bibit salsam aquam.

Nam de aliis mortuis cum loquitur Homerus, non ait illos periisse; sed ut quisque a corpore seiunctus est, ire ad domos Plutonis. Inde ait Synesius[17] epist. 4. factum, ut cum ab Homero mortui in infernis excitentur, minor Aiax nunquam introducatur, ὡς τῆς ψυχῆς οὐκ οὔσης ἐν Ἅιδου, *ut cuius anima in inferno non fit,* quia omnino aquis perierit. Ad quam rem faciunt verba ista Heracliti[18] citata ab nostris eruditis, ψυχῇσι θάνατος ὕδωρ γίνεται: *animis aqua est mors.* Aristoteles, 3. Ethic. de viris fortibus, qui moriuntur in mari, ait, καὶ τὸν θάνατον τὸν τοιοῦτον δυσχεραίνουσιν: *ferunt moleste tale genus mortis.* [marg: Mori in bello honestissimum.] et addit postea, velle illos cadere in bello, quam mortem in bello vocat honestissimam, adhibita hac ratione, quia cadunt, ἐν μεγίστῳ καὶ καλλίστῳ κινδύνῳ: *in maximo et pulcherrimo periculo*: qua laude ait carere illos, qui obeunt in mari. Apto hic verba Nazianzeni[19] orat. 1. ubi inter ea quae accidunt in tempestate, tum hoc subiicit: καὶ τῆς ἀνδρείας καιρὸν οὐκ ἔχοντες· *nullam habent occasionem ostendendae virtutis.* Haec res adeo vulgata fuit, ut milites quidam (narrat ibidem Synesius) statuerint sibi necem sua manu consciscere, ne naufragio perirent, quia mors aquarum exitialis erat animae. Verba Synesii, πρὸς τὸν ἀέρα τὴν ψυχὴν ἐρυγεῖν, ἀλλὰ μὴ πρὸς κῦμα χανόντας. *Volebant animam difflare in aërem, non exstingui in aquis.*

Laceravi locum Synesii, quia longus. Ad hanc veterum persuasionem pertinere arbitror Plutarchi locum de primo frigido, ubi ait, Homerum non fabulose, sed physice opposuisse fluvium Vulcano, Neptunum Apollini: atque Aeschylum dixisse παῦε ὕδωρ δίκην πυρός: *compesce aquam, ignis poenam.* Itaque hoc naturali involucro[20] aspirarunt illi ad explicandas inimicitias aquae cum ignea anima. [marg: Persarum supplicandi mos.] Additque apud Persas fuisse supplicandi genus acerrimum, et securum repulsae, si supplex cum igne in fluvium descendens, minaretur ignem se in eum abiecturum, nisi impetraret, quod petebat. Fiebat enim compos voti, sed puniebatur propter comminationem, ut pote iniustam, et naturae contrariam.[21] Quod tametsi conferri queat ad ignem Deum Persarum, non video cur non etiam ad rem, in qua sum. Huc trahit Delrius versus Albinovani:[22]

Thus he for his part perished, after he had drunk the salt water.

For when Homer speaks of other dead people, he does not say that they perished but rather that as each is separated from his body, that he goes to the house of Pluto. Thus it happens, Synesius[17] explains in *Epistle* 4[.131], that when the dead are roused by Homer in the underworld, the lesser Ajax is not at any point brought on, 'since his soul [*psyche*] was not in Hades', because he had utterly perished in the waters. Those words of Heraclitus[18] cited by our learned men are relevant to this matter: 'water is death to souls.' Aristotle in the third book of the *Ethics* [*NE* 3.1115b3] says about courageous men who die at sea '<and> such a kind of death is disagreeable to them' [marginal note: Death in battle is most honourable.], and he adds afterwards [*NE* 3.1115b31] that those men wish to fall in battle, which death in battle he calls most honourable, giving the reason that they fall 'in the greatest and most beautiful danger', praise which he says those who die at sea go without. I add here the words of the Nazianzene[19] from his first oration [*Apol.* 35.488.17], where among the things that occur in a storm he includes the following: 'and they have no opportunity to show their valour.' This phenomenon was so ubiquitous that certain soldiers (according to Synesius, in the same work) decided to die by their own hand, so as not to die in shipwreck, because a watery death destroyed the soul. Synesius' words [*Epist.* 4.138]: 'They wished to breathe out their soul into the air, not have it smothered in the waters'.

I have truncated the Synesius passage, since it is long. I think that a passage from Plutarch's 'On the Principle of Cold' [*Mor.* 950e] is relevant to this notion of the ancients, where he says that it was as a natural philosopher and not as a poet that Homer set the river in opposition to Vulcan, and Neptune to Apollo, and that Aeschylus said [fr. 360 Radt] 'stop water, the punisher of fire.' So, those [authors] aimed to explain the enmity of water with the fiery soul by means of this natural wrapping.[20] [marginal note: Persian custom of making an appeal.] And he [Plut. *Mor.* 950f] adds that the Persians had a very effective and refusal-proof method of making an appeal: if a suppliant were to descend into a river holding fire and threaten to throw the fire into the river unless he got what he was asking for. So, he would get what he was praying for, but he would be punished for the threat, since it was unjust and against nature.[21] Even though this story could be related to the Persians' fire-God, I don't see how it isn't also relevant to the point I am explaining. Delrius brings verses of Albinovanus[22] to bear on the matter [10–11 Morel]:

Seque feris credunt per inertia fata marinis
Iam non felici laniandos sorte relinqui

Item locum Senecae, et Alexandri Aetoli.[23] Vide illum in Agamem. Huc spectat Ovidius lib. 1. Trist. eleg. 2.

Non mortem[24] *timeo, genus est miserabile lethi,*
Demite naufragium, mors mihi munus erit.

Sed de hac re loquor infra ad locum alium.[25]

3. TALIA VOCE REFERT] Mutavit Homericum,

εἶπε πρὸς ὃν μεγαλήτορα θυμόν[26]
secum locutus est ad generosum animum.

Nam tempestas Homeri ad unum tantum Ulyssem destinatur, neque alterius fit mentio; igitur secum loquatur[27] necesse est: Maro in Troianos omnes tempestatem concitat, et ideo ab omnibus audiri Aeneas debet, ideo *voce*. Nullus itaque est pleonasmus.

4. O TERQUE QUATERQUE BEATI] [marg: Numerus finitus pro infinito.] Ponit numerum finitum pro infinito. Commentatio Macrobii de septenario tantum numero,[28] quem et Beroaldus sequitur et Petr. Bongus, ad Virgilii locum inanis omnino est. Hic tantum monuisse sit satis, locum tracto 12. Aeneid ad illud,

Terque quaterque manu pectus percussit honestum.[29]

Transfer huc.

And they think they are being left by the sluggish fates to wild sea creatures,
to be torn apart now in an unhappy lot.

Likewise he cites a passage of Seneca and of Alexander the Aetolian[23]. Consult the former [Seneca] in the *Agamemnon*. Ovid has an eye on the same point in the second elegy of the first book of the *Tristia* [1.2.52]:

I do not fear death,[24] *it is a miserable kind of death,*
Take away shipwreck, [and] death will be a gift to me.

But I shall speak of this matter below at another point.[25]

3. SPOKE OUT LOUD AS FOLLOWS] He has changed the phrase from Homer:

He spoke by himself to his magnanimous spirit.[26]

For the storm in Homer is directed against just one man, Ulysses, and no mention is made of anyone else; therefore he has to speak[27] to himself; Maro rouses the storm against all the Trojans, and therefore Aeneas should be heard by everyone, which is why [he writes] 'out loud.' Therefore there is no redundancy.

4. O THRICE AND FOUR TIMES BLESSED] [marginal note: A finite number for an infinite one.] He inserts a finite number for an infinite one. Macrobius' comment [which is] only about the number seven,[28] which both Beroaldus and Petrus Bongus follow, is utterly irrelevant to the Virgilian passage. Let it suffice that I have merely given a warning here; I treat the passage in [my commentary on] *Aeneid* 12 [12.155]:

And three and four times she struck her fair breast with her hand.[29]

Bring that to bear here.

Commentary

1 *Queis* = *quibus* (dative), with *contigit*. Modern editions use the spelling *quis*.

2 *Aeneid* line-numbers are higher by four than in our standard Virgil editions, as La Cerda considers the four-line pre-proem of the *Aeneid* genuine (*Ille ego qui* . . .).

3 I have translated *anima* as 'soul' and *animus* as 'spirit' throughout.

4 Here La Cerda summarizes the storm scene that has immediately preceded (*Aen.* 1.81–91 in standard numeration). The line quoted immediately precedes our passage.

5 Other poets such as Homer; contrast Odysseus' storm-fear at *Od.* 5.389 and 419.

6 In a Stoicizing vein, Cicero thinks of some heroes as having ascended to the stars (*Dream of Scipio, De re publica* 6.15). La Cerda may also be applying a Christian sensibility, as he does to the *Fourth Eclogue*.

7 La Cerda often notes the affective power of the narrative, with reference to tragic models and Aristotelian modes of interpretation.

8 Diomedes: the wily commentator glosses over Aeneas' ignominious rescue by his mother from otherwise certain death at Diomedes' hands (*Iliad* 5.297–318). Diomedes omits the same event in his reminiscence of their encounter at *Aen.* 11.282–4.

9 *pugnaverit* . . . *victus fuerit* . . . *pugnaverit*: the subjunctives attribute the implied judgement of praise to Virgil; *voluerit* and *potuerit* are perfect subjunctives of result.

10 La Cerda appreciates Virgil's expressive sound-painting and imagines the effect of the poem being read out loud.

11 River in Troy. La Cerda assumes basic familiarity with mythical details.

12 La Cerda humorously deflects the charge of omission by saying he wishes to avoid being thought pedantic.

13 Sebastianus Corradus' edition with commentary of *Aeneid*, book 1, Florence 1555, not listed in the syllabus of more recent authors in the prolegomena, which does include [Petrus] Nannius, Germanus [Valens PP], [M. Antonius] Delrius, [Philippus] Beroaldus, Petrus Bongus, all mentioned in the notes below.

14 A verb such as 'explains' is omitted.

15 Quintus of Smyrna, author of the imperial Greek epic *Posthomerica*, of which the only manuscript was found in Calabria. Aldus Manutius published the *editio princeps* in 1504 and attributed the poem to 'Quintus Calaber'.

16 La Cerda changes δ' ἄρ' (Greek 'and then') to *inquit* (Latin 'he said'). Modern editions read κατεκλάσθη for La Cerda's κατέκλαστο (a form not attested in Greek). We know very little about which editions of classical authors La Cerda used, but in any case he sometimes tacitly adapts or truncates quotations.

17 Synesius (*c.* 373–414 CE), a Neoplatonist Christian bishop of Ptolemais in Lybia. La Cerda has already been paraphrasing Synesius' fourth epistle before introducing him with *inde*.

18 Heraclitus, the pre-Socratic philosopher, fragment 36 DK, which La Cerda may have known from Philo of Alexandria (*De aeternitate mundi* 111.2) or Aristides Quintilianus (*De musica* 2.17.89), or he may have found the quotation in a commentary on Aristotle, whom he cites next.

19 Gregory of Nazianzus, a fourth-century archbishop of Constantinople and author of theological works.

20 The 'veil' (often *integumentum*) of allegory, which hides the true philosophical meaning.

21 In the Persians' fire-worshipping culture (see also Strabo, *Geography* 15.3.14) the suppliant obtains their demand, because the onlookers wish to preserve the fire from water at all costs; but in turn the suppliant is punished for their disrespectful threat.

22 Albinovanus Pedo, Augustan poet, quoted by Seneca the Elder, *Suas.* 1.15.

23 A Hellenistic Greek poet and grammarian.

24 Most modern editors read *letum* for *mortem*.

25 La Cerda's unspecific cross-references can be hard to track down.

26 A Homeric formula.

27 Present subjunctive in result clause without *ut*, after *necesse est*.

28 Macrobius, *Commentary on the Dream of Scipio* 6.44 (from a discussion of the number seven as the sum of three and four): 'Virgil, schooled in all of the arts, when he wished to express that men were fully blessed in all respects, called them "O thrice and four times blest!"' (tr. W. H. Stahl). Macrobius

championed schematic allegorical readings of Virgil, which became a staple of medieval learning, but of which La Cerda is sceptical.

29 La Cerda *ad Aen.* 12.155 adds little to what he says here. He thinks that Macrobius' numerology is nonsense and that the rhetorical explanation *Numerus finitus pro infinito* in the marginal note is sufficient. I am very grateful to Carlotta Dionisotti for discussing this extract with me.

15

Vitalist Philosophy from a Long-lost Author

Anne Conway (1631–79), *Principia Philosophiae Antiquissimae & Recentissimae*, Excerpts from Chapter VII

Laurynas Adomaitis

Introduction

There are two stories to be told about Anne Conway's *Principles of the Most Ancient and Modern Philosophy*. The first is about its author, Lady Anne Conway née Finch. She was born in London, daughter of the lawyer and parliamentarian Sir Heneage Finch. We have no information about her early education. Formal higher education was also generally not available to seventeenth-century European women. However, Conway made contact with the famous Cambridge philosopher Henry More via her half-brother John Finch. More instructed Conway through their correspondence (1650–78), some of which survives today (ed. Nicolson / Hutton 1992).

In his letters, More translated key passages from Descartes' Latin works for Conway, which suggests that she could not read Latin on her own. In 1651 she married Viscount Edward Conway, who continued to support her intellectual interests. Since her teens, she had suffered from extreme headaches, and at times she would remain bedridden for months. Her disease led her to meet some of the most influential physicians and natural philosophers of her time, including William Harvey and Francis Mercury van Helmont, with whom she also developed a close relationship. She spent the last years of her life incapacitated and in extreme pain, but kept her bright mind until her death (see Hutton 2004: 215–19).

The other story is about the text of the *Principles*. It first appeared as part of an anonymous collection of short Latin works called *Opuscula philosophica* ('*Short philosophical treatises*', Amsterdam 1690) as *Principia philosophiae antiquissimae & recentissimae*. Yet we know that Conway did not write in Latin, so it must have been a translation (Conway's original is lost).[1] Two years later it appeared translated back into English. The new English edition mentioned that its author was an 'English countess, a Woman learned beyond her Sex' (Conway 1692: [3]). The Latin edition did not refer to an author at all. For a long time, it was not accepted that the treatise was written by Conway. Jacob Friedrich Reimmann attributed the book to van Helmont (1725: 520). He was followed by an influential historian, Johann Jakob Brucker, who wrote: 'it is a book attributed by Johann Wilhelm Petersen to some illustrious English woman but Reimmann affirms that van Helmont was its real and genuine author by the testimony of Leibniz' (1742: 723). Little did Reimmann and Brucker know that Gottfried Wilhelm Leibniz not only recognized Conway as the true author (his copy of the book has 'La comtesse de Konnouay' inscribed on it, see Hutton 2004: 2), but had also explained in a letter: 'My views in philosophy approach somewhat closely those of the late Countess of Conway' (A1.14.450). Despite this, Conway's philosophy only experienced resurgence with the recent turn to the history of women philosophers, propagated by scholars like Eileen O'Neill (1998).

Conway's *Principles* contains a systematic treatment of the vitalist doctrine. Her vitalism means that every being is alive and there is no dead matter. To establish this, she argues that no dead matter would be created by God:

> For since God is infinitely good and communicates his goodness to all his creatures in infinite ways, so that there is no creature which does not receive something of his goodness, and this as fully as possible, and since the goodness of God is a living goodness, which possesses life, knowledge, love, and power, which he communicates to his creatures, how can any dead thing proceed from him or be created by him, such as mere body or matter?
>
> Conway 1996: 46–7

Conway's argument relies on several suppositions about the nature of God. According to her, some of God's attributes are communicable during creation and some are not. All communicable attributes are such that, when transferred to the created world, they would not change its essence. For example, God is immutable, but that attribute cannot be communicated to the created world: 'creatures are changeable because otherwise they would be God himself' (Conway 1996: 24). Other attributes, which do not collapse different essences or substances into one, can be and are communicated from God to the created world.[2] However, according to Conway, there is no communicable attribute of God that would warrant the creation of dead matter: 'The communicable attributes are that God is spirit, light, life, that he is good, holy, just, wise, etc. Among these communicable attributes there are none which are not alive and life itself' (Conway 1996: 46). Therefore, every creature must be at least to a certain degree alive and must have a certain degree of light.

Furthermore, this argument implies that there is a similarity relation between God and the created world:

> When anything gives being to another, as when God and Christ give being to creatures (indeed, true essence comes from them alone), they are similar to some extent. For it is impossible for a creature not to have some similarity to its creator or to agree with it in certain attributes and perfections.
>
> Conway 1996: 47–8

This similarity relation would be broken by dead matter which, according to Conway, has no resemblance to the creator. The similarity relation was important for Conway because 'love necessarily occurs because of the similarity or affinity' (Conway 1996: 47). So, in order to love his creations, God must be in some sense similar to them.[3]

Importantly, Conway extends her argument that love necessarily implies similarity to the case of spirit and body. According to her, if body and spirit are so strongly united, there must be love between them, and since love implies similarity, then the body and spirit must be similar to each other. This position was antagonistic to the influential view at the time that body and spirit are essentially different substances. Conway discusses the love and similarity between body and spirit in the selected passage of the *Principles*.

Notes

1 The translator is yet to be identified. There have been suggestions that it was van Helmont (Broad 2002: 68–9). Jasper Reid has argued instead that it was Christian Knorr von Rosenroth (Reid forthcoming).

2 Mercer has identified that this argument has a neo-Platonic influence. According to the neo-Platonic theory of emanation, 'for a being A that is more perfect than a being B, A can emanate its attribute f-ness to B in such a way that neither A nor A's f-ness is depleted in any way, while B has f-ness, though in a manner inferior to the way it exists in A' (Mercer 2019: 57).

3 An implication of this doctrine is that, when creatures die, they do not become dead matter but undergo a transition into another type of being. Conway calls this process 'transmutation'.

Bibliography

Broad, J. (2002), *Women Philosophers of the Seventeenth Century*, Cambridge.

Brucker, J. J. (1742), *Historia critica philosophiae a mundi incunabulis ad nostram usque aetatem deducta*, Vol. 4, part II, Leipzig.

[Conway, A.] (1690), 'Principia philosophiae antiquissimae & recentissimae', in *Opuscula philosophica*, Amsterdam: 1–144.

[Conway, A.] (1692), *The Principles of the most Ancient and Modern Philosophy*. Translated by J. C., London.

Conway, A. (1982), *The Principles of the Most Ancient and Modern Philosophy*. Edited by Peter Loptson, The Hague.

Conway, A. (1996), *The Principles of the Most Ancient and Modern Philosophy*. Translated and edited by Allison P. Coudert and Taylor Corse, Cambridge.

Conway, A. (2019), *Principia philosophiae antiquissimae & recentissimae*, http://dev.cambridge-platonism.divinity.cam.ac.uk/view/texts/normalised/Conway1690.

Feingold, M. (1996), 'When Facts Matter', *Isis*, 87(1): 131–9.

Gordon-Roth, J. (2018), 'What Kind of Monist Is Anne Finch Conway?', *Journal of the American Philosophical Association*, 4(3): 280–97.

Hutton, S. (2004), *Anne Conway: A Woman Philosopher*, Cambridge.

Leibniz, G. W. (1923–), *Sämtliche Schriften und Briefe*. Edited by the Berlin-Brandenburgische Akademie der Wissenschaften and Akademie der Wissenschaften zu Göttingen, Berlin (referenced by series number, volume and page).

Llull, R. (1959–67, 1975–), *Raimundi Lulli Opera Latina*, Palma, later Turnhout (cited as ROL).

Mercer, C. (2019a), 'Anne Conway's Metaphysics of Sympathy', in E. O'Neill and M. P. Lascano (eds), *Feminist History of Philosophy*, 49–73, Cham.

More, H. (1987), *The Immortality of the Soul*, Dordrecht.

Nicolson, M. H. and S. Hutton, eds (1992), *The Conway Letters: The Correspondence of Anne, Viscountess Conway, Henry More, and their Friends 1642–1684. Revised edition*, Oxford.

O'Neill, E. (1998), 'Disappearing Ink: Early Modern Women Philosophers and their Fate in History', in J. A. Kourany (ed.), *Philosophy in a Feminist Voice: Critiques and Reconstructions*, 17–61, Princeton.

Reid, J. (forthcoming), 'Anne Conway and her Circle on Monads', *Journal of the History of Philosophy*.

Reimmann, F. (1725), *Historia universalis Atheismi et Atheorum*, Hildesheim.

Thomas, E. (forthcoming), 'Anne Conway as a Priority Monist: A Reply to Gordon-Roth', *Journal of the American Philosophical Association*.

Source of the Latin text

The edition of the Latin text is based on the comparison between Loptson (Conway 1982) and the Cambridge online (Conway 2019) editions, as well as the *editio princeps* ([Conway] 1690). The choices of reading are my own. The translation is my individual contribution and does not necessarily correspond to the forthcoming translation of which I am a co-editor.[1]

Note

1 A new English translation of the *Principles* is in preparation by Andrew Arlig, Christia Mercer, Jasper Reid and Laurynas Adomaitis.

Latin text

CAPUT VII.[1]

. . .

§. 3. . . . Supposito hoc Lapide Lydio[2] iam ad substratam materiam convertemur: videlicet, ut examinemus: annon spiritus & corpus unius sint naturae & substantiae, adeoque in se invicem convertibiles? Quaero igitur:[3] quaenam sit causa, quod anima sive spiritus hominis tantopere amet[4] corpus, adeoque cum ipso sit unita, tamque invita ab ipso discedat,[5] ut animas quorundam compertum sit[6] manifeste super corpora sua, et penes illa substitisse, postquam corpus esset mortuum, donec istud corrumperetur & resolveretur in pulverem. Ratio huius amoris haec esse nequit, quod spiritus vel anima dederit distinctam corpori essentiam, vel corpus spiritui. Haec enim esset creatio sensu stricto,[7] et proprie dicta: haec autem soli competit Deo & Christo, dare nempe rebus essentiam. Ergo id necessario fiet propter suam, quam inter se invicem habent, similitudinem, vel aliquam inter naturas earum affinitatem. Vel si dicatur esse certam quandam in corpore bonitatem,[8] quae spiritum commoveat, ut illud amet, haec sane bonitas necessario respondebit rei cuidam in natura animae, quae ipsi similis est, alias enim in illam ferri non posset. Imo dicant ergo nobis; quaenam sit illa bonitas in corpore propter quam anima tantopere istud amat? Vel in quibus attributis sive perfectionibus corpus simile est spiritui, si corpus nihil est, nisi truncus mortuus, et massa quaedam, quae omnino sit incapax ullius vitae & perfectionis gradus? Si dicant: corpus concordare cum anima vel spiritu in ratione Entis, id est, quod sicut illa habet entitatem, ita eandem & hoc habet; hoc refutatum iam est in Argumento priore. Si enim hoc ens nulla habet attributa sive perfectiones, in quo conveniat cum entitate spiritus, tunc merum saltem est figmentum. Deus enim nullum creavit ens nudum, quod merum tantum ens sit, et nulla habeat attributa, quae de ipso praedicari possint. Et praeterea Ens tantum est Terminus Logicus et notio, quam Logici vocant Genus generalissimum,[9] quod in nuda et abstracta notione sua non est in rebus ipsis, sed saltem in conceptu sive intellectu humano. Et propterea quodlibet Ens verum natura est quaedam singularis, de qua affirmari queant haec vel illa attributa.[10] Iam quaenam sunt illa attributa corporis, in quibus simile sit spiritui? Examinemus principalia corporis attributa, quatenus distinctum est a spiritu. Iuxta illorum sensum, qui tantopere disceptant corpus et spiritum tam infinite in natura distare, ut alterum nunquam fieri possit alterum, illa attributa sunt haec: quod corpus sit impenetrabile ab

English translation

CHAPTER VII.[1]

. . .

§. 3. . . . Supposing this Lydian stone,[2] we shall now return to the underlying matter, namely, to examine whether or not spirit and body are of one nature and substance and thus convertible into each other? Thus I ask:[3] what is the reason that the soul or the spirit of a person loves[4] the body so much, and is so united with it, and leaves it so unwillingly,[5] that the souls of certain beings have been known[6] to clearly subsist over and near their bodies after the body had been dead [and] until it is corrupted and turned into dust? The reason of this love cannot be that the spirit or soul has given to the body a distinct essence, nor the body to the spirit. For this would be properly speaking creation in the strict sense.[7] But that belongs only to God and Christ, namely, to give essence to things. Therefore, it [i.e. the love between body and soul] will necessarily happen because of the similarity that they have with each other, or some affinity between their natures. Or again, if it is said that there is a certain goodness in the body[8] that moves the spirit to love it, this goodness will clearly correspond to something in the nature of the soul that is similar to it; otherwise, [the body] could not be moved towards it. Therefore, by all means, let them tell us: what is that goodness in the body on account of which the soul loves it so much? Or again, in what attributes or perfections is the body similar to the spirit, if the body is nothing but a dead trunk and some mass that is completely incapable of any degree of life and perfection? If they say: the body agrees with the soul or spirit by the reason of Being, that is, because, just as the latter has entity, so the former has it, too; this is already refuted in the previous argument. For if this being [i.e. that of the body] has no attributes or perfections whereby it might come together with the entity of the spirit, then it is just mere fancy. Surely God has not created any bare being, which would be *just* a being and would have no attributes that could be predicated of it. And moreover, 'being' is just a logical term and notion, which the logicians call the most general genus,[9] which in its bare and abstract notion is not [found] in things themselves, but only in human conceptions or intellects. And because of that, every actual being is a certain singular nature, to which can be ascribed some attributes or others.[10] Now, what are those attributes of a body in which it is similar to a spirit? Let's examine the principal attributes of a body [and] to what degree it is distinct from a spirit. Following the opinion of those who argue so vigorously that body and spirit differ so infinitely in their nature that one can never become the other, these attributes are the following: that a body is impenetrable by any other bodies, so that even its parts cannot penetrate each other. Then

omnibus corporibus aliis, ita ut etiam partes eius sese penetrare nequeant. Porro aliud etiam attributum corporis est, esse discerptibile sive divisibile[11] in partes. Attributa autem spiritus, prout isti eundem definiunt, sunt penetrabilitas et indiscerptibilitas, ita ut spiritus unus penetrare possit alium, ut etiam mille spiritus consistere possint intra se invicem, nec plus tamen occupent spatii, quam spiritus unus. Praeterea spiritus tam est simplex et unus in seipso, ut non possit discerpi vel actualiter dividi in partes a se invicem segregatas. Si iam haec attributa corporis et spiritus invicem comparentur, tantum abest, ut sibi invicem sint similia, vel ut aliquam habeant naturae analogiam, (in quo tamen verum consistit amoris et unitatis fundamentum, sicut dictum est) ut plane sibi sint contraria; imo nihil concipi potest in toto universo tam rei alicui contrarium,[12] quam corpus et spiritus sunt in notione istorum hominum. Pura enim et puta contrarietas hic est in omnibus attributis eorum; quia impenetrabilitas et penetrabilitas magis sibi invicem contraria sunt, quam nigrum et album, sive calidum et frigidum, quod enim nigrum est, fieri potest album, et quod calidum est, fieri potest frigidum; sed prout isti dicunt: quod impenetrabile est, non fieri potest penetrabile; imo Deus et Creatura non tam infinite differunt in essentia sua a se invicem, quam isti Doctores corpus differre faciunt a spiritu. Multa enim sunt attributa, in quibus Deus et Creaturae eius[13] invicem concordant: nullum autem invenire possumus, in quo corpus ullo modo conveniat cum spiritu et per consequens nec cum Deo, qui spirituum est summus et purissimus; quare etiam nulla poterit esse Dei creatura, sed merum non ens, sive figmentum.[14]

another attribute of the body is to be discerpible or divisible[11] into parts. On the other hand, the attributes of the spirit, according to the way these people define it, are penetrability and indiscerpibility, so that one spirit can penetrate another, [and] that even a thousand spirits can consist inside each other, and they would not occupy more space than a single spirit. Also, the spirit is so simple and unified in itself that it cannot be discerpted or actually divided into parts separated from each other. Now if these attributes of body and spirit are compared with each other, they are so far from being similar to each other, or having some analogy of nature (where, still, lies the true foundation of love and unity, as was said), that they are plainly contrary to each other. In fact, nothing in the whole universe can be conceived so contrary to some other thing,[12] as body and spirit are in the notion of these people. For it is a pure and clear contrariety, [that is a contrariety] in all of their attributes, because impenetrability and penetrability are more contrary to each other than black and white, or hot and cold, for what is black can become white and what is hot can become cold. But, according to what they say, what is impenetrable cannot become penetrable. Indeed, God and the Creature do not differ from each other in their essence so infinitely as these teachers make body differ from spirit. For there are many attributes in which God and his creatures[13] agree with each other. But we can find none in which body in some way agrees with spirit, and by consequence also with God, who is the highest and the purest of spirits. Hence it [the body] will surely not be able to be any creature of God, but a mere non-being or fancy.[14]

Commentary

1 In chapter VII of the *Principles* Conway is arguing against her dualist contemporaries, who thought that body and spirit are essentially different. Conway's position is that instead they are essentially similar and differ only in degree. In this excerpt, she challenges her opponents – the dualists – to explain how there could be love between body and spirit if the two were as different as they claim.

2 *Lapide Lydio*: a black variety of jasper (basanite) used by jewellers as a touchstone for testing gold. Conway is metaphorically referring to her previous discussion of the causes of love. She has argued that the true basis for love is similarity: 'love necessarily occurs because of the similarity or affinity' (Conway 1996: 47). Now, given that the spirit loves its body, she asks what similarity could be the basis of this love. The definition of love is a touchstone in a sense that it will help to discern the true explanations of the unity of body and spirit from false arguments.

3 *Quaero igitur*: extensive portions of Conway's work are written in a polemical voice. It often becomes an imagined interlocution with opponents. The polemical passages are characterized by phrases like *si quis dicat* ('if someone should say'), *si quis negare velit* ('if someone should want to deny'), *ego respondeo* ('I respond'), *iam quaero* ('I now ask') etc.

4 *amet*: in claiming that the body loves the spirit and vice versa Conway is using the notion of love in the way she had previously defined it, i.e. as a case of similarity and shared goodness. Having established that love arises from similarity, she deduces from this that the greatest love comes from shared goodness, because 'there is no greater similarity than between good and good' (Conway 1996: 47).

5 *ab ipso discedat*: the image of death as the leaving and separating of spirit has been present in philosophy at least since Plato (cf. *Phaedo* 64c), and Conway uses this imagery in her description of death elsewhere (Conway 1996: 43).

6 *compertum sit*: it is unclear what examples Conway is referring to. Most of her cases of natural history come from van Helmont, but he began actively publishing his works only after Conway's death. So it is likely that she came across such examples in conversation with him. Conversation in general is held to be an important medium in the scientific and philosophical discourse of the seventeenth century (see Feingold 1996: 134–9).

7 *creatio sensu stricto*: creation in the strict sense is the process through which a substance is given its essence. According to Conway, that does not happen within the created world, which as a whole has one and the same essence.

8 *bonitatem*: it is characteristic of Conway to refer to the various attributes as types of goodness. This follows her conception of creation as the process in which God communicates his attributes as much as possible to the created world, and since God has no badness, all of the communicated attributes are varieties of goodness.

9 *Genus generalissimum*: the most general genus is that which cannot be a species of anything. But according to Porphyry it is *substantia* ('substance') and not *ens* ('being'). In Aristotelian logic overall being is not a genus, since it is not directly predicated (*Posterior Analytics* 92b14; *Metaphysics* B.3, 998b22). Thus Conway's claim that the most general genus is *ens* ('being') is not uncontroversial and certainly not accepted by many *Logici* ('logicians'). One famous exception was Ramon Llull (1232–1315), who insisted specifically on *ens* ('being') as the most general notion, e.g. *Centum Formae* in *Ars Brevis* (ROL 1984: 232) and *Ars generalis ultima* (ROL 1986: 325). Llull's logical theories were propagated by Peter Ramus (1515–72) and his followers well into the seventeenth century. Thus Conway might be referring to this tradition.

10 As discussed in the introduction, Conway argues that there is a similarity relation between a creature's body and spirit. This implies that they must be similar in their attributes. Here Conway is considering a possible response from her opponents that body and spirit are similar in that they are both *something*, i.e. they both exist. Conway's answer is that *pure* existence is just an abstract notion invented by the logicians, rather than a real attribute of either body or spirit. Therefore, the similarity of body and spirit cannot be built on this foundation.

11 *discerptibile sive divisibile*: although *divisibilitas* ('divisibility') is a commonly known attribute, *discerptibilitas* ('discerpibility') comes specifically from Henry More's philosophy. More introduces it as follows: 'By Actual Divisibility I understand Discerpibility, gross tearing or cutting one part from another' (More 1987: 27). More distinguishes between divisibility as virtually having parts and discerpibility as being actually divided; according to him these categories are not equivalent (More 1987: 41). In other words, not everything that has parts (is divisible) can actually be divided (is discerpible).

12 *nihil concipi potest in toto universo tam rei alicui contrarium*: clearly there is some irony in Conway's language when she describes the position of her opponents, which she wants to present as absurd.

13 *Deus et Creatura . . . Deus et Creaturae eius*: Conway seems to be using the notion of *creatura* ('the Creature') and *creaturae* ('creatures') in two different ways. By the first she means the whole of the created world as it is distinguished from the two other entities (*entitates*) – God and Christ; whereas the second seems to encompass the set of all individual created beings (*entia*). For the discussion of these two meanings of *creatura* see Gordon-Roth (2018) and Thomas (forthcoming).

14 In the end, Conway reaches a conclusion that, if body and spirit are essentially different (as her opponents suppose), then there can be no coherent relation between them. Also, if body and spirit have contrary attributes, then body should be mere dead matter, but dead matter cannot be created by God, who only creates beings at least in some way similar to himself. In the *Principles* Conway goes on to develop the idea that bodies and spirits differ only in degree but not essentially, and hence that every body has a degree of spirituality and life.

16

A New Approach to Studying Old Documents

Jean Mabillon (1632–1707), *De Re Diplomatica*, Extracts

Alfred Hiatt

Introduction

At the opening of *De re diplomatica* ('*On diplomatics*') Jean Mabillon (1632–1707) stated his intention to inaugurate a 'new kind of antiquarian art' (*novum antiquariae artis genus*). By compiling detailed observations on the nature of medieval documents, based in many cases on first-hand examination, Mabillon set out to provide a firm basis for differentiating between genuine and forged material therein, or as he put it, for the *discrimen veri ac falsi in vetustis monumentis* ('discernment of truth from falsehood in old records'). The fact that *De re diplomatica* is still cited by medievalists today as the foundation stone of the scientific study of historical documents is a measure of Mabillon's success.

Jean Mabillon was a Benedictine monk of the congregation of St Maur, a union of French Benedictine monasteries that included the royal abbey of St Denis and St Germain-des-Prés in Paris. As a result, Mabillon had access to the outstanding collections of documents and manuscripts contained in the archives of these and other monasteries. The Maurists specialized in scholarship, and in the last quarter of the seventeenth century Mabillon became their leading intellectual. Prior to the publication of *De re diplomatica*, he had already completed an edition of the works of St Bernard of Clairvaux (1667), co-edited (with Luc d'Achery) the opening volumes of the *Acta Sanctorum* ('*Deeds of the Saints*') of the Benedictine order, eventually published in nine volumes between 1668 and 1701, and commenced publication of the *Vetera Analecta* ('*Ancient Selections*', 1675–85), a collection of miscellaneous medieval texts with commentary. Later works included the *Annals* of the Benedictine order in six volumes (1690–1710); the *Museum*

Italicum (1687–9), a collection of diverse ecclesiastical texts with special relevance for the history of the Latin liturgy, based on Mabillon's study of documents in Italian collections; and the *Traité des études monastiques* ('*Treatise on monastic studies*', 1691), a salvo in Mabillon's dispute with Armand de Rancé, reformist abbot of the Cistercian abbey at La Trappe. These works show Mabillon's devotion to his order and its history, factors of significance when considering *De re diplomatica*.

The spark for *De re diplomatica* was the publication in 1675 of the Jesuit Daniel van Papenbroeck's attack on the veracity of a number of medieval documents, including those contained in the archives of St Denis, in a treatise that appeared as a preface to the edition of the Society of Bollandists' *Acta Sanctorum* ('*Deeds of the Saints*') for the month of April.[1] Mabillon accused Papenbroeck and other scholars, such as the Englishman John Marsham, of adopting an excessively harsh approach to the criticism of early documents, thereby tainting swathes of genuine material with the suspicion of falsehood. As Mabillon emphasized in his introduction to *De re diplomatica*, the history of churches, monasteries, private individuals and families depended on the authority of historical records. Hence, he argued, the systematic examination of documents was of considerable importance to the state as well as the Church.

From its first appearance in 1681, *De re diplomatica* made a monumental contribution to historical and antiquarian studies, attracting both fervent praise and strong criticism. Within Mabillon's lifetime, several works appeared that were directly or indirectly influenced by *De re diplomatica*, written by scholars with diverse national and religious affiliations. These works included José Pérez de Rozas' *Dissertationes ecclesiasticae* ('*Ecclesiastical Dissertations*', Salamanca 1688), which used historical documents as the basis for the study of the ecclesiastical and political history of Spain; Gottfried Wilhelm Leibniz's (see Text 18) two-volume *Codex Juris Gentium Diplomaticus* ('*Diplomatic Codex of the Laws of Nations*', Hanover 1693–1700); George Hickes's monumental study of northern antiquities, the *Linguarum Vett. Septentrionalium Thesaurus Grammatico-Criticus et Archaeologicus* ('*Grammatico-Critical and Archaeological Thesaurus of the Ancient Northern Languages*', Oxford 1705); and the Maurist Bernard de Montfaucon's *Palæographia Græca, sive De ortu et progressu literarum Græcarum* ('*Greek Palaeography, or On the Rise and Progress of Greek Letters*', Paris 1708). *De re diplomatica* received criticism, at one extreme, from Jesuit scholars such as Bartolomy Germon, who argued that all extant Merovingian charters were later forgeries, and Jean Hardouin, who claimed that nearly all of classical Latin literature had been invented during the Middle Ages. Such claims were wildly exaggerated, but all post-medieval historians had to grapple with the fact that a significant proportion of medieval records, particularly those of early medieval popes and kings, comprised either outright forgeries or documents altered by interpolations or other types of intervention. From a far more moderate position than those of either Germon or Hardouin, Hickes, too, suggested that in *De re diplomatica* Mabillon may have been acting in the interests of his order by promoting a relatively lenient approach to the detection of forged documents. Such criticisms were energetically refuted in the second edition of *De re diplomatica* (1709), overseen by Mabillon's disciple Thierry Ruinart, and in the monumental *Nouveau Traité de Diplomatique* (*'New Treatise of Diplomatic'*) of the Maurists Charles-François Toustain and René-Prosper Tassin (Paris 1750–5). Although the manuals of 'diplomatic' (on this term see note 1 below) produced by nineteenth-century scholarship eventually supplanted *De re diplomatica* as a resource, Mabillon's position as a founder of the discipline remained intact, having been consolidated by his eighteenth-century followers.

De re diplomatica consists of six books. The first three consider the age, material, script, style and authenticating devices of historical documents. Book 4 comprises an excursus on the French royal palaces and estates where kings had promulgated documents, while books 5 and 6 provide a conspectus of annotated 'specimens' of old documents, consisting of facsimile engravings designed to illustrate their scripts, and to enable scholars to compare and evaluate records.

The following extracts are taken from books 1 and 3 of Mabillon's work. In the first extract Mabillon introduces *De re diplomatica* and explains its motivation and significance. In the second and third he discusses the materials on which medieval documents were written, and outlines a history of different scripts in Italy and in France. In the final extract Mabillon concludes his discussion of documents by setting out a number of guidelines for the examination of *vetusta monumenta*.

Note

1 The *Acta Sanctorum* is a collection of saints' lives and related materials begun in the early seventeenth century, based on the study and editing of original texts found in medieval manuscripts. The term Bollandist derives from the enterprise's association with the Jesuit scholar Jean Bolland, editor of the first volume in the collection.

Bibliography

Aris, R. (1995), 'Jean Mabillon', in Helen Damico and J. B. Zavadil (eds), *Medieval Scholarship: Biographical Studies on the Foundation of a Discipline*, Vol. 1, 15–32, New York.

Barret-Kriegel, B. (1988), *Les historiens et la monarchie*, Vol. 1: *Jean Mabillon*, Paris.

Bischoff, B. (1990), *Latin Palaeography: Antiquity and the Middle Ages*, trans. D. Ó Cróinín and D. Ganz, Cambridge.

Boyle, L. E. (1984), *Medieval Latin Palaeography: A Bibliographical Introduction*, Toronto.

Brown, M. P. (1990), *A Guide to Western Historical Scripts from Antiquity to 1600*, London.

Fichtenau, H. (1992), 'Diplomatiker und Urkundenforscher', *Mitteilungen des Instituts für Österreichische Geschichtsforschung*, 100: 9–49.

Hiatt, A. (2009), 'Diplomatic arts: Hickes against Mabillon in the Republic of Letters', *Journal of the History of Ideas*, 70: 351–73.

Hurel, D.-O., ed. (2003), *Érudition et commerce épistolaire: Jean Mabillon et la tradition monastique*, Paris.

Leclant, J., A. Vauchez and D.-O. Hurel, eds (2010), *Dom Jean Mabillon, figure majeure de l'Europe des lettres*, Paris.

Leclercq, H. (1953–7), *Mabillon*, 2 vols, Paris.

McDonald, P. (1979), 'Mabillon and the birth of diplomatics', in *Sciences religieuses / Studies in Religion*, 8: 441–8.

Mélanges et documents publiés à l'occasion du 2e centenaire de la mort de Mabillon (1908), Paris.

Source of the Latin text

The Latin text is taken (with some adjustments to spelling and punctuation) from the first edition of *De re diplomatica*:

De re diplomatica[1] *libri vi. In quibus quidquid ad veterum Instrumentorum antiquitatem, materiam, scripturam, et stilum; quidquid ad sigilla, monogrammata, subscriptiones, ac notas chronologicas; quidquid inde ad antiquariam, historicam, forensemque disciplinam pertinet, explicatur et illustratur*, Paris 1681.

'Six Books on Diplomatics[1]. *In which whatever pertains to the antiquity, material, script and style of old documents; whatever [pertains] to seals, monograms, signatures and indications of chronology; whatever, consequently, to antiquarian, historical and legal science, is set in order and illustrated.'*

Latin text

Liber Primus, Caput I

[p. 1] I. Novum antiquariae artis[2] genus aggredior, in qua de veterum instrumentorum ratione, formulis et auctoritate agitur. Praecipuam eis fidem, si modo vera et genuina fuerint, tribuendam esse censent omnes, maxime quantum ad rei transactae circumstantias et ad res chronologicas attinet, quae nullo aliunde certiori testimonio, quam eiusmodi monumentis resciri et confirmari possunt. Verum iidem ipsi,[3] qui hoc instrumentorum genus probant, quaedam in eis falsa, suspecta, interpolata circumferri causantur: et dum in istis discernendis haerent, etiam indubitatis fidem temere abrogant aliquando. At valde mirum esset, si in tanta autographorum et exemplorum varietate, quae ex tam longa annorum serie, per tot diversarum nationum manus ad nos transmissa sunt, adulterina aut vitiosa nulla reperirentur.[4] Sed inquirendum, quam late pateat hoc malum, et si qua tandem arte ipsi occurri possit: ne rei litterariae illa pars, quae potiorem sibi auctoritatem merito vindicat, vanis exceptionibus atque censuris impune violetur.

Quanta sit istius artis utilitas ac necessitas, nemo non videt: cum non solum ecclesiastica et civilis historia, sed maxime privatorum hominum, ecclesiarumque fortunae plurimum pendeant ex eiusmodi monumentis.[5] Quam ob rem magnopere interest ad antiquariam forensemque disciplinam haec tractatio, magnamque a re publica gratiam inierit, quisquis certas et accuratas tradiderit conditiones ac regulas, quibus instrumenta legitima a spuriis, certa et genuina ab incertis ac suspectis secernantur . . .

English translation

Book 1, Chapter 1

I. I undertake a new kind of antiquarian art,[2] which concerns the nature, 'formulae' and authority of old documents. Such documents, as all agree, should be assigned particular trust provided that they are true and genuine. This is especially the case insofar as regards the circumstances of business transacted and matters of chronology, which can be known and confirmed by no more certain evidence than by records of this kind. However, the very same people[3] who examine this kind of document allege that false, suspect and interpolated [material] is scattered about within them, and while they are intent on distinguishing such material, they sometimes also rashly annul trust in [documents] of unquestioned veracity. Yet it would be very surprising if nothing forged or corrupt were found amid such a great variety of originals and copies [of documents], passed down to us over the course of so many years, through so many hands of diverse peoples.[4] But it is necessary to investigate how widely this evil extends, and whether in the end it can be obviated by any method, lest that portion of texts which deservedly claims superior authority for itself should with impunity be harmed by empty objections and condemnations.

None can fail to see how great is the utility and necessity of this method, since not only ecclesiastical and secular history, but especially the fortunes of private individuals, and of churches, heavily depend on records of this kind.[5] For that reason, this treatise is of great relevance to antiquarian and legal science, and whoever delivers firm and accurate conditions and rules, by which legitimate documents may be divided from spurious ones, the certain and genuine from the uncertain or suspect, will win great esteem from the state . . .

Liber Primus, Caput VIII

[p. 31] I. Cum iam de diplomatum, aliorumque instrumentorum antiquitate, deque falsorum origine constet, ad alia verorum a falsis discrimina veniendum est. Quapropter a diplomatum antiquitate progredior ad eorum materiam; inquisiturus qualis fuerit materia, in qua, et ex qua illa scripta sunt ab annis mille et trecentis,[6] quo ex tempore veterum instrumentorum, quae ad res maxime ecclesiasticas pertinent, antiquitas superius definita est. Mirum vero est, quam varia ac multiplex apud antiquos fuerit materia,[7] in qua olim excepta scriptura est ... Ex his omnibus materiis quinque tantum in quaestionem hic venire possunt: nempe charta membranacea seu coriacea; corticea ex ligno et papyro Aegyptiaca; plumbea; et nostra communis.[8] Nam chartae nomine olim veniebat, quidquid codicibus aut excipiendae scripturae aptum esset, ut viri docti observarunt, quae appellatio etiam traducta est ad diplomata, quae a charta, materia videlicet sua, chartae dictae sunt.[9]...

[p. 32] III. Ad membranae qualitatem accedunt piscium pelles, in quibus scripta fuisse diplomata quaedam Puricellus contestatur.[10] Is in libro de Ambrosianae Mediolanensis ecclesiae monumentis, agens de diplomate Hugonis et Lotharii Italiae Regum, ait eius *archetypum aureis* esse *litteris conscriptum*, et quidem *in corio piscis*. Quod quidem numquam sibi venturum fuisse in mentem confitetur, *nisi iam pridem alii, quo tempore qualitas membranae characterisque discerni facilius poterat, eamdem rem a semetipsis observatam memoriae prodidissent. Quippe duo nobis,* inquit, *praeterea suppetunt archetypi eius exemplaria, ex eo postmodum transscripta, et auctoritate publica rite recognita et comprobata, in quibus litteras illas esse aureas, et in corio piscis exaratas affirmatur*. Unum Mediolani anno Domini M CCC XXII coram Cathelollo de Medicis Vicario generali, alterum sexto inde anno in burgo Casalis Sancti Evasii coram Henrico de Sancto Stephano confectum.[11] ... Et fortasse non desunt alibi etiam eiusmodi piscium membranae, quas ab ovinis curiosus indagator facile discernet. Certe nonnullas vidimus, quae ad illas potius quam ad ovinas accedere videntur. Ceterum ne quis dubitet de hoc corii piscini usu in scribendis vetustis instrumentis, occurrit illud quod apud Cedrenum legimus,[12] nempe Basilisco Imperatore ortum fuisse Constantinopoli incendium, quod basilicam devoravit, in qua fuit bibliotheca, librorum millia CXX continens, quos inter erat etiam *draconis intestinum, τοῦ δράκοντος ἔντερον pedes CXX longum, cui Homeri poemata, Ilias et Ulyssea, aureis litteris fuerant inscripta,* [p. 33] *cum historia rerum ab Heroibus gestarum*. Et id piscinis illis membranis sane auctoritatem conciliat.

Book 1, Chapter 8

I. Having now dealt with the antiquity of diplomas and other documents, and the origin of forgeries, it is necessary to move on to other means of discerning genuine [documents] from false [ones]. On that account, I proceed from the antiquity of diplomas to their material. I will investigate of what sort the material was, on which and from which these [documents] were written, going back 1300 years,[6] which was the time defined above as antiquity for old documents that pertain especially to ecclesiastical matters. Now it is remarkable how varied and manifold among the ancients was the material on which writing used to be received.[7] . . . From all these materials only five can come into question here: namely, leaves of skin or leather; vegetable material from wood and from Egyptian papyrus; lead; and the [kind of paper that is] standard for us.[8] For, as learned men have observed, it used to be the case that whatever material was used for books or for receiving writing went by the name of *charta*. This name was also transferred to diplomas, which are called charters from *charta*, that is, from their own material.[9]. . .

III. The skins of fish, on which Puricellus testifies that some diplomas were written, bear resemblance to the quality of parchment.[10] That man says, in his book on the records of the church of Ambrose in Milan, when discussing a diploma of Hugh and Lothar, Kings of Italy, that its 'original (is) written in golden letters', and indeed 'on the skin of a fish'. He confesses that this possibility would never have occurred to him 'unless long ago, at a time when the nature of the skin and its letters could be discerned more easily, others recorded the same thing, which they themselves had observed'. 'Indeed,' he says, 'two further copies of that original are at hand, transcribed from it at a later date, and duly inspected and approved by public authority: in which [copies] it is affirmed that those letters were golden and written on the skin of a fish.' One [copy] was produced in Milan in the year of the Lord 1322 in the presence of Catellolo de' Medici, the Vicar General; another six years later in Casale Monferrato of St Evasius in the presence of Henry of St Stephen.[11] . . . And perhaps fish skins of the same kind also survive elsewhere, which the curious investigator will easily distinguish from sheepskins. Certainly we have seen some [skins] that seem more similar to those [fish skins] than to sheepskin. Furthermore, in case anyone has doubts about this use of piscine skin in writing old documents, that which we read in Cedrenus comes to mind,[12] namely that in Constantinople during the reign of Emperor Basiliscus a fire arose, which destroyed the basilica in which there was a library containing 120,000 books. Among the books were 'the intestines of a serpent (*draco*), *tou drakontos enteron*, 120 feet long, on which the poems of Homer, the *Iliad* and *Odyssey*, were inscribed in golden letters, with a *History of the Deeds of Heroes*'. And that indeed provides authority for these piscine skins.

Liber Primus, Caput XI

[p. 46] II. Ex praemissis omnibus scripturae generibus, ad propositum nostrum pertinent quatuor dumtaxat priores species, nempe Romana vetus, Gothica, Langobardica, et Saxonica. Romana illa obtinuit aureis saeculis[13] apud Romanos et Italos, viguitque ad saeculum v, quo tempore cum Gothi Italiam sub iugum suum adduxissent, etiam Gothicis litteris Romanas aliquantisper vitiarunt. Tum saeculo vi Langobardis in Italiam effusis,[14] successit Langobardica scriptura ad communem usum. Romana illa sic corrupta in libris describendis aliquandiu viguit, nempe ad saeculum viii. Nam post id tempus Romana ad solos ferme librorum titulos reservata est, exceptis nonnullis libris ad pompam descriptis in gratiam principum personarum. Sic ergo Langobardica obtinuit apud Italos ad saeculum xii, quo ex tempore in politiorem illum modum sensim deducta est, quo nunc est Romana recentior. Haec apud Italos.

III. Gothica usi sunt in Hispania Vesigothi, Saxonica Britanni seu Anglosaxones.[15] At quo genere Galli, Germani, et alii populi Septemtrionales? Gallis scripturae genus proprium ante Francorum adventum[16] fuisse constat, sicut idioma. Sed ex illis temporibus nulla nobis relicta sunt monumenta, praeter nonnullos titulos sepulcrales, ex quibus priscum Gallorum alphabetum eruere tentavit Boterovius in suo libro de re monetaria.[17] Hoc alphabetum, quodcumque illud est, suo loco exhibebimus. Post Francorum in Gallias accessum Galli duplici scripturae genere usi videntur, altero Romano, quale in plerisque vetustioribus codicibus reperitur, altero minutiori in diplomatibus et quibusdam libris conscribendis, quod uniforme ubique in diplomatis et chartis sub Merovingica stirpe[18] fuisse observavimus. Hanc scripturam *Francogallicam* seu *Merovingicam* appellare licet, quae *barbara* iam dudum ob litterarum asperitatem ac difficultatem dicta est.[19] Haec paullatim politior evasit Carolinis temporibus,[20] quibus duae maxime scripturae species apud nostrates obtinuerunt: una ad Italicae nostrae formam accedens, qualis in diplomatibus Caroli M. nonnullis, omnibus Ludovici Pii et Caroli Calvi deprehenditur, quae ob id *Carolina* appellari potest; altera, in libris describendis et synodicis litteris[21] adhiberi solita, quae a minutae Romanae forma paullum recedit. Haec de Gallis . . .

Book 1, Chapter 11

II. Of all the above-mentioned types of script, only the four earlier forms pertain to our project here, namely Old Roman, Gothic, Lombardic and Saxon. That Roman [script] prevailed among the Romans and [other] peoples of Italy during the golden age,[13] and it flourished until the fifth century, at which point the Goths brought Italy under their yoke and for a time corrupted Roman [letters] with Gothic letters. Then in the sixth century, following the Lombard invasion of Italy,[14] Lombardic script entered in turn into common use. The Roman [script], corrupted in this way, flourished for some time [as a script] for copying books, namely up to the eighth century. For after that time Roman [script] was reserved for the most part just for the titles of books, apart from some books copied for display, in honour of important personages. In this way, then, Lombardic [script] prevailed among the peoples of Italy until the twelfth century, from which time it was gradually brought towards that more polished mode [of writing] that is the origin of the more contemporary Roman [script]. So much [for scripts] among the Italian peoples.

III. The Visigoths in Spain employed Gothic [script]; the Britons or Anglo-Saxons [used] Saxon [script].[15] But what kind [of script] did the Gauls, Germans and other northern peoples [use]? As with language, it is known that there had been a type of script peculiar to the Gauls prior to the arrival of the Franks.[16] But no records survive for us from those times, other than some inscriptions on tombs, on the basis of which, in his book on coinage, Boterovius[17] attempted to elicit the ancient alphabet of the Gauls. We shall display this alphabet, whatever it might be, in its place. After the entry of the Franks into Gaul, the Gauls seem to have used two kinds of script: one Roman, of the kind that is found in many old manuscripts; the other a smaller script, [used] in writing diplomas and certain books, which we observe to have been [used] consistently everywhere in diplomas and charters under the Merovingian line.[18] This script, which formerly was called 'barbarian' on account of the unpolished and difficult nature of its letters, is rightly named 'Francogallic' or 'Merovingic'.[19] It gradually became more polished in Carolingian times,[20] during which two forms of script in particular prevailed among our countrymen. One, resembling our Italic [script], such as is discerned in some diplomas of Charlemagne and in all [diplomas] of Louis the Pious and Charles the Bald, on account of which it can be named 'Caroline'. The other, which departs slightly from the form of Roman minuscule, was used customarily in books and in synodical letters.[21] So much about the Gauls . . .

Liber Tertius, Caput VI[22]

...

[p. 241] II. Magna prudentia, eruditione ac moderatione summa opus esse, ut vetera instrumenta legitime examinentur; nec cuivis illotis manibus[23] id tentandum.

III. Semper iudicandum in partem favorabilem, ubi res longa possessione firmata est, ut leges civiles et canonicae praecipiunt.[24]

IV. Non ex sola scriptura,[25] neque ex uno solo characterismo, sed ex omnibus simul de vetustis chartis pronuntiandum. Neque enim unum est in uno saeculo, unave provincia scripturae genus, sed varia, ut de nostro experiri licet, nec possunt omnes unius saeculi scripturae ad amussim repraesentari.

V. Unum aut alterum defectum, modo essentialis non sit, legitimis autographis obesse non debere, cum in sinceris diplomatibus nonnullis, quae vidimus,[26] quidam occurrant eiusmodi leviores defectus ...

VI. Historicorum aut inscriptionum testimonia legitimis chartis non ita praeiudicare debere, ut illorum praeferatur auctoritas. Siquidem errata non levia auctoribus etiam aequalibus subrepunt aliquando ...

[p. 242] VII. Additiones Incarnationis, Indictionis, glossematum,[27] aliorumque similium, maxime in exemplis seu apographis,[28] non officere instrumentorum veritati ...

VIII. Puniendos utique falsarios, atque eos, qui falsis instrumentis dolo malo[29] abutuntur, sed revincendos etiam pseudocriticos, qui quodlibet temere falsi insimulant ...

Book 3, Chapter 6[22]

...

II. In order to examine old documents legitimately, great prudence, erudition and the highest level of moderation are required. It should not be attempted by anyone with unwashed hands.[23]

III. A claim should always be judged favourably where the matter is confirmed by lengthy possession, as civil and canon laws instruct.[24]

IV. Pronouncements on old charters should not be made on the basis of script alone,[25] nor from a single characteristic, but from all things [taken] together. For in any century, and in any province, there is not just one type of script in use, but several, as can be proven by our own [era]. Nor can all the scripts of a single century be accurately displayed.

V. [The presence of] one or two defects, provided they are not fundamental ones, should not be prejudicial to legitimate original documents, since in some genuine diplomas, which we have seen,[26] some relatively insignificant defects of this sort do occur ...

VI. The evidence of historians or inscriptions ought not to be prejudicial to legitimate charters, as if the authority of the former were preferable. For serious errors sometimes creep into even contemporaneous authorities ...

VII. The addition of [the era of] Incarnation, indictions, glosses[27] and other similar matter, especially in copies and transcripts,[28] should not detract from the truth of documents ...

VIII. Forgers, and those who misuse false documents with evil intent,[29] should by all means be chastised; but pseudo-critics, who rashly assert the falsity of whatever they please, should also be refuted ...

Commentary

1 A *diploma* was in classical Latin an official letter authorizing travel (effectively a passport) or more generally a legal document certifying rights and privileges. In the Middle Ages the term continued to be used to signify an official document, particularly one issued by royal or papal authority. Mabillon coined *diplomaticus* as an adjective describing the scholarly study of old documents. The association of 'diplomatic' with diplomacy appears to derive from Leibniz's *Codex Juris Gentium Diplomaticus* ('*Diplomatic Codex of the Law of Nations*', 1693–1700), a work heavily influenced by *De re diplomatica*.

2 The adjective *antiquarius* was of classical and medieval usage (Isidore, *Etymologiae* 6.14), while Jerome uses the term *ars antiquaria* in one of his letters (*Ad Florentinum* 5.2.4), in the context of the copying of manuscripts. Mabillon's 'new type' of antiquarian art refers to the study of medieval, rather than classical, materials on scientific principles. He seems to use *ars* and *disciplina* as synonyms, with an emphasis on the systematic examination of old records.

3 Mabillon is referring specifically to the Jesuit scholar Daniel van Papenbroeck, whose work he names on the following page and in subsequent chapters of *De re diplomatica*, and more generally to historians who have taken a partisan and hypercritical approach to medieval documents.

4 Mabillon uses hypozeugma, adding emphasis to the main clause by positioning it at the end of a series of phrases, in this case drawing attention both to the quantity of medieval documentation and to the improbability of its complete purity.

5 Mabillon points out that, since the claims to antiquity of churches, and the wealth, title and privileges of many private individuals, depend on the validity of old records (*monumenta*), assertions of widespread forgery of such records threaten the stability of the state. Mabillon's statement is not empty, since medieval royal diplomas continued to have legal validity in France up to the time of the Revolution. The potency of medieval and pseudo-medieval documents in late-seventeenth-century France was revealed in 1695, when Mabillon himself, along with his disciple Thierry Ruinart and the historian and jurist Étienne Baluze, was duped into authenticating forged documents purporting to demonstrate the descent of the Cardinal de Bouillon, Emmanuel-Théodose de la Tour d'Auvergne, from the Dukes of Aquitaine and the Counts of Auvergne.

6 In chapters 3, 4 and 5 of book 1, Mabillon amassed evidence for the usage of royal, papal and private documents from as early as the fourth century; the use of such documents from the sixth century was, he concluded, irrefutable.

7 Mabillon's original note at this point reads '*Vide Hermannum Hugonis de primar. scribendi orig. et Alexand. ab Alex. genial. dier. lib. 2 cap. 30.*' He refers to Hermann Hugo, *De prima scribendi origine et universa rei literariae antiquitate* ('*On the earliest origin of writing and the general antiquity of literature*') (Antwerp 1617), e.g. chapters 10, *De materia in qua scriptum antiquissime* ('On material used for writing in very ancient times'), and 11, *De primo usu chartae, eiusque variis generibus et appellatione* ('On the first use of paper, and on its various types and names'), pp. 89–101; Alexander ab Alexandro [Alessandro Alessandri], *Genialium dierum libri VI* ('*Six Books of Festive Days*') (Paris 1586), book 2, chapter 30, fols 108r–10r.

8 Mabillon identifies five major material supports for writing: parchment (i.e. animal skin prepared as a writing surface), paper made from wood, papyrus, lead (as used in seals) and paper made from rags, the last the standard material in his day.

9 Mabillon may have in mind here the discussion of *charta* in Hugo, *De prima scribendi origine*, chapter 11, which collects various authorities on the topic. The term *charta* developed from its classical meaning of a leaf of papyrus, and by extension the writing that appeared on papyrus, to its post-classical sense of a formal document, usually written on parchment, and usually sealed or attested in some other way (e.g. by signature or witness list).

10 Mabillon's original note: '*Puricell. pag. 282 et 283.*' He refers to Joannis Petrus Puricellus [Giovanni Pietro Puricelli], *Ambrosianae Mediolani Basilicae, ac monasterii, hodie Cistertiensis Monumentorum Singularis Descriptio* ('*Notable Description of the Records of the Church and Monastery, now Cistercian, of St Ambrose in Milan*') (Milan 1645; repr. Leiden 1722), cols 130–2, nos 164–5.

11 The document in question – a grant of Hugh and Lothar, Kings of Italy, in favour of the monastery of St Ambrose of Milan, dated 942 – is of disputed authenticity. It survives in a badly damaged eleventh-century copy as well as in the two fourteenth-century confirmations described by Puricellus, *Descriptio*, cols 131–2, no. 165. Puricellus seems to have mistaken the eleventh-century copy for the original. Few subsequent scholars have given credence to the possibility that the lost original was actually written on fish skin, otherwise unknown as a material for documents in the medieval West, and it has been suggested that the confirmation's phrase *in corio pissis* (*sic*) should be understood as 'on purple parchment' (*I diplomi di Ugo e di Lotario di Berengario II e di Adalberto*, ed. Luigi Schiaparelli, Rome 1924, no. 64, pp. 189–93).

12 Mabillon's original citation: '*Cedren. pag. 286 edit. Basil.*' Georgius Cedrenus, *Annales, sive Historiae ab exordio mundi ad Isacium Comnenum*

usque Compendium (*'Annals, or Epitome of History from the Beginning of the World to Isaac Comnenus'*) (Basel 1566), 288–9.

13 Mabillon's golden age seems to encompass the period of the Roman Empire from its inception up to the barbarian invasions of the fifth century. Mabillon's evidence for script up to the fifth century came from inscriptions, such as the two bronze tablets he reproduced at the start of book 5 of *De re diplomatica*, but he also drew on the references to documents he found in authors such as Cicero, Tacitus, Augustine and Jerome.

14 The Goths famously sacked Rome in 410 and, under Theodoric the Great, took control of the Western Roman Empire in 489. The Lombards, another Germanic people, entered northern Italy in 568, where they established a kingdom. The script misleadingly identified by Mabillon as 'Lombardic' is now recognized as 'Beneventan', from its use in the Duchy of Benevento. It did not originate with the Lombards, being like most 'national' hands a development of the cursive script used in late Roman provincial chanceries. Beneventan script remained dominant in southern Italy until the end of the twelfth century, when it was replaced by the Caroline-based 'proto-Gothic' script. Contrary to Mabillon's suggestion, northern and central Italy rapidly adopted Caroline script in the years after *c.* 800.

15 The Visigoths (Western Goths) established a kingdom in Spain from the mid fifth century until the Muslim conquests of the early eighth century. The Angles and Saxons began to enter Britain in the mid fifth century. As in his remarks on Lombardic script (see n. 14) and Merovingian script (see n. 19), Mabillon overestimated the independence of 'national' scripts such as Visigothic and Saxon. Both derive directly from Roman models, though they possess distinctive features.

16 The Franks, a confederation of German tribes, first entered Gaul in the third century, although a Frankish kingdom in the northern parts of Gaul was not consolidated until around 496, during the reign of Clovis (481–511).

17 Mabillon refers to Claude Bouteroüe's *Recherches curieuses des monoyes de France depuis le commencement de la monarchie* (*'Curious inquiries into the Moneys of France from the Beginning of the Monarchy'*, Paris 1666), where an alphabet of 'the first race' of the Gauls is displayed on p. 379. This alphabet is printed in *De re diplomatica*, book 5 (p. 347), along with 'Caroline or Francic', Gothic and Runic alphabets. It comprises a mixture of Latin and Greek letter forms (in which, along with an Old Italic script similar to Etruscan, all surviving ancient Gaulish inscriptions are expressed). Bouteroüe was vague about the sources for his alphabet, which presumably included

inscriptions on coins as well as the inscriptions on stone mentioned by Mabillon. His alphabet can be compared with those reproduced in *Recueil des Inscriptions Gauloises*, ed. Paul-Marie Duval et al., 4 vols (Paris 1985–2002).

18 The Merovingians were the ruling dynasty of the Frankish kingdom from Clovis until the middle of the eighth century.

19 Mabillon here describes Merovingian cursive script, before going on to distinguish two forms of writing used by the Carolingians. Mabillon's Merovingian script is actually a derivative of the Roman cursive script which developed from the mid fourth century. It is a visually striking, compressed and 'spidery' script, notable for elongated ligatures, particularly in the opening lines of documents.

20 The Carolingians (descendants of Charles Martel) took power from the Merovingians, first under Pippin III (r. 751–68), whose son Charlemagne (r. 768–814) expanded Frankish rule to include Saxony and parts of northern Italy and north-eastern Spain. Charlemagne was succeeded by his son Louis the Pious (r. 814–40); Louis' son Charles the Bald ruled the West Frankish kingdom from 840 to 877. Mabillon outlines a distinction between what more recent palaeographers have termed 'chancery hand' and 'book hand' (the latter including uncial and minuscule hands).

21 Letters of a synod (a meeting of priests, with authority to decide legal or administrative matters) or church council.

22 Mabillon couches his list of guidelines for the study of ancient documents in indirect discourse, marked by the use of accusative-infinitive constructions and gerundives.

23 A proverbial expression used to mean undertaking an activity without appropriate preparation.

24 Mabillon refers to the two main branches of law defined and studied during the Middle Ages, and of enduring influence thereafter, encompassing secular (civil) and ecclesiastical (canon) jurisdictions.

25 Although by the word *scriptura* Mabillon is clearly referring to script rather than Scripture, his phrase alludes to the Protestant catchphrase *ex sola scriptura* ('on the basis of Scripture alone') and indicates the confessional loyalties of his work. Mabillon, that is, wrote at one and the same time from the positions of a Benedictine monk loyal to the order of St Maur, a Catholic, and an intellectual dedicated to the establishment of scientific principles and to scholarly dialogue across confessional lines.

26 Mabillon goes on to give two examples, one of a charter of Philip I of France (r. 1060–1108), in which the Roman numeral M was initially omitted and subsequently added above the line, the other of a document of Archbishop William of Rheims dated 1167 in numerals but 1166 in words.

27 Mabillon refers to additions of dates expressed in the form of years from the Incarnation of Christ or indictional cycles of fifteen years.

28 Mabillon distinguishes between original or 'autograph' documents written at the time of the deed and later copies and transcripts, which are more likely to contain additions of one kind or another.

29 Here as elsewhere Mabillon uses traditional legal language, *dolus malus* being a standard Roman law term for intentional deceit.

17

Newton on Theology

Isaac Newton (1642–1727), Theological Section from the General Scholium to the *Principia Mathematica*

Pablo Toribio[1]

Introduction

Isaac Newton (1642–1727) is one of the greatest figures in the history of science. He made groundbreaking discoveries in physics and mathematics, including the law of universal gravitation, the laws of motion, the heterogeneity of white light and the development of infinitesimal calculus. He was additionally deeply engaged with alchemy, both theoretical and practical. Moreover, Newton was devoted throughout his whole adult life to private study of the Bible (especially the Book of Revelation), the early history of the Christian Church and the chronology of ancient nations. In the final three decades of his life he combined these intellectual endeavours with his position as guardian and then master of the Royal Mint as well as the presidency of the Royal Society.

As a young man, Newton was constantly exposed to Latin: first during his primary education at the Free Grammar School of Grantham (Westfall 1980: 55–7) and then at Trinity College, Cambridge, where students were supposed to 'speak Latin all the time they were in Hall' (Iliffe 2017: 74). Much of the scholarly literature Newton was reading and engaging with was written in Latin, and he consequently used it to a considerable extent in his own productions, particularly in the fields of natural philosophy, mathematics and church history. In his manuscript notes shifts are frequently found from English to Latin and vice versa, mostly depending on the sources being discussed. From the late 1690s onwards, however, when Newton entered the public sphere and moved to London, his overall Latin production decreased significantly.

Newton may have chosen to write in Latin his masterpiece, *Philosophiae naturalis principia mathematica* ('*Mathematical principles of natural philosophy*', 1687), not only owing to the status of the ancient language as scholarly lingua franca, but also because the work was in many regards intended as a response (Smith 2008) to René Descartes' *Principia philosophiae* ('*Principles of philosophy*', 1644). As for the choice of English for Newton's second major work, the *Opticks* (1704), reasons related to the contents have been suggested. For Grafton (1996: 206) 'even Sir Isaac Newton, who used his fluent Latin as the appropriate dress for the great baroque world picture of the *Principia*, used English for the pullulating experimental details of his *Opticks*'. Cohen (2001: 41) argued that this choice 'would seem to be a kind of admission by Newton of the imperfect or incomplete nature of the *Opticks*'. In any case the work was soon translated into Latin in an augmented edition under Newton's own supervision (*Optice*, 1706).

For Newton writing was largely 'a question of finding the right words, and specifically of finding matter-of-fact, nonmetaphoric words' (Coetzee 1992: 187). His meticulousness in choosing his wording is certainly confirmed by the vast numbers of drafts that make up his manuscript legacy.[2] This meticulousness, however, did not always militate against accidental mistakes: phrases such as *de origine schismatico* (instead of *schismatica*, 'on the schismatic origin', see Toribio 2013: 129–30) or *rei alicuius incorporei* (instead of *incorporeae*, see n. 10 below) are striking but not utterly exceptional.

Although a systematic study on Newton's Latinity is still to be undertaken, some of its features are apparent, such as its remarkable lack of classical allusions: when classical literature is referred to, it serves no ornamental function, but is rather used as evidence for historical claims. Newton's writing displays a tendency towards concision and terseness that is very well exemplified in this selection. Here, his striking taste for asyndeton is perceivable, as is his sparse use of connectors, in spite of the complexity of his chain of thought. In relation to this, it is possible to observe the frequent occurrence of lists, parallelisms and tricolons, such as the beautifully worded one on God's inaccessibility to human senses (*more minime humano, more minime corporeo, more nobis prorsus incognito*).

The General Scholium included in the second (1713) and third (1726) editions of the *Principia* contains some of Newton's very rare public statements on theology. This brief but extremely rich piece brings together crucial aspects of Newton's natural philosophical and theological thought. The presentation of gravity in the *Principia* as a force acting at a distance, without any apparent mechanical cause, aroused serious criticisms from Gottfried Wilhelm Leibniz (see Text 18) and others: they considered that Newton was 'using the enormous cultural prestige of mathematics to reintroduce occult principles' (Shapin 1996: 63; see Snobelen 2001: 174). In the General Scholium Newton counter-attacked with criticisms of both conventional mechanical philosophy and philosophical conceptions identifying God with Nature.

The Scholium begins by describing how the movements of celestial bodies cannot be accounted for with Descartes' mechanical hypothesis. As Newton put it, it is not the task of a natural philosopher to 'invent' hypotheses in order to account for gravity (*hypotheses non fingo* ['I do not invent hypotheses'], he famously writes towards the end), but to deduce 'propositions' from phenomena and to make them general 'by induction'. This self-imposed methodological framework allows Newton to claim (at the end of this selection) that discussions about God do belong to natural philosophy, provided that they are based on the observation of natural phenomena. In keeping with this, the discussion about God is introduced by a typical enunciation of the argument of design (Shapin 1996: 142–8), according to which the perfect constitution of nature bears witness to the existence of a Creator. With the characterization of God that follows, Newton makes it clear that he is by no means implying that nature is alive and endowed with occult qualities; on the contrary, Newton's God is the personal God of the Bible, who rules over his creation as an absolute monarch. In his further description of God, several lines of thought arising from Newton's decades-long research programme on biblical exegesis and the history of the early Church and ancient religions converge.

Of particular interest are Newton's claims about the word 'God': for Newton this is a relative term, only definable by reference to the entities said to be subordinate to the one who is called 'god'. The implications of this reasoning are widely attested in Newton's theological manuscripts: there are true and false gods (depending on their ascendancy being true or false), and higher and lower gods. The highest God is by definition only one, and for Newton this is the God of the Bible, God the Father only. Christ is not the highest God: however, he is true God, in as much as the ascendancy which he has received from the Father is a true one. Orthodox Trinitarianism can therefore be legitimately seen as an implied, secondary target of the theological section of the General Scholium: in fact, it was occasionally read that way in the early eighteenth-century (Snobelen 2005: 275–83).

Notes

1 I have written this section as a researcher of the ILC, CSIC (Madrid) and as a member of project FFI2017-86726-P, funded by the Spanish AEI / FEDER (European Union). I am grateful to William M. Barton for his careful revision of an earlier version of the introduction.

2 The draft material for the General Scholium is mostly held in Cambridge University Library (henceforward CUL), in MS Add. 3965, and can be viewed online via the Cambridge Digital Library. For transcriptions and translations of many of Newton's manuscripts see the websites of *The Newton Project*, *The Newton Project Canada* and *The Chymistry of Isaac Newton*.

Bibliography

Casini, P. (1984), 'Newton: The Classical Scholia', *History of Science*, 22 (1): 1–58.

Coetzee, J. M. (1992), 'Isaac Newton and the Ideal of a Transparent Scientific Language (1982)', in D. Attwell (ed.), *J. M. Coetzee: Doubling the Point. Essays and Interviews*, 184–92, Cambridge MA.

Cohen, I. B. and A. Whitman (1999), *Isaac Newton: The Principia: Mathematical Principles of Natural Philosophy. A New Translation. Preceded by a Guide to Newton's Principia by I. Bernard Cohen*, Berkeley.

Cohen I. B. (2001), 'The Case of the Missing Author: The Title Page of Newton's *Opticks* (1704), with Notes on the Title Page of Huygen's *Traité de la lumière*', in I. B. Cohen and J. Z. Buchwald (eds), *Isaac Newton's Natural Philosophy*, 15–45, Cambridge MA.

Grafton, A. (1996), 'The New Science and the Traditions of Humanism', in J. Kraye (ed.), *The Cambridge Companion to Renaissance Humanism*, 203–23, Cambridge.

Iliffe, R. (2017), *Priest of Nature: The Religious Worlds of Isaac Newton*, Oxford.

Koyré, A., I. B. Cohen and A. Whitman (1972), *Isaac Newton's Philosophiae naturalis principia mathematica: 3rd ed. with Variant Readings*, London.

Levitin, D. (2016), 'Newton and Scholastic Philosophy', *British Journal for the History of Science*, 49(1): 53–77.

Motte, A. (1729), *The Mathematical Principles of Natural Philosophy. By Isaac Newton. Translated into English by Andrew Motte*, Vol. 2, London.

Pococke, E. (1650), *Specimen historiae Arabum, sive Gregorii Abul Farajii Malatiensis de origine et moribus Arabum succincta narratio*, Oxford.

Shapin, S. (1996), *The Scientific Revolution*, Chicago / London.

Smith, G. (2008), 'Newton's *Philosophiae Naturalis Principia Mathematica*', in E. N. Zalta (ed.), *The Stanford Encyclopedia of Philosophy* (http://plato.stanford.edu/archives/win2008/entries/newton-principia/).

Snobelen, S. D. (2001), 'God of Gods, and Lord of Lords: The Theology of Isaac Newton's General Scholium to the Principia', *Osiris*, 16: 169–208.

Snobelen, S. D. (2005), 'Isaac Newton, Socinianism, and the One Supreme God', in M. Mulsow and J. Rohls (eds), *Socinianism and Arminianism: Antitrinitarians, Calvinists and Cultural Exchange in Seventeenth-Century Europe*, 241–98, Leiden.

Toribio, P. (2013), *Isaac Newton: Historia ecclesiastica (de origine schismatico ecclesiae papisticae bicornis). Edición crítica, traducción y estudio*, Madrid.

Westfall, R. (1980), *Never at Rest: A Biography of Isaac Newton*, Cambridge.
Whiston, W. (1728), *Sir Isaac Newton's Corollaries from His Philosophy and Chronology, in His Own Words*, London.

Source of the Latin text

The text that follows is based on the third edition of the *Principia* (see facsimile with apparatus in Koyré, Cohen and Whitman 1972: 759–65). Punctuation has been standardized in places. Capitalization remains the same as in the original. Previous English translations include Whiston (1728: 6–10), Motte (1729: 388–92) and Cohen and Whitman (1999: 940–3).

Latin text

...Elegantissima haecce solis, planetarum et cometarum compages non nisi consilio et dominio entis intelligentis et potentis oriri potuit. Et si stellae fixae sint centra similium systematum, haec omnia simili consilio constructa suberunt *Unius* dominio: praesertim cum lux fixarum sit eiusdem naturae ac lux solis, et systemata omnia lucem in omnia invicem immittant, et ne fixarum systemata per gravitatem suam in se mutuo cadant, hic eadem <ad> immensam ab invicem distantiam posuerit.[1]

Hic omnia regit non ut anima mundi,[2] sed ut universorum dominus. Et propter dominium suum dominus deus Παντοκράτωρ[3] dici solet. Nam deus est vox relativa et ad servos refertur: et deitas est dominatio dei, non in corpus proprium, uti sentiunt quibus deus est anima mundi, sed in servos. Deus summus est ens aeternum, infinitum, absolute perfectum: sed ens utcunque perfectum sine dominio non est dominus deus. Dicimus enim deus meus, deus vester, deus Israelis, deus deorum et dominus dominorum, sed non dicimus aeternus meus, aeternus vester, aeternus Israelis, aeternus deorum; non dicimus infinitus meus vel perfectus meus. Hae appellationes relationem non habent ad servos. Vox deus passim significat dominum,[4] sed omnis dominus non est deus. Dominatio entis spiritualis deum constituit, vera verum, summa summum, ficta fictum. Et ex dominatione vera sequitur deum verum esse vivum, intelligentem et potentem; ex reliquis perfectionibus summum esse vel summe perfectum.

Aeternus est et infinitus, omnipotens et omnisciens, id est, durat ab aeterno in aeternum et adest ab infinito in infinitum; omnia regit et omnia cognoscit, quae fiunt aut fieri possunt. Non est aeternitas et infinitas, sed aeternus et infinitus; non est duratio et spatium, sed durat et adest. Durat semper et adest ubique, et existendo semper et ubique durationem et spatium constituit. Cum unaquaque spatii particula sit *semper* et unumquodque durationis indivisibile momentum *ubique*, certe rerum omnium fabricator ac dominus non erit *nunquam*, *nusquam*. Omnis anima sentiens diversis temporibus et in diversis sensuum et motuum organis eadem est persona indivisibilis. Partes dantur successivae in duratione, coexistentes in spatio, neutrae in persona hominis seu principio eius cogitante; et multo minus in substantia cogitante dei.[5] Omnis homo, quatenus res sentiens, est unus et idem homo durante vita sua in omnibus et singulis sensuum organis. Deus

English translation

...This most elegant structure of the Sun, the planets and the comets could not have originated without the decision and dominion of an intelligent and powerful being. And if the fixed stars are the centres of similar systems, all these, built by a similar decision, will be subjected to the dominion of *One*: especially since the light of the fixed [stars] is of the same nature as the light of the Sun, and all systems exchange light with all others, and [since], in order to avoid systems of the fixed [stars] mutually falling upon each other on account of their gravity, He has placed them at an immense distance from each other.[1]

He governs all things not as the soul of the world,[2] but as Lord of everything. And because of his dominion, the Lord God is usually called *Pantokratōr*.[3] For 'God' is a relative word and is used with reference to servants, and deity is God's domination not over his own body, as those for whom God is the soul of the world believe, but over servants. The highest God is an eternal, infinite, absolutely perfect being, but a being, however perfect, without dominion is not the Lord God. For we say 'my God', 'your God', 'God of Israel', 'God of gods' and 'Lord of lords', but we do not say 'my eternal', 'your eternal', 'eternal of Israel', 'eternal of gods'; we do not say 'my infinite' or 'my perfect'. These names have no relation to servants. The term 'God' means everywhere 'lord',[4] but every lord is not a god. It is the domination of a spiritual being that makes a god: a true [domination makes] a true [god], the highest [domination makes] the highest [god], a false [domination makes] a false [god]. And from his true domination it follows that the true God is alive, intelligent and powerful; from his other perfect qualities it follows that he is the highest, or perfect in the highest way.

He is eternal and infinite, almighty and all-knowing, that is, he lasts from everlasting to everlasting, and is present from infinity to infinity; he governs all things and knows all things that happen or can happen. He is not eternity and infinity, but eternal and infinite; he is not duration and space, but lasts and is present. He lasts forever and is present everywhere, and by existing always and everywhere he establishes duration and space. Since each particle of space exists *always* and each indivisible moment of duration exists *everywhere*, the maker and lord of all things will certainly not exist *at no time, nowhere*. Every perceiving soul is the same indivisible person through different times and in the different instruments of its senses and movements. There are successive parts in duration, coexisting [parts] in space, [but] neither [of these sorts of] parts is in the person of a human being or in its thinking principle; and much less [are there parts] in the thinking substance[5] of God. Every human being, insofar as it is a perceiving thing, is one and the same human being during its whole life in each and every instrument of its senses. God

est unus et idem deus semper et ubique. Omnipraesens est non per *virtutem* solam, sed etiam per *substantiam*: nam virtus sine substantia subsistere non potest.[6] In ipso continentur[7] et moventur universa, sed sine mutua passione. Deus nihil patitur ex corporum motibus, illa nullam sentiunt resistentiam ex omnipraesentia dei.[8]

Deum summum necessario existere in confesso est, et eadem necessitate *semper* est et *ubique*. Unde etiam totus est sui similis, totus oculus, totus auris, totus cerebrum, totus brachium, totus vis sentiendi, intelligendi et agendi,[9] sed more minime humano, more minime corporeo, more nobis prorsus incognito. Ut caecus non habet ideam colorum, sic nos ideam non habemus modorum, quibus deus sapientissimus sentit et intelligit omnia. Corpore omni et figura corporea prorsus destituitur, ideoque videri non potest, nec audiri, nec tangi, nec sub specie rei alicuius corporeae[10] coli debet. Ideas habemus attributorum eius, sed quid sit rei alicuius substantia minime cognoscimus. Videmus tantum corporum figuras et colores, audimus tantum sonos, tangimus tantum superficies externas, olfacimus odores solos et gustamus sapores: intimas substantias nullo sensu, nulla actione reflexa[11] cognoscimus; et multo minus ideam habemus substantiae dei. Hunc cognoscimus solummodo per proprietates eius et attributa et per sapientissimas et optimas rerum structuras et causas finales, et admiramur ob perfectiones; veneramur autem et colimus ob dominium. Colimus enim ut servi, et deus sine dominio, providentia et causis finalibus nihil aliud est quam fatum et natura. A caeca necessitate metaphysica, quae utique eadem est semper et ubique, nulla oritur rerum variatio. Tota rerum conditarum pro locis ac temporibus diversitas ab ideis et voluntate entis necessario existentis solummodo oriri potuit.[12]

Dicitur autem deus per allegoriam videre, audire, loqui, ridere, amare, odio habere, cupere, dare, accipere, gaudere, irasci, pugnare, fabricare, condere, construere. Nam sermo omnis de deo a rebus humanis per similitudinem aliquam desumitur, non perfectam quidem, sed aliqualem tamen. Et haec de deo, de quo utique ex phaenomenis disserere ad philosophiam naturalem pertinet.

is one and the same God always and everywhere. He is omnipresent not only through his *power*, but also through his *substance*, since power cannot subsist without substance.[6] In him everything is contained[7] and moves itself, but without their mutually affecting each other. God is not affected in any way by the movements of bodies, [and] these do not experience any resistance from God's omnipresence.[8]

It is acknowledged that the highest God necessarily exists, and by the same necessity he is *always* and *everywhere*. Therefore he is also all similar to himself: all eye, all ear, all brain, all arm, all ability to perceive, to understand and to act,[9] but in a manner in no way human, in a manner in no way corporeal, in a manner completely unknown to us. As a blind person does not have any idea of the colours, so we do not have any idea of the ways in which the most wise God perceives and understands everything. He lacks any body or corporeal shape whatsoever, and therefore he cannot be seen, or heard, or touched, nor should he be worshipped under the form of any corporeal thing.[10] We have ideas of his attributes, but we do not know at all what the substance of any thing is. We see only shapes and colours of bodies; we hear only sounds; we touch only external surfaces; we smell only odours and taste only flavours: by no sense, by no reflection[11] do we know their inner substances, and much less do we have any idea of God's substance. We know him only through his properties and attributes, as well as through the most wise and excellent constructions and final causes of things, and we admire [him] on account of his perfect qualities; but we venerate and worship [him] on account of his dominion. Indeed, we worship [him] as servants, and a god without dominion, providence and final causes is nothing but fate and nature. From a blind metaphysical necessity, which is certainly the same always and everywhere, no variation of things originates. The whole diversity of created things in different places and times could only originate from the ideas and will of a necessarily existing being.[12]

On the other hand, God is allegorically said to see, to hear, to speak, to laugh, to love, to hate, to desire, to give, to receive, to feel joy, to get angry, to fight, to produce, to establish, to build, since all language about God is taken from human realities by way of a certain similarity, no doubt imperfect, but still of some kind. And [I will say] that much about God – to discuss him from phenomena certainly does belong to natural philosophy.

Commentary

1 *et ne fixarum . . . posuerit*: The whole phrase was inserted in the 1726 edition after a full stop. The misleading punctuation in the original has caused all previous English translations to render the clause an independent item, in spite of the fact that, as implied by the subjunctive *posuerit*, *cum* ('since') still applies. The omission of *ad* with the resulting loose double accusative construction is also most probably accidental, as suggested by some of Newton's drafts (see CUL, MS Add. 3965, fol. 468v). Elsewhere Newton took Lucretius, *De rerum natura* 5.91–109 as evidence that the possibility of different star systems falling upon each other on account of their gravity was a genuinely held fear in the ancient world (Casini 1984: 27–8).

2 The reference is to the widespread Platonic doctrine of the 'soul of the world', according to which the world is a living being endowed with soul and intelligence (Plato, *Timaeus* 30bc). See further n. 7.

3 *Newton's note a*: 'Id est Imperator universalis.' ('That is, "universal emperor"').

4 *Newton's note b*: 'Pocockus noster vocem *dei* deducit a voce Arabica *du*, et in casu obliquo *di*, quae dominum significat. Et hoc sensu principes vocantur dii: *Psalm*. LXXXII, 6 et *Ioan*. X, 35. Et Moses dicitur deus fratris Aaron et deus regis Pharaoh (*Exod*. IV, 16 et VII, 1). Et eodem sensu animae principum mortuorum olim a gentibus vocabantur dii, sed falso propter defectum dominii.' ('Our Pococke derives the term *deus* from the Arabic term *du* (and in the oblique case *di*), which means "lord". And in this sense princes are called gods: *Psalm* LXXXII, 6 and *John* X, 35. And Moses is called god of his brother Aaron and god of the King Pharaoh (*Exodus* IV, 16 and VII, 1). And in the same sense the souls of dead princes were called gods by the Gentiles in ancient times, but falsely, due to their lack of dominion.')

Newton refers to the celebrated Oxford Orientalist Edward Pococke (1604–91), who does discuss the Arabic term *du* as meaning 'lord' (Pococke 1650: 104), but does not establish any connection between this term and the Latin *deus*. The biblical passages listed next refer to cases where people other than God are called gods: Moses in Exodus, the 'mighty' (princes and judges) in Psalm 82 (Vulgate 81):6; the latter is quoted in John 10:35. These two references are erroneously rendered as Psalm 84 and John 10:45 in the original.

5 *substantia cogitans* or 'thinking substance' is a typically Cartesian phrase referring to personal identity. Newton draws a parallel between God's 'thinking substance' and the human 'thinking principle', which Newton gives

here as a synonym for *persona*. The correspondence implies that God is also a single 'person', thereby contradicting the doctrine of the Trinity, which postulates a single substance and three persons. If the printed wording is at odds with Trinitarian orthodoxy, there is manuscript evidence that Newton even envisaged a much bolder version: *et multo minus in persona Dei*, 'and much less in the person of God' (CUL, MS Add. 3965, fol. 539r).

6 As shown by Levitin (2016: 70–3), this is a commonplace attack on the concept of 'virtual extension', which scholastic philosophers had applied to souls and other incorporeal entities. For anti-scholastic philosophers like Newton, the possibility of something being only virtually extended was nonsensical.

7 *Newton's note c*: 'Ita sentiebant veteres, ut Pythagoras apud Ciceronem, *de Natura deorum*, lib. I; Thales; Anaxagoras; Virgilius, *Georgic.* lib. IV, v. 220 et *Aeneid.* lib. VI, v. 721; Philo, *Allegor.* lib. I sub initio; Aratus in *Phaenom.* sub initio. Ita etiam scriptores sacri ut Paulus in *Act.* XVII, 27, 28; Iohannes in *Evang.* XIV, 2; Moses in *Deut.* IV, 39 et X, 14; David, *Psal.* CXXXIX, 7, 8, 9; Salomon, *I Reg.* VIII, 27; *Iob*, XXII, 12, 13, 14; *Ieremias* XXIII, 23, 24. Fingebant autem idololatrae solem, lunam et astra, animas hominum et alias mundi partes esse partes dei summi et ideo colendas, sed falso.' ('The ancients believed this, as Pythagoras in Cicero, *On the nature of the gods*, book I; Thales; Anaxagoras; Virgil, *Georgics*, book IV, v. 220 and *Aeneid*, book VI, v. 721; Philo, *Allegories*, book I, at the beginning; Aratus, *Phaenomena*, at the beginning. So also the sacred writers, such as Paul in Acts, XVII , 27, 28; John in his *Gospel*, XIV, 2; Moses in *Deuteronomy*, IV, 29 and X, 14; David, *Psalm* CXXXIX, 7, 8, 9; Solomon, *I Kings* VIII, 27; Job, XXII, 12, 13, 14; *Jeremiah*, XXIII, 23, 24. Moreover, idolaters imagined that the Sun, the Moon and the stars, the souls of people and other parts of the world were parts of the highest God and therefore to be worshipped, but [this was] false.')

The classical references here include passages where the world is presented as a living, divine being (according to the doctrine of the *anima mundi* ['soul of the world'], idolatrous in Newton's eyes). The Apostle Paul's famous reference to Aratus in Acts 17:28 works as a bridge between the classical references and the biblical ones. The latter depict God as exceeding the dimensions of heaven and earth (1 Kings 8:27), and at the same time being present everywhere (Psalm 139 [Vulgate 138]:7). The last sentence insists again on ancient idolatry conflating God and his creation.

8 Of course, this does not mean that physical bodies are not affected by God's *will*, but only by the incorporeal quality of His omnipresence.

9 Newton is here probably echoing his own reading of the second-century heresiologist Irenaeus of Lyon (*Against the heresies* 2, 13, 3): 'He is simple & not compound. He is all & equal to himself, all sense, all spirit, all perception, all Ennoea, all λόγος [*logos*, 'word'], all ear, all eye, all light. He is all sense which cannot be separated from itself, nor is there any thing in him which can be emitted from anything else. Thus does Irenaeus represent & confute the Metaphysicks of the Gnosticks.' (Newton's drafts in Jerusalem, National Library of Israel, Yahuda Ms. 15.7, fol. 128r).

10 The original reads *sub specie rei alicuius corporei*, as if the feminine noun *res* were masculine or neuter. Translators have implicitly corrected *corporei* into *corporeae*: 'under the representation of any corporeal thing' (Whiston 1728: 9; Motte 1729: 391), 'in the form of something corporeal' (Cohen and Whitman 1999: 942). The correction also appears in editions of the Latin text following Newton's death.

11 *actio reflexa* usually means 'reflex act' (as in Descartes: see Shapin 1996: 48–9). Here Newton must have intended the meaning of the scholastic phrase *actus reflexus*: 'reflection' based on perceptions through the senses.

12 This reuses the argument of intelligent design, stated at the beginning of this section, against atheism. The previous sentence (*A caeca necessitate metaphysica* . . .) also implies opposition to any philosophy equating God to his creation. For Newton, the only truly Christian philosophy of nature is the one allegedly resulting from his world view: one that confirms God's intelligent control over nature as a separate entity.

18

Damnation and Divine Justice

Gottfried Wilhelm Leibniz (1646–1716), *Confessio Philosophi*, Extract

Lucy Sheaf

Introduction

Gottfried Wilhelm Leibniz (1646–1716) has aptly been called the last universal genius. His enduring renown rests largely on his discovery of differential calculus, his theory of monads and his claim that ours is the best of all possible worlds. Another important legacy is his coining of the term 'theodicy'.[1] In Leibniz's view, the chief task of the theodicist is to show that God's permitting evil is consistent with God's being perfectly just. The *Confessio philosophi* ('*The philosopher's confession*') is Leibniz's first substantial contribution to his lifelong theodicy project. It is an early work, dating from between the autumn of 1672 and the spring of 1673, and is in dialogue form. Two speakers are involved: the Theologian and the Philosopher. Leibniz never published the *Confessio philosophi*, but there is reason to think that he hoped to do so.[2] The central theme is signalled in the opening speech, when the Theologian declares: *Nunc exspectat nos spinosa tractatio de Iustitia Dei* ('Now a thorny discussion about the justice of God awaits us').[3]

To a significant extent, the 'thorniness' of the discussion will be due to a sustained focus on damnation. The question why the God of classical theism permits not only suffering in this life, but also eternal misery is an awkward one for any Christian philosopher who accepts the doctrine of eternal damnation.[4] Yet it is particularly problematic for Leibniz, as he consistently defines justice in relation to love. In his early writings – including the *Confessio philosophi* – the just person is defined as 'one who loves everyone', while love is defined as 'delight in the happiness of another'.[5] Soon after hearing the definitions just cited, the Theologian asks: *Si Deus omnium felicitate delectatur, cur non omnes fecit felices; si amat omnes, quomodo tam multos damnat*? ('If God is delighted by the happiness of everyone, why did he not make everyone happy? If he loves everyone, how is it that he damns so many?').[6] The Theologian appears to be gesturing towards the following problem: given that love involves delighting in the happiness of another person, and that the damned are devoid of happiness, is it not impossible for God to love the damned? If so, God cannot be said to love everyone – and thus cannot be said to be just. Leibniz's theodicy must therefore be deemed a failure. Strangely, the Theologian does not pursue this line of argument in the subsequent discussion, which instead addresses other theodician problems.[7]

In the *Confessio philosophi* Leibniz is particularly concerned with the implications of his thoroughgoing determinism.[8] Committed as he is to the Principle of Sufficient Reason – the principle that nothing occurs without a sufficient reason why it is so and not otherwise[9] – he insists that there are sufficient reasons for the acts of the will. He also maintains that these reasons are to be found *outside* the will. In his scheme we are constituted in such a way that we always seek our own good (real or apparent). Since it is our intellect that allows us to perceive various goods, to compare them and to come to a judgement about the course of action which best serves our own good, the intellect has a decisive role in determining our will. However, it must also be noted that the intellect is in turn determined by the circumstances of our lives. 'Circumstances' is to be construed broadly here: under this heading Leibniz includes not only such things as our being members of a particular family and community, but also innate dispositions and temperament. Crucially, Leibniz holds that the circumstances of our lives are ultimately controlled by God: in creating a world that is fully determined, God *ipso facto* brings about the circumstances that determine all our actions. Given this deterministic scheme, Leibniz is vulnerable to the objection that we lack the freedom required for moral responsibility. If so, then God's punishing mortal sin with eternal misery would appear to be a gross injustice. The Theologian presses this very point when he articulates the 'complaint of the damned', which is the centrepiece of this extract.

In the person of the Philosopher, Leibniz seeks to show that the complaint of the damned is groundless. To a large extent, his efforts are focused on showing that determinism does not preclude our having free will.[10] As Leibniz sees things, the damned cannot reasonably complain about a fate that they have freely chosen. The Theologian professes himself unsatisfied by this response, as it does little to quell concerns about God's role in damnation. It is easy to share these misgivings, but we must recall that the *Confessio philosophi* is a youthful work and that Leibniz's thinking on the problem of evil evolved significantly.[11]

Notes

1 'Theodicy' is an amalgam of the Greek words θεός (*theos*, 'God') and δίκη (*dikē*, 'justice'). It was apparently used by Leibniz for the first time in 1696, and with little comment. See Rateau 2008: 317–22.

2 See R. Sleigh's comments in Leibniz 2005: 32. There is illuminating discussion of the circumstances of composition in the three critical editions listed in the bibliography.

3 Leibniz 2005: 26.

4 See M. M. Adams 1993.

5 Leibniz holds that properties can be attributed to God and to human beings univocally (i.e. in one and the same sense). He therefore intends these definitions of *the just* and of *love* to apply not only to human beings, but also to God, and to be understood in precisely the same sense in both cases.

6 Leibniz 2005: 32.

7 No doubt the most plausible explanation for this lacuna is that Leibniz assumes that the definition of love as 'delight in the happiness of another' is not to be taken at face value. The definition in question is first introduced in the *Elementa juris naturalis* ('*Elements of natural law*', 1670–1), where Leibniz suggests that 'delighting in the happiness of another' can be construed as 'willing the good of another'. See for example Leibniz 2003: 294. Given that willing another person's good or happiness is sufficient for loving them, there is no great difficulty in saying that God loves the damned, since God can will or strive for the good even of those who are enduring eternal misery.

8 For present purposes, determinism is the view that every act of the will has causes external to the will itself. In contemporary discussions, the view that the will is undetermined is characterized as 'libertarianism'. This view can be traced back to Augustine, but Leibniz generally associates it with Luis de Molina (1535–1600). For Leibniz's dismissal of the Molinist conception of freedom of the will see Leibniz 2005: xxxiii–xxxix; 158, n. 73; 171, n. 2. There is a comprehensive discussion of Leibniz's determinism in R. M. Adams 1994: Part 1.

9 Leibniz gives various formulations of this principle. Key texts are cited and discussed in Rodriguez-Pereyra 2018: 48–59.

10 See Parkinson 1999.

11 See Rateau 2008 and Sleigh's introduction in Leibniz 2005. In both the *Confessio philosophi* and the later *Theodicy* (1710) Leibniz devotes considerable attention to the question of whether God's permitting some to endure eternal damnation precludes God's being perfectly just. These sustained discussions suggest that Leibniz was well aware that the doctrine of eternal damnation aggravates the problem of evil enormously.

Bibliography

Adams, M. M. (1993), 'The Problem of Hell: A Problem of Evil for Christians', in E. Stump (ed.), *Reasoned Faith: Essays in Philosophical Theology*, 301–27, Ithaca NY / London.

Adams, R. M. (1994), *Leibniz. Determinist, Theist, Idealist*, Oxford.

Adams, R. M. (2005), 'Moral Necessity', in D. Rutherford and J. Cover (eds), *Leibniz: Nature and Freedom*, 181–93, Oxford.

Adams, R. M. (2014), 'Justice, Happiness, and Perfection in Leibniz's City of God', in L. Jorgensen and S. Newlands (eds), *New Essays on Leibniz's Theodicy*, 197–217, Oxford.

Antognazza, M. R. (2009), *Leibniz: An Intellectual Biography*, Cambridge.

Leibniz, G. W. (1875–90), *Die Philosophischen Schriften von Gottfried Wilhelm Leibniz*, Vol. 6. Edited by C. I. Gerhardt, Berlin.

Leibniz, G. W. (1965), *Monadology and Other Philosophical Essays*. Edited and translated by P. Schrecker and A. M. Schrecker, Indianapolis.

Leibniz, G. W. (1967), *Confessio philosophi. Ein Dialog*. Edited and translated by O. Saame, Frankfurt.

Leibniz, G. W. (1970), *Confessio philosophi – La profession de foi du philosophe*. Edited and translated by Y. Belaval, Paris.

Leibniz, G. W. (2003), *Frühe Schriften zum Naturrecht*. Edited and translated by Hubertus Busche, Hamburg.

Leibniz, G. W. (2005), *Confessio philosophi. Papers Concerning the Problem of Evil, 1671–1678*. Edited and translated by R. Sleigh, New Haven / London.

Leibniz, G. W. (2011), *Dissertation on Predestination and Grace*. Edited and translated by M. Murray, New Haven/London.

Lodge, P. (2017), 'Eternal Punishment, Universal Salvation and Pragmatic Theology in Leibniz', in L. Strickland, E. Vynckier and J. Weckend (eds), *Tercentenary Essays on the Philosophy and Science of Leibniz*, 301–24, Cham.

Parkinson, G. H. R. (1999), 'Sufficient Reason and Human Freedom in the *Confessio Philosophi*', in S. Brown (ed.), *The Young Leibniz and His Philosophy*, 199–222, Dordrecht / London.

Rateau, P. (2008), *La question du mal chez Leibniz: fondements et élaboration de la Théodicée*, Paris.

Rodriguez-Pereyra, R. (2018), 'The Principles of Contradiction, Sufficient Reason, and Identity of Indiscernibles', in M. R. Antognazza (ed.), *The Oxford Handbook of Leibniz*, 45–64, Oxford.

Rutherford, D. (1995), *Leibniz and the Rational Order of Nature*, Cambridge.

Rutherford, D. (2001), 'Leibniz and the Stoics: The Consolations of Theodicy', in M. Latzer and E. Kremer (eds), *The Problem of Evil in Early Modern Philosophy*, 138–64, Toronto.

Strickland, L (2009), 'Leibniz on Eternal Punishment', *British Journal for the History of Philosophy*, 17: 307–31.

Source of the Latin text

I have used the text in Robert Sleigh's critical edition of the *Confessio philosophi* (Leibniz 2005) as the basis for my own, making only minor changes to spelling and punctuation. Words underlined in the original manuscript are italicized here.

Latin text

PHILOSOPHUS. O ergo stultos nos, qui spretis naturae Deique privilegiis, chimaeras quasdam imperceptibiles postulamus, nec rationis usu contenti, vera radice libertatis, nisi potestas brutalitatis fiat, satis nos liberos esse non putamus![1] Quasi non summa libertas sit et intellectu suo et voluntate perfectissime uti, ac proinde a rebus ad agnoscenda, intellectum, ab intellectu ad amplectenda vera bona, voluntatem cogi . . . Certe Dei libertas summa est, etsi errare in delectu optimorum non possit[2] . . .

THEOLOGUS. Ergo peccatum omne ab errore.

PH. Fateor.

TH. Ergo peccatum omne excusandum.

PH. Minime, nam in mediis tenebris illabente quadam velut per rimas luce, evadendi ratio in potestate est, modo uti velimus.

TH. Sed cur alii volunt uti, alii non volunt.

PH. Quia non volentibus ne in mentem quidem venit, se uti cum fructu posse, aut ita in animo est quasi non esset, id est absque *reflexione* sive *attentione*, ut videntes non videant, audientes non audiant.[3] In quo sita initia sunt *negatae gratiae*, ac velut scriptura sacra appellat indurationis.[4] Quotusquisque nostrum non millies audivit illud: *dic cur hic* seu *respice finem* sive *vide quid agas*,[5] et tamen certum est una sola sententia eiusmodi recte percepta, et quibusdam velut legibus poenisque severe sancitis constanter praefixa, hominem unumquemque, velut oculi quodam ictu, *momentanea metamorphosi*, fore infallibilem et prudentem et beatum, supra omnia paradoxa sapientis Stoicorum.[6]

TH. Nonne ergo omnes mali denique sunt in ultima resolutione censendi infelices, quia obversantem sibi tam facilem expeditamque felicitatis viam non animadvertere?

PH. Fateor.

TH. Et miserandi.

PH. Non possum negare.

TH. Et malitiam infortunio debentes.

English translation

PHILOSOPHER. So how foolish we are, we who demand certain imperceptible chimeras, having spurned the privileges of nature and of God. Not content with the use of reason – the true root of freedom – we think that we are not sufficiently free unless the power of brutishness is given [to us].[1] As if it is not the height of freedom to use both one's intellect and one's will perfectly, and accordingly for the intellect to be compelled by things to recognize true goods, and for the will to be compelled by the intellect to embrace them ... Certainly the freedom of God is supreme, even though he could not err in his choice of the best[2] ...

THEOLOGIAN. Therefore all sin [comes] from error.

PH. I agree.

TH. Therefore all sin is to be excused.

PH. By no means, for thanks to a certain light breaking in, as it were, through the cracks in the midst of the darkness, the means of escape is in our power, provided we are willing to use this.

TH. But why is it that some are willing to use [this means of escape], and others are not willing?

PH. Because in those who are not willing, it does not even come into their mind that they are able to use [this means of escape] fruitfully; or it is present in their mind just as if it were not there, that is, without *reflection*, or *attention*, so that seeing they do not see, hearing they do not hear.[3] In this we find the beginnings of the *rejection of grace* – and, as sacred scripture calls it, 'hardening'.[4] How many of us have not heard a thousand times this 'Say why [you are] here' or 'Consider the end' or 'Watch what you do'?[5] And yet it is certain that, once a single saying of this kind is correctly understood and, as it were, constantly set before [us] by means of certain laws and punishments that are strictly enacted, each human being, as though in a blink of an eye, *by an instant metamorphosis*, will become infallible and prudent and blessed, beyond all the paradoxes of the wise man of the Stoics.[6]

TH. Surely, then, in the final analysis all wicked persons must be considered unhappy, because they did not heed the path of happiness that presented itself to them as so easy and so free of obstacles.

PH. I agree.

TH. And they are to be pitied.

PH. I cannot deny [that].

TH. And they owe their wickedness to misfortune.

PH. Manifestum: est enim ultima ratio voluntatis extra volentem. Et demonstratum est in seriem rerum,[7] seu harmoniam universalem[8] haec denique omnia refundi.
TH. Et similes insanis.
PH. Prope verum, sed non omnino. Insani recolligere sese et cogitare illud: *dic cur hic*, quo omnis prudentia continetur . . . ne si velint quidem possunt . . .
TH. Ergo similes saltem erunt quarta ut aiunt luna natis,[9] male educatis, seductis conversatione, coniugio perditis, adversitate efferatis, qui se negare non possunt sceleratos, habent tamen cur sive de fortuna, sive de hominibus, desperatae vitae occasione, querantur.
PH. *Ita est omnino, imo ita necesse est esse. Nemo ipse se volens malum fecit, alioquin antequam fieret esset.*
TH. At vero *nunc animis opus est, nunc pectore firmo, ventum ad supremum est*,[10] venimus ad fastigium difficultatis nec sentientes. Si te hic fortuna non deseret, in perpetuum vicisti. Nam obiicit se nobis indeclinabilis illa, et (quicquid etiam cavillemur) iusta species querimoniae damnatorum: ita natos sese, ita in mundum missos, in tempora, in homines, in occasiones incidisse, ut non potuerint non perire; occupatam praemature vitiosis cogitationibus mentem, fuisse quae foverent malum, quae stimularent; defuisse quae liberarent, quae retinerent, velut conspirantibus in miserorum interitum fatis. Si qua monita salubria intervenerint, attentionem eos, atque illam ipsam *reflexionem*, sapientiae animam – illud: *dic cur hic*; illud: *Respice finem* – maximum *gratiae* donum, quo solo recte percepto evigilamus, destituisse. Quam iniquum illud, in communi somno aliquos excitari, caeteros mactationi relinqui! Si necesse erat tot creaturas perire, si non aliter constabat ratio mundi, at sorte fuisse ducendos infelices.
PH. Ita factum est quoque, idem enim est fato aliquid seu sorte, et ob harmoniam universalem contingere.
TH. Ne interpella quaeso, dum omnia audias. Quam crudele enim, miseriam, qui fecerit, immotum intueri[11] patrem, qui male genuerit, qui pessime educaverit, puniendum ipsummet, etiam punire velle. Maledicent naturae

PH. Evidently. For the ultimate ground of the will is outside the one willing. And it has been demonstrated that in the end, all these things flow back into the series of things,[7] or the universal harmony.[8]
TH. And [the wicked] are similar to the insane.
PH. [That is] almost true, but not entirely. Even if they wanted to, the insane cannot collect themselves and think of that 'Say why [you are] here', in which all prudence is contained . . .
TH. So clearly they will be like those born on the fourth day after the new moon, as they say,[9] badly educated, led astray through the company they keep, destroyed by a marriage, embittered by adversity. They cannot deny that they are wicked, but still they have reason to complain about fortune, or about [their fellow] human beings, the cause of their desperate lives.
PH. *It is exactly so. Indeed, it is necessary that it is so. Nobody willingly has made themselves wicked. Otherwise they would have been* [*wicked*] *before they became* [*wicked*].
TH. But *now we need our wits about us, now we need a firm heart. The crux has been reached.*[10] We have come to the chief point of difficulty without even realizing it. If fortune does not desert you here, you have won forever. For that [complaint] of the damned presents itself to us, which cannot be ignored, and which is a legitimate kind of complaint, whatever quibbles we may now raise. [They complain] that they were born in such a way, were sent into the world in such a way, came upon [such] times, persons, [and] occasions, that they could not but perish; that their mind was occupied too early with sinful thoughts, that those circumstances that fostered evil, that stimulated it, were in place [for them], but not those circumstances that would have freed [them], would have restrained [them]; that it was as though the fates were conspiring in the destruction of the wretched. If some edifying influences did intervene, their attention failed them, as did that very *reflection*, the soul of wisdom – that 'Say why [you are] here', that 'Consider the end' – the greatest gift of *grace*. [And yet] it is only by means of properly grasping these [maxims] that we remain vigilant. How unjust it is for some in the common sleep to be roused, while others are abandoned to the slaughter! If it was necessary for so many creatures to perish, if the foundation of the world would not otherwise have held, then the wretched should have been chosen by lot.
PH. It was in fact done in this way, for it is the same if something comes about by fate or lot and [if it comes about] on account of the universal harmony.
TH. Please don't interrupt, until you have heard everything. For how cruel it is for the father who brought about their misery – [the father] who caused an unfortunate birth, who provided the worst upbringing – to gaze on [their misery] unmoved,[11] [and] for him even to will their punishment, when

rerum, ut perderet fecundae, Deo aliorum miseria felici, sibi quod extingui non possint,[12] seriei universi, quae se quoque implicuit, denique ipsi illi aeternae immutabilique possibilitati Idearum, primae scaturigini malorum suorum;[13] harmoniae universalis, et in ea existentiae rerum, determinatrici, ac proinde in non alium ex tot possibilibus statum universi erumpenti, quam <quo> ipsorum miseria, ut aliorum felicitas scilicet conspectior esset, contineretur.[14]

PH. Satis tragice, non aeque iuste. ... Propone igitur tibi hominem damnandum, fac eius oculis animoque, quantus horrore ac profunditate est, infernum exhiberi, adde ipsimet monstrari angulum illum, aeternis eius, si sic agat, tormentis destinatum. Poteritne queri vivus vidensque de Deo aut natura rerum, damnationis suae causis?[15]

TH. Non poterit tunc quidem, quia statim responderi ei potest, posse eum, si velit, non damnari.

PH. Hoc volebam scilicet. Ponamus igitur, eundem nihilominus pergere, et (ex hypothesi) damnari. Poteritne tunc ullo iuris colore recurrere ad easdem querelas iam tum explosas, poteritne miseriam suam alteri imputare quam voluntati suae?

TH. Vicisti potius quam satisfecisti.[16]

it is he himself who should be punished. They shall curse the order of things, apt for their destruction; [they shall curse] God who is happy at the misery of others; [they shall curse] themselves because they cannot be annihilated;[12] [they shall curse] the series of the universe, which also involved them; and finally [they shall curse] that very eternal and immutable possibility of the Ideas, the primary source of their misfortunes,[13] which determines the universal harmony and the existence of things in it, and accordingly breaks out, from among so many possible [states], into none other than the state of the universe in which their misery is contained, so that, to be sure, the happiness of others may be more conspicuous.[14]

PH. That is rather dramatic, but it is not equally justified ... Call to mind, then, a person who is damnable; have hell revealed to his eyes and to his mind, in all its horror and depth. Imagine further that the corner of hell is shown to him which is destined for his eternal torment, if he acts in this way. Could he complain, seeing this in his lifetime, about God or the order of things, the causes of his damnation?[15]

TH. Indeed, he could not complain then, because one could immediately respond to him that if he willed, he could avoid being damned.

PH. That is certainly what I meant. Let us imagine then that that person nonetheless continues [to act wickedly] and (hypothetically) is damned. Will he then be able – with any hint of justification – to have recourse to those complaints that have already been overthrown, [and] will he be able to attribute his misery to anything but his own will?

TH. You have overcome [me], rather than satisfied [me].[16]

Commentary

1 Leibniz's target here is the libertarian or Molinist view of freedom of the will, according to which our will is undetermined. He dismisses this rival view as a 'chimera' because he takes it to involve a violation of the Principle of Sufficient Reason and to be inconsistent with a proper appreciation of our nature as rational beings.

2 Before he wrote the *Confessio philosophi*, Leibniz was already committed to the view that God wills to bring into existence the best possible world. See, for example, the letter to Magnus Wedderkopf of 1671 (Leibniz 2005: 3–5). Both Leibniz's claim that ours is the best possible world and Voltaire's parody are notorious. The former is widely misunderstood. See R. M. Adams 2014: 200–3 and Rutherford 1995: 22–67 for a helpful discussion of Leibniz's position.

3 Cf. John 12:40 and Isaiah 6:9.

4 In the Old Testament *induratio* signifies a lack of openness to God, which is both culpable and obstinate. While it is generally the Israelites' 'hardness of heart' which is at issue (see, for example, Jeremiah 7:26; 17:23; Psalm 94:8), the most notable case is the hardening of Pharaoh's heart by God, when he refuses to release the Israelites from slavery (Exodus 4:21; 7:3 etc.). The implication that God is directly responsible for Pharaoh's hardness of heart has long troubled biblical scholars and theologians. In a piece written between 1701 and 1706 Leibniz suggests that God's role is limited to bringing about the circumstances that lead to the hardening of Pharaoh's heart: God does not administer some kind of 'anti-grace' (*cuiusdam anti-gratiae influxus*). See Leibniz 2011: 136.

5 For the provenance of these maxims see Otto Saame's comments in Leibniz 1967: 177–8, n. 146.

6 Leibniz seems to be assuming that these sayings enable us to recall that we will be judged after death and thus motivate us to remain virtuous. He also takes it for granted that, thanks to our God-given 'innate light' (*lumen innatum*), we can understand that the world is governed by a most perfect mind, rather than by the kind of 'blind necessity' which he associates with the (neo-)Stoics. For Leibniz's attitude to (neo-)Stoicism see Rutherford 2001. Leibniz outlines his understanding of the *lumen innatum* in §§ 97–100 of the *Causa Dei* of 1710 (Leibniz 1875–90: 453–4; translation in Leibniz 1965: 135–6).

7 Leibniz frequently characterizes our world as a 'series of things'. In the *Confessio philosophi* he describes God as the first term of this series; the series is thus a necessary emanation of the divinity. This rather Spinozistic account

is subsequently revised: in his later writings Leibniz indicates that God is *outside* the series of things which constitutes our world, and emphasizes that there is an infinity of possible worlds that God could have brought into existence. See Rateau 2008: 150–5; R. M. Adams 1994: 20–1.

8 In Leibniz's writings 'universal harmony' denotes the actual world insofar as it represents an unsurpassably harmonious whole. The question how 'harmony' should be understood in this context is a complex one. See Rutherford 1995.

9 Saame notes a German tradition associating the fourth day after a new moon with bad luck. See Leibniz 1967: 179, n. 152.

10 *ventum ad supremum est*: Virgil, *Aeneid* 12.803. The words are uttered by Jupiter, as he urges Juno to accept that her struggle to thwart Aeneas is futile. Whatever Leibniz's intentions relating to this citation, it is an effective means of signalling that the Theologian is about to make his most rhetorically powerful speech.

11 Leibniz is committed to the doctrine of divine impassibility. Cf. Leibniz 2005: 60.

12 In Leibniz's scheme God delights in the universal harmony, and the misery of the damned is an indispensable part of this harmony. Earlier in the *Confessio philosophi* the Philosopher argued that God's delighting in the universal harmony *as a whole* does not entail God's delighting in *each part* of that harmony: God takes no delight in sin or in the misery with which it is punished. See Leibniz 2005: 48.

The suggestion that the damned curse themselves because they cannot be annihilated should not be taken to imply that God is unable to annihilate them, but rather that God will not in fact annihilate them, because their continued existence is indispensable to the perfection of the world, in which God delights.

13 Leibniz espouses 'a theistic modification of Platonism, sponsored in antiquity by Philo and Augustine, and generally accepted in the Middle Ages. On this view, the reality in which necessary truths … are grounded is the ensemble of ideas in the mind of God' (R. M. Adams 1994: 180). For Leibniz, God's willing to actualize our world must ultimately be explained by reference to God's perfect apprehension of these truths or Ideas.

14 In suggesting that there is an aesthetic rationale for God's punishment of sin – i.e. that such punishment is permitted because it increases the overall harmony of the world – Leibniz is developing a line of thought found in Augustine. See R. M. Adams 2014: 207, n. 60.

15 It could be objected that a loving God would give all those in danger of being damned the kind of vision of hell which is described here. Leibniz would no doubt argue that such an intervention would be unnecessary, as we already have innate knowledge of God and of the fact that we will be judged after death. Furthermore, Leibniz holds that, thanks to the faculty of imagination that God has given us, we are able to form representations of heaven and hell that are sufficiently vivid to deter us from succumbing to mortal sin. Cf. Leibniz 1999: 2328–9.

16 The Theologian is clearly not persuaded that it is sufficient merely to establish that the damned freely committed mortal sin. Later in the dialogue, he raises the question why our world should involve damnation at all (Leibniz 2005: 100). In his mature work Leibniz consistently argues that God was morally necessitated to create the best possible world, notwithstanding that such a world includes the damnation of certain individuals. There is some evidence that Leibniz came to have doubts about the adequacy of this response. On this point see R. M. Adams 2014, Lodge 2017 and Strickland 2009. For the notion of 'moral necessity' see R. M. Adams 2005.

19

A School Play

Gottlob Krantz (1660–1733), *Memorabilia Bibliothecae Publicae Elisabetanae Wratislaviensis*, Excerpts from Acts I and IV

Jacqueline Glomski

Introduction

In May 1698 the boys of St Elizabeth's School in Wrocław performed a play that described the contents of their school's library. The script had been written by their teacher, Gottlob Krantz, who was celebrating ten years as the librarian of the Bibliotheca Publica Elisabethana.

St Elizabeth's Library was formed from the collections of a Silesian nobleman, Thomas Rehdiger (Rhediger) (1540–76). Rehdiger had attended St Elizabeth's School and then studied at both Wittenberg and Paris. Afterwards, for fifteen years, he led a peripatetic lifestyle, travelling through the Netherlands, France, Italy and Switzerland, collecting books and art without sparing any expense. Just before his premature death in Cologne, Rehdiger stated that his collections should return to his family in Wrocław, but also that they should be opened to the public. The transfer of the books and objects to Silesia (an area across modern Poland, Czech Republic and Germany) took five years. The library was first kept in a private house, but was moved, with the agreement of the town council, to the Auditorium Theologicum above the choir of St Elizabeth's Church. Still, the formal establishment of the library was delayed by administrative quarrels, and it did not open as a public institution until 1661. During the seventeenth century the library was augmented by donations from the town clerk Chrysostomus Schultze, the notary Matthias Machner and the military officer Albrecht von Säbisch (Sebisch). The library would be transferred from the school to the new Wrocław city library in 1865 and then to the university library in 1945, where the books that have not been destroyed by natural disaster or removed by pillage remain today.

Gottlob Krantz was the son of a Lutheran pastor, and studied at Königsberg and Leipzig. He came to work at St Elizabeth's School in 1686, where he taught history, rhetoric, mathematics and physics. Krantz was appointed professor and librarian in 1688, and would rise to become pro-rector in 1700 and then rector in 1709. In that year he would also become inspector of all the Protestant schools in Wrocław. St Elizabeth's School was the most outstanding *gymnasium* in Wrocław and played a primary role in the scholarly and cultural life of a city that had come to cultural prominence with the humanist movement in the sixteenth century and enjoyed a flowering of literature in the seventeenth. The school had been founded at the end of the thirteenth century as a parish school, teaching the typical medieval *trivium* (grammar, logic, rhetoric) and *quadrivium* (arithmetic, geometry, music, astronomy), but had been transformed in the late sixteenth century into a Lutheran *gymnasium*, that aimed specifically to prepare students for a higher education at a university. The school had a strong humanist tradition: the celebrated Silesian scholar Laurentius Corvinus (1465–1527) was the rector from 1497 to 1503, and the standard of Latin instruction was high, as evidenced by the Latin spoken by the characters in *Memorabilia Bibliothecae Publicae Elisabetanae Wratislaviensis* ('*Memorabilia of St Elizabeth's Public Library at Wrocław*').

In producing school plays, Krantz was following the example of Corvinus, who had staged two classical plays in the Wrocław town hall, Terence's *Eunuchus* and Plautus' *Aulularia*, in 1500 and 1502, respectively. Moreover, the tradition of pupil plays in German Protestant schools had existed since the time of Philip Melanchthon, and after St Elizabeth's became Protestant, the frequency of performances increased. Late-seventeenth-century school plays were designed for the boys not only to master elegant Latin (and German) style, but also to practise oratory and to learn about public life, in preparation for taking up their roles in society.

Krantz intended his play to introduce the pupils – and their audience – to the library and its history as well as to familiarize them with the academic subjects connected to the objects in the library's collections. The library contained – as was usual at this time – works of art, coins and samples from the natural world, in addition to books. At the point of Krantz's writing, the library held more than 6,000 printed books and 300 manuscripts. The book section was strong in the classics, but also in history, theology and mathematics, and the manuscripts covered all topics. Rehdiger's art collection had been augmented with rare prints and drawings from the von Säbisch bequest, which contributed minerals and shells as well. Krantz's text referred to all these categories.

The play itself is written in prose, in four acts that cover the itinerary of the protagonist *Curiosus* ('Curious') through the library's departments of visual and plastic arts, of natural sciences, of numismatics and, finally, of printed books and manuscripts. In the first three acts *Curiosus* is guided by an apparent expert – in Acts One and Three by *Historicus* ('Historian'), and in Act Two by *Physicus* ('Natural Scientist'). These two guides field *Curiosus*' questions and interpret and expand the answers of subject-specialist interlocutors.

Consequently, the play is formed of intellectual, academic dialogues, and there is no dramatic action as such. The only hint of a plot is *Curiosus*' quest to satisfy his curiosity. In Act One *Historicus* and *Pictor* ('Painter'), *Sculptor* ('Engraver') and *Plastes* ('Modeller') comment on the major works of art contained in St Elizabeth's collections (paying particular attention to the history behind the individuals depicted in the portraits), generally discuss artistic techniques and genres (such as engraving and etching), and make remarks on the famous artists of the Renaissance and seventeenth century (such as Albrecht Dürer and Peter Paul Rubens). In Act Two *Curiosus* is given detailed information on the minerals and stones found in the library by *Metallifossor* ('Metal Miner'), while *Nauta* ('Sailor') describes the marine samples, with *Physicus*, *Mathematicus* ('Mathematician') and *Metallifossor* adding scientific facts. Act Three concerns the coin collection of the library, with *Ethicus* ('Ethicist') and *Antiquarius* ('Antiquary') explaining that coins are collected and displayed because the images impressed on them represent in a potent way – through symbols – the virtues and vices, customs, rituals and mentalities of antiquity. *Historicus* states simply that the display of coins is 'nothing but history'. These three, together with *Geographus* ('Geographer'), clarify for *Curiosus* the meanings of the images on various coins and provide further historical background, particularly on ancient Rome. In Act Four *Curiosus* appears to guide himself, speaking first to *Typographus* ('Printer') and *Bibliopegus* ('Bookbinder') about early printing and bookbinding, before proceeding to the subject areas of the library, where *Philologus* ('Scholar') gives the layout of the library and joins in with *Theologus* ('Theologian'), *Politicus* ('Political Scientist'), *Historicus* and *Medicus* ('Doctor') to highlight the theological, political, legal, historiographical, medical and natural science (including alchemy) books and manuscripts.

The play is prefaced by a verse prologue that chronicles the history of scholarship, introduced by *Eruditio* ('Learning') and *Tempus* ('Time'), followed by a strophe spoken by each century after Christ, from the first to the seventeenth, describing the continuing struggle against barbarism and mentioning such scholars and writers as Galen, Priscian, Avicenna, Thomas Aquinas, Petrarch and Poggio Bracciolini. Between this prologue and the first act Krantz has inserted a short poem in German in praise of wisdom. Furthermore, to vary his piece, Krantz has placed verse *interscenia* ('interludes') after the first, second and third acts, and an epilogue after the fourth. The themes of these verse pieces support the conversations found in the acts preceding them. So, the first *interscenium* consists of an interchange between *Pictura* ('Painting'), *Sculptura* ('Engraving') and *Plastice* ('Modelling'), which praises these arts, describing their techniques. In the second *interscenium* *Faunus* and *Triton* address each other, claiming that the other's realm (land or sea) should be more admired for the wonders it contains. In the third *interscenium Avaritia* ('Greed') attacks *Antiquitas* ('Antiquity') for her love of old coins, claiming that her efforts are wasteful of money, and asserting that old coins should be melted down and stamped out into new ones. *Antiquitas* responds that she sees the wars and heroic deeds as well as the peaceful, prosperous times of the past; she argues that coins can portray the events of history more elegantly than writing, and she accuses *Avaritia* of being a barbarian. In the final epilogue *Ars scriptoria* ('Art of Writing') complains that she is exhausted because, in the present barbaric age, she is forced to copy out a great number of stupid books. *Typographia* ('Printing') announces that she has come to the rescue, and explains that with 'tin words' (*stannea verba*) she can make many copies of a text in a short time. Her craft has kindled a learned zeal, and many intellectuals are now correcting corrupted classical writings: wisdom will be restored, and libraries will be enlarged with a growing number of books.

Krantz's choice of a description of a library as a topic for a school play may seem unusual – most of the school plays of the time were based on classical or biblical motifs, or on historical figures and events (with a political lesson stressed; see Text 13), or were even comedies. However, Krantz's emphasis on the value of learning situates his text well within the tradition of these plays, which always possessed a moralistic / didactic slant, and which were intended also to develop oratorical skills. In any case, *Memorabilia Bibliothecae Publicae Elisabetanae Wratislaviensis* can be thought of as a pageant and, in this sense, is reminiscent of humanist dialogues of the fifteenth and sixteenth centuries (see Text 3), which often relied on dramatic presentation. On a personal level, Krantz's text expresses his pride in his school and its remarkable collection of historical books and objects, and in his town and the outstanding philanthropy of its citizens, who have continued to foster the public library through donations from their own collections. Krantz's play reflects his intellectual interests in polymathy (the grasp of every academic subject) and *historia literaria* (the history of scholarship), two trends current in eastern German academic institutions in the late seventeenth century. Krantz's Latin style is learned and correct, and typically Baroque – full of emotion and exaggeration, and employing a vocabulary containing post-classical expressions and neologisms that permit him to describe early modern cultural and technological innovations. The passages here have been selected to give the reader a flavour of the play – the beginning of Act One, which introduces *Curiosus* and his quest, and the beginning of Act Four, concerning the library's early printed books.

Bibliography

Biber, A. (1931), 'Thomas Rehdiger', in F. Andreae, E. Graber and M. Hippe (eds), *Schlesische Lebensbilder*, Vol. 4: *Schlesier des 16. bis 19. Jahrhunderts*, 113–24, Wrocław.

Davies, N. and R. Moorhouse (2002), *Microcosm: Portrait of a Central European City*, London.

Gajek, K., ed. (1994) *Das Breslauer Schultheater im 17. und 18. Jahrhundert*, Tübingen.

Garber, K. (2014), *Das alte Breslau: Kulturgeschichte einer geistigen Metropole*, Cologne.

Glomski, J. (1996), 'Book Collecting and Bookselling in the Seventeenth Century: Notions of Rarity and Identification of Value', *Publishing History*, 39: 5–21.

Kulak, T (1997), *Wrocław: Przewodnik historyczny*, Wrocław.

Kundmann, J. C. (1741), *Academiae et scholae Germaniae praecipue Ducatus Silesiae cum bibliothecis in nummis*, Wrocław.

Scheibel, J. E. (1810), 'Notices of What Is Remarkable in the Elizabethian Library at Breslau', in *Memoirs of the Life of Sir John Froissart: To Which Is Added, Some Account of the Manuscript of his Chronicle in the Elizabethian Library at Breslau, and a Complete Index*, by T. Johnes, 79–100, Hafod.

Schmidt, J. (1841), 'Gottlob Krantz', *Schlesische Provinzialblätter*, 114: 293–301.

Sordet, Y. (2009), 'Le baptême inconscient de l'incunable: non pas 1640 mais 1569 au plus tard', *Gutenberg Jahrbuch*, 84: 102–5.

Steinberg, S. H. (1996), *Five Hundred Years of Printing*, London and New Castle DE.

Wachler, A. W. J. (1828), *Thomas Rehdiger und seine Büchersammlung in Breslau*, Wrocław.

Source of the Latin text

The text is given, with spelling and punctuation standardized, according to the unique printing: Gottlob Krantz, *Memorabilia Bibliothecae Publicae Elisabetanae Wratislaviensis*, Wrocław (Johann Georg Steck) 1699.

Latin text

Introitus I. (pp. 18–19)

Curiosus:[1] Gratulor mihi,[2] viri optimi, de prasentia vestra exoptatissima, et quod sermonibus vestris aures et animum pascere liceat,[3] in sinu gaudeo. Animus noster, qui in rerum terrestrium varietate curiosiora inquirere satagit, vix amabilius contemplationum suarum obiectum invenire potest, quam artes vestras naturae imitatrices, quae curiosum spectatorem nunquam sine delectatione dimittunt.

Historicus: Quod curiosa artis pictoriae aut plastices opera mentem et oculos oblectent,[4] nullus[5] dubito; immo et curiositati tuae[6] artificum horum seu stylo seu penicillo satisfieri posse[7] spero. Sed quid ego, artium harum ignarus, voto tuo conferre valeam, vix perspicio.

Curiosus: Non pingendi aut fingendi, sed loquendi causa huc accessimus, vir doctissime, et ut illi de pretiosis artificum operibus optime disserere, sic, te interprete, discere poterimus,[8] quae rerum in orbe gestarum monumenta, pictorum plastarumque operibus impressa, posteritati relicta sint. Nec ingratum artificibus nostris erit si artium suarum incunabula et antiquum decus sermonibus tuis explicata audient.

Pictor: Delineatio corporum et accuratior artis nostrae cognitio omnes hucusque intentionis meae vires sibi poposcerunt, ita ut pictoriae artis initia et progressum inquirere minime licuerit. Felicem vero me hodie praedicarem, si, tuo beneficio, vir eruditissime, hunc cognitionis meae defectum supplere liceret.

Historicus: Operosum est quod poscis, amice, immo, ob perpetuum fere scriptorum dissensum, vix satis explicabile; quae tamen succurrunt, paucissimis[9] exponam. Primum picturae initium Plinius Gygi cuidam Lydo tribuit, qui, in Aegypto degens, corporis sui ad ignem stantis umbram carbone circumscripsisse dicitur.[10] Ex hoc linearis pictura originem sumsisse creditur, quae inter antiquissimos diu floruit, donec Polygnotus Atheniensis lineas circumscriptas colore quodam explere inciperet.[11]

English translation

Act I.

Curious:[1] I am happy,[2] noble fellows, on account of your most longed-for presence, and I rejoice in my breast that I am permitted to gratify my ears and my mind with your discussions.[3] My mind, which is busy inquiring into the more curious things among the variety of earthly objects, is scarcely able to find a more agreeable object of contemplation than your arts, imitators of nature, which never leave the curious beholder without delight.

Historian: I do not doubt at all[5] that the interesting works of pictorial or plastic art are pleasing to your mind and eyes;[4] indeed, I also hope that your curiosity[6] can be satisfied[7] by the pen or pencil of these artists. But I scarcely perceive how I, ignorant of these arts, am able to fulfil your wish.

Curious: It is not for the purpose of painting or sculpting that we have come here, most learned man, but for speaking, and just as they [i.e. historians] [were able][8] to write in the best way about the precious works of artists, likewise, with you as an interpreter, we will be able to learn which tokens of earthly deeds have been left to posterity, expressed through the works of painters and sculptors. And it will not be disagreeable to our artists if they hear about the origin and ancient glory of their arts explained in your words.

Painter: The sketching of bodies and a more accurate acquaintance with our art have demanded for themselves all my powers of attention up to this point, so that I have not been able to inquire at all into the beginnings and development of pictorial art. But I would declare myself happy today, if, through your kindness, most learned man, I could make up for this weakness in my knowledge.

Historian: What you demand, friend, is difficult, indeed scarcely able to be explained sufficiently, on account of the almost continuous disagreement of writers; however, I shall set forth, in just a very few [words],[9] the things that come to mind. Pliny attributes the very beginning of painting to a certain Lydian, Gyges, who, living in Egypt, is said to have outlined with charcoal the shadow of his own body standing by a fire.[10] From this, linear painting is believed to have taken its origin, which flourished for a long time among the most ancient peoples, until Polygnotus the Athenian began to fill in outlines with some colour.[11]

Introitus IV. (pp. 72–3)

Curiosus. Satisfecistisne desiderio meo, boni viri, et in Bibliotheca Elisabetana artium vestrarum cimelia[12] perlustrastis?

Typographus. Satisfecimus, patrone, et thesaurum rerum memorabilium exspectatione nostra maiorem ibi invenimus, omniaque quae captum nostrum non superant, quantum licebat, inquisivimus.

Curiosus. Quid itaque tibi videbatur de artis typographicae speciminibus hic inventis?

Typographus. Mirabar tantam characterum diversitatem, artisque nostrae incunabula,[13] incrementa, summamque demum perfectionem non sine gaudio deprehendebam. Vidi antiquissimam typorum simplicitatem, quibus[14] maiores literae non nisi calamo addi poterant, quique,[15] monachorum scribendi methodum imitantes, tam characteris aequalitate nimia quam distinctionum defectu et abbreviationum molestia lectori taedium creant. Nec tamen omnia saeculi XVti monumenta his defectibus laborare vidi, sed pro artificum varietate etiam characteres varios deprehendi. Biblia inspexi italica, duobus voluminibus sat magnis comprehensa, Venetiis Anno 1471 membranis purissimis impressa,[16] quibus[17] quidem maiores literae titulique pro more aevi desunt; minutus tamen character adeo purus, adeo distinctus et elegans est ut multos nostri temporis typos superare mihi videatur. Nec nomina sua, nisi rarius, antiquiores typographi addiderunt; in tanta scilicet officinarum paucitate vix necessarium ducebant hoc, quod fama satis divulgabat, chartae[18] imprimere.

Act IV.

Curious: Have you fulfilled my wish, good fellows, and have you surveyed the treasures[12] of your arts in the Elizabethan Library?

Printer: We have fulfilled it, patron, and we have found there a treasure-house of remarkable things, greater than our expectation, and we have investigated all the things that do not exceed our comprehension, as much as we could.

Curious: And so, what did you think about the examples of the art of printing found here?

Printer: I was amazed at such a diversity of typefaces; and not without joy, I discovered the beginnings,[13] the increments of growth and lastly the ultimate perfecting of our art. I saw the earliest simplicity of printing types, in which capital letters could not be added except by pen,[14] and which, imitating the method of writing by monks, create weariness for the reader by both an excessive indifferentiation of typeface and by a lack of word divisions, and by the nuisance of abbreviations.[15] On the other hand, I saw that not all the monuments of the fifteenth century suffered from these defects, but, in line with the diversity of craftsmen, I also found typefaces of different kinds. I inspected an Italian Bible, contained in two quite large volumes, printed at Venice in 1471 on the purest parchment,[16] which, indeed, is lacking[17] capital letters and titles, according to the custom of the age; still, its small typeface is so clear, so distinct and elegant that it seems to me to surpass many of the printing types of our time. And neither have the older printers, except rather rarely, given their names; of course, with such a scarcity of [printing] workshops they hardly considered it necessary to print on paper that which fame would publish widely.[18]

Commentary

Act I.

Here, at the start of the play, *Curiosus* introduces himself and establishes his method of inquiry: *Historicus* will interpret for him the works of art found in St Elizabeth's collection. An emphasis is thus placed on history, rather than on aesthetics, with the characters relating to a greater extent historical details concerning artists and artistic genres than providing descriptions of the objects they are discussing. *Curiosus* sets the tone by stating that he is not here to paint or sculpt but to talk and to learn about the 'tokens of earthly deeds (i.e. history) left to posterity' and by immediately demanding information on the origins of the visual arts.

1 In the seventeenth century *curiosus* referred to an intellectual who studied (or collected) material objects, not just written texts, and so could refer to someone who had (or desired to have) expertise as a connoisseur. A 'curiosity' was an object that sparked intellectual interest and/or that was potentially collectable. In the case of books and manuscripts, the adjective *curiosus* could indicate a particular historical significance, or simply connote the physical beauty of an item (see Glomski 1996).

2 *sibi gratulari*: 'to call oneself happy; to congratulate oneself'.

3 *quod . . . liceat*: the object of *gaudeo*; *quod* can be translated as 'that' or 'because'.

4 *quod . . . oblectent*: the object of *dubito*; *quod* can be translated as '(the fact) that'.

5 *nullus*: has adverbial force here ('not at all').

6 *curiositati tuae*: dative case with *satisfieri*.

7 *satisfieri posse*: the passive infinitive is used here in an impersonal construction, which can be translated in the active voice with a personal subject.

8 *ut . . . poterimus*: supply *potuerunt* after *disserere*.

9 *paucissimis*: supply *verbis*; *paucis* can be used as an idiomatic expression for 'in just a few words' or 'very briefly'; see, for example, Cicero, *Pro Cluentio* 160; Sallust, *Iugurtha* 17.7; Tacitus, *Annales* 1.52 (for further examples see *OLD* s.v. *paucus* 6b).

10 Pliny the Elder, *Natural History* 7.57 (56).

11 Quintilian, *Institutio oratoria* 12.10.3. Polygnotus was a native of the Greek island of Thasos, but was admitted to Athenian citizenship; he painted at Athens in the middle of the fifth century.

Act IV.

Krantz begins his fourth and final act of the play, which covers the library's books, with a discussion of early printing and bookbinding that references items from St Elizabeth's collection. As in the previous passage, the accent is on history: *Typographus* describes fifteenth-century typefaces, mentioning the library's Italian Bible of 1471; but after this passage, he rattles off a list of fifteenth- and sixteenth-century printers, before returning to notable examples of rare books from the collection. Krantz's antiquarian interests (already revealed in the previous act, which dealt with the library's numismatic collection) come to the fore in this act. Not only will he have the character *Bibliopegus* give an overview of the historic bookbindings in the library, but he will devote the second half of the act to an inventory of the library's manuscripts. The play will finish with a prayer, voiced by *Theologus*, for the library to be kept safe for the benefit of learned men, and for it to be increased by the generosity of donors.

12 *cimelia*: from the Greek κειμήλιον, 'treasure'; not a classical word, but in use from the Middle Ages.

13 The term *incunabula* (meaning 'cradle', and, by extension, 'infancy') is still used today (in English also 'incunable') to refer to books printed before 1501, that is, in the infancy of printing. The term was promoted by Bernhard von Mallinckrodt in his treatise *De ortu et progressu artis typographiae* ('*On the rise and progress of the art of printing*', Cologne 1639/40), but it was actually first used by the Dutch doctor and philologist Hadrianus Junius (Adriaan de Jonghe) in the second edition of his *Batavia* (written in 1569, published in Leiden in 1588) (see Sordet 2009).

14 *quibus* is dative dependent on *addi*.

Krantz is referring here to the fact that during the incunabula period (i.e. fifteenth century), coloured, decorative initials, in imitation of those found in medieval manuscripts, generally had to be inserted by hand by a rubrisher, after the sheets were printed. Woodcut initials came into common use in the sixteenth century, with elaborate, engraved initials appearing only in more expensive books from late in that century until the second half of the seventeenth century, when all the leading European printers began to use them.

15 *quique*: *qui* + *que*, not a form of *quisque*.

Typographus alludes to the fact that the first printers tried to make their work, as much as possible, resemble handwriting, in imitation of medieval scribes. Early printing was considered a cheaper substitute for manuscripts and inferior to them. Even so, the reading public, conservative as to the presentation of reading matter, demanded conformity to existing conventions, and in any case, with no other models to follow, readers would need some time to adjust to the possibilities of the new technology. Gothic, the typeface of early printing, because of its dense appearance, has always been considered more difficult to read than roman (see the following note). A medieval scribe, in drawing one letter to fit after another, altered shapes in the process of creating an appropriate spacing between letters, but with printing, letters became standardized, and a typeset page appeared more even than a page of handwriting.

16 This is the Bible translated into Italian by Niccolò Malermi, with additions by Hieronymus Squarzaficus, printed at Venice by Vindelinus de Spira (Wendelin of Speyer), 1 August 1471, ISTC no. ib00640000. According to the ISTC (Incunabula Short Title Catalogue), part one, printed (as Krantz states) on vellum, is still held at the University of Wrocław Library (https://data.cerl.org/istc/ib00640000).

Typographus is praising 'antiqua' or 'roman' typeface, which had first been developed during the years 1465 to 1467 by the German printers Konrad Sweynheym and Arnold Pannartz, working in Italy, and perfected in 1470, in Venice, by the French printer Nicolas Jenson. Fifteenth-century typefaces imitated handwritten scripts (see Text 16), and roman approximated the handwriting of Renaissance humanist scribes. Its rival was 'gothic', which came from the medieval 'textura' scripts that were used in Germany, where printing with movable type was invented. Gothic type was allegedly so termed by the Italian humanists to suggest barbarism. Gothic is also known as 'black letter' or 'Fraktur' and is found in English vernacular printing from the fifteenth to the early eighteenth century and in printing in German up to the mid twentieth century.

17 *quibus*: dative case with *desunt*.

18 *chartae*: dative case (*imprimo* is construed with the accusative [here, *hoc*] and dative).

With the invention of printing, a whole group of expressions came into being to describe the new technology. Besides *imprimo* (originally meaning 'to press into' and by extension 'to engrave', 'to stamp' or 'to mark'), the verb *excudo* ('to strike') could be used for 'to print' (or *recudo*, to 'reprint' a text).

The nouns *typographia*, a combination of the Greek τύπος (*typos*, 'impression') and γραφή (*graphē*, 'drawing' or 'writing'), and *chalcographia* (or *calcographia*), from the Greek χαλκός (*chalcos*, 'metal') added to γραφή, were commonly employed for 'printing' or 'typography'. To distinguish printed books from handwritten ones, the noun *manuscriptum*, which is not attested in classical times and which in the Middle Ages referred to a 'charter' or 'signed document', was employed. Furthermore, the phrase *editio princeps* (or *prima editio*) came to be used to denote the first printing of a text that had previously existed only in manuscript form.

Index of Names

This index includes the names of early modern authors, of the ancient authors and biblical books referred to as inspirations and precedents and of the historical figures the early modern authors interacted with; it covers the general introduction as well as the introductions and commentaries to the selected texts.

www.ingramcontent.com/pod-product-compliance
Lightning Source LLC
Chambersburg PA
CBHW071202100726
47908CB00002B/477

9781350157293